Wendy Robinson was born in England in Heswall, Wirral and was brought up and educated in Wallesey before training as a nurse and midwife in Liverpool. She worked for a year in Malawi with VSO (the organization for Voluntary Services Overseas) before going on to form and run a local support group for parents of children with autism in Reading. She was also the welfare officer for Mid Counties Autistic Society for several years. Wendy qualified as an aromatherapist in 1998 and she currently works with many autistic adults in this field. *Gentle Giant* is her first book, although pieces of her poetry have been published previously.

Gentle Giant

THE INSPIRING STORY
OF AN AUTISTIC CHILD

Wendy Robinson

ELEMENT
Shaftesbury, Dorset • Boston, Massachusetts • Melbourne, Victoria

First published in the UK in 1999 by
Element Books Limited
Shaftesbury, Dorset SP7 8BP

Published in the USA in 1999 by
Element Books, Inc.
160 North Washington Street, Boston MA 02114

Published in Australia in 1999 by
Element Books and distributed
by Penguin Australia Ltd
487 Maroondah Highway, Ringwood,
Victoria 3134

The author and publishers wish to thank IMP Ltd for permission to reproduce
lyrics from 'Wonderful Baby': words and music by Don McClean. EMI
Catalogue Partnership/EMI Unart Catalog Inc./Yahweh Tunes Inc., USA.
Worldwide print rights controlled by Warner Bros. Publications Inc/IMP Ltd.
Reproduced by permission of IMP Ltd.

Plate section photographs © Wendy and Paul Robinson, with the exception of
Plate 5 of Zoe Denham © Jean and David Denham

Cover design by Mark Slader
Text design by Roger Lightfoot
Typeset by Bournemouth Colour Press
Printed and bound in Great Britain by Creative Print and Design (Wales)

British Library Cataloguing in Publication
data available

Library of Congress Cataloging in Publication
data available

ISBN 1 86204 304 3

To Paul and Julian

Contents

Acknowledgements

The friends we made through Grant were numerous. If your name does not appear in this book, it is no reflection on that friendship or the valuable part played in Grant's life.

My book would be much too long if I included you all: if you played a part you will know who you are and we thank you for it.

I would like to thank my personal proof-readers: Glenda Hemken, who put her English skills to test on my work; Margaret Macleod, Health Visitor, who viewed my book through the professional eye; Jo Swinn, who has the parental experience as the mother of autistic twins; and Edna Robinson, my mother-in-law whose years of being secretary to an eminent military historian made her input invaluable.

Lastly I could not have written this book without the help of my husband, Paul, who patiently and painstakingly read and reorganized some of my language, not to mention the correction of my spelling!

Like bringing up Grant, it has been a team effort.

Introduction

'Autistic? What is that?' asked a lady with a pound coin already poised above my collection box. 'I had a cousin who was *artistic* – a sensitive member of the family; she painted beautiful pictures.' The coin dropped to the bottom of my box and I smiled and shook my head. '*Autistic* not *artistic* – they are children who have severe communication problems.' The lady's eyes glazed: 'Oh,' she said, 'my sister was shy too.'

I sighed and handed her a leaflet and she went on her way, reading the information that we had tried to simplify into a clear message explaining the condition. How I would have preferred her confused interpretation.

The normally busy street emptied and I lowered my heavy box to bring back the circulation to my numbing fingers. My mind drifted back twenty years to a hospital bed bathed in warm sunshine. I felt bruised and battered but very happy. I now had two little boys, Julian who was three and a half and this little bundle that we would call Grant Michael who was just four hours old. The day was Wednesday, 26 March 1975, just five days before Easter. I fitted the radio headphones over my ears, picked up my snuffling baby, rocked him and admired his beauty. He was so perfect. His hair was dark blond and softly waved on top; his face round and not at all distorted from that first traumatic journey that begins life's story.

I put the child to my breast – he needed little help to acquire his first breakfast – and I lay back to enjoy this initial bonding with my precious gift from God. A delightful song by Don McLean began on the radio and I couldn't help but listen to the words:

> Wonderful baby living on love,
> The sandman says maybe he'll take you above
> Up where the girls fly on ribbons and bows
> Where babies float by just counting their toes …
>
> Wonderful baby I'll watch while you grow
> If I knew the future you'd be first to know
> But I know of nothing of what life's about
> Just as long as you live you will never find out
> Wonderful baby …

Why did listening to these words bring back the unease that I had felt throughout this pregnancy? Now, twenty years on, how significant the words of this pretty song were. Grant had lived on the love of so many people. Without their love how would we have survived the tremendous difficulties those early years brought? The sandman did come to take him above, but only after twenty frustrating years locked in an autistic world. We reached in every way we could to try and pull him out from behind the invisible brick wall that lay between him and us but, despite our efforts and the love and enthusiasm of so many, we could never do it. The wall was tough, but there were cracks that allowed us occasionally to peep at the person within. Sometimes he pushed aside a brick and looked out, but this was brief and he soon slid it back again. I want this story of our son to describe to you some of the intense efforts we made to reach the boy inside the perfect shell – Grant the person. Those who got really close to him saw that person underneath; he was very beautiful, loving and gentle. In his latter years he gained the nickname 'Gentle Giant'. I would like to share some of our feelings experienced in living and working with Grant as we led him along his path of life. The life path that had only little openings and a sandman at the end that took him to where he would know the answers.

I want our story to help others with their God-given task. To instil hope in new methods and fresh insight into this intensely difficult condition. No parents should ever give up hope of helping their child, but sometimes we do need to stand back and accept what we have and love them for what they are.

One

As a midwife, I had delivered many babies and assisted women in all stages of pregnancy and labour. I had helped ease and alleviate the many aches and pains that women have to endure through the seemingly endless nine months. I had mopped brows, lent my hands to give human presence and comfort through the agonizing pains of labour, and wept with couples at the pure joy of new life. We midwives called producing our own children Part III of our training. Personally I think every midwife should experience 'Part III', as first-hand knowledge can only lead to sympathetic understanding and consequently better practice.

I did, however, feel that during pregnancy you could act as an invalid and enjoy being nurtured, or get on with life and endure the accompanying discomforts, of which I am sure I had my fair share. The rewards at the end would be worth it. As for childbirth, you either screamed your head off or bore it bravely; I was determined to take the latter course.

I loved being pregnant, and felt I had an inner glow. In September and into my sixth month my husband, Paul, and I went camping in the mountains of Scotland with my bump large and active. I slept on the ground because I was too cold on the camp bed, the icy Scottish air circulating the light metal structure far too well.

We thrilled at the magnificent views from the top of one of Scotland's highest peaks, which we reached by cable car, but opted to walk down so that we could take in the air and the scenery. The descent took much longer than we had anticipated as we had to stop at ten-minute intervals while I experienced strong 'Braxton Hicks' contractions. These are false contractions that women can get in pregnancy from quite an early stage, usually quite painless but sometimes can be severe. They are also a bit unnerving when you are 3,500 feet up a mountain and completely alone! However, Paul and I laughed happily and said that the baby wished to see the mountain and the wonderful views! (Julian, now twenty-six, loves the mountains and spends many weekends walking, climbing or cycling in ranges throughout Europe.)

During the last two weeks of my pregnancy, it being near to Christmas, we attended a few parties and I danced merrily; I could never sit still to music. Two other very pregnant friends sat demurely on a settee nurturing their bumps, just as I should have been at that stage.

Then came *my* time and I learnt labour was extremely painful, but just about managed not to scream. Then gazing with wonder and delight at the sticky bundle in the hospital cot by my side, I had a pulmonary embolism and knew it. The pains in my head and chest were intense. I believed I was going to die, and would not have the pleasure of bringing up my baby.

I should have died, but didn't. I was still needed in this world. God had a part for me to play, tasks for me to perform. Fortunately, the bit of technology needed for my survival was found at the RAF hospital at Halton in Buckinghamshire, 40 miles from our home. This is where I woke up, in a dialysis unit. My baby was with me but on a floor below in the Maternity Wing. My breasts were engorged with the milk my baby should be receiving and I felt and was constantly sick.

The embolus, which consisted of fluid, had been sucked, very unusually, from the amniotic fluid that surrounds the baby and into my main blood vessels. It had then journeyed via the lungs to the kidneys. These had been put out of action and the drugs given to control the sky-high blood pressure, noted after the birth, had not been excreted by the kidneys, therefore putting me into a coma.

The day I received my first dialysis was Christmas Eve. Julian had been born in the early hours of 20 December. After five days in a coma I awoke that Christmas morning, feeling alive again, thanks to the elimination of toxins within me, flushed out by the amazing machine. Later I was wheeled down to the Maternity floor where my baby was placed in my arms. It was the most perfect and blessèd Christmas gift.

After several miserable sessions on the dialysis machine, my only-sleeping kidneys bounced back into action. Never have I experienced in my nursing career such pure joy at seeing a full urine bag hanging from the side of a bed! Before long I was back in the local hospital and in early February baby Julian and I were discharged home to my grateful husband.

Two years later I was ready to begin again!

This time getting pregnant and keeping it proved difficult. After just eight months of trying we visited our General Practitioner. Because of my past experience with Julian's birth, he considered that an early referral to a fertility clinic was advisable. I soon became pregnant, but suffered an early miscarriage. After weeks of cold douches and baggy underpants on Paul's part, and my first packet of fertility drugs still to be opened, I managed to conceive again. The pregnancy was supported with hormone injections as a second miscarriage threatened. It continued, but unlike my first pregnancy I was miserable and sick. I felt constantly uneasy and bothered, and couldn't really understand why. Should I have risked a second pregnancy and the chance of my husband being left a widower with a small son to bring up? I spent long hours in the bath stroking my bump and cooling the water with my tears.

March arrived with an abundance of daffodils and crocuses. I chose the church festival of Easter to bring my baby into the world this time. Amazingly my blasé attitude of 'the midwife who knows it all' did come into action again. I started my contractions while shopping and, far from rushing home, I stopped to talk to a friend in the local W H Smith. While Julian happily looked around the toys and books we chatted.

'Maybe we should return home,' I told her. 'I am having contractions every three minutes!'

My friend looked horrified and bade a very hasty farewell as she didn't share my profession and didn't wish to learn new skills now! So in the early hours of the next morning Grant Michael was born. I happily had all that was going to make the birth as smooth as possible, opting for an epidural anaesthetic and low forceps to facilitate delivery. No heroics this time!

Paul was with me to comfort, support and dig my nails into throughout the birth. However, he was somewhat concerned about the length of time that our new baby son turned from blue to pink, and often queried this later in Grant's life as a possible cause of his condition. I, however, never believed this to be a concern, having watched many babies take some time to get that pink flush as their new lungs and circulation began their function of providing oxygen to all the body cells.

We were delighted to have a second son as our first-born, Julian, was a good bright boy who often made us laugh. He needed a lot of adult stimulation and thrived on talking, questioning and learning. He did the latter very speedily. He loved numbers and we counted most things whatever or wherever they were. Sometimes I even found his brightness quite embarrassing as I couldn't help being a very proud, boasting, boring mother. I was so thrilled with his abilities.

At three and a half he was asking how many lots of twenty went into the minutes of a clock! I almost hoped that this new baby might not be as bright so that I wouldn't have anything to boast about.

I was such a proud mother with two lovely little boys and a doting husband and father. I felt so lucky and very happy, feeling that I had what I wanted in life.

I adored breast feeding Grant as I had felt so cheated with Julian, my illness making feeding him myself out of the question. Grant, however, took to the breast like a duck to water and the memories of those precious moments will last forever. I thrilled at feed times to sit with my feet up with my pretty baby contentedly sucking. I fed on demand day and night and, like so many other mothers, became exhausted! He never gained any pattern and by three months he became prone to frequent attacks of colic and I had to resort to gripe water and dummies. I sought help from a severe but admired health visitor. She tried hard to advise with his feeding problems. Grant, however, never settled to any pattern and our nights were always very disturbed.

I took him for his six-week check-up at the Health Centre. We had to wait in a queue of three other mothers with babies of the same age. We chatted, babes in arms, theirs quiet and mine fidgeting, his arms, legs and head moving constantly. He was not hungry or distressed. Consequently this became my first real worry about him, even though it was only of short duration. On reflection, from his autistic viewpoint, I had taken him into a potentially threatening situation. At a later stage of his life in a comparable situation he would just run and continue running until caught.

Time passed uneventfully and early milestones were achieved when they should have been, or perhaps just a little later than usual. There was one short-lived worry that was significant when Grant was four months old. I became concerned about his hearing as I felt he didn't always turn as he should to sounds. I did some simple tests and decided that I was worrying unnecessarily.

Two

When Grant was four months old I tape-recorded his sounds while he was lying on the lounge carpet cooing happily at his bright toys around him. They were lovely normal baby noises appropriate for his age. He vocalized a lot and was an adorable, smiley, contented baby. He loved being carried around on my back in a baby harness while I attended to the daily chores.

In the summer of 1975 we rented a cottage on the Fife coast in a delightful village. The back door led to a small yard and onward to a high gate that opened straight on to a picturesque beach. It was a lovely holiday. While Julian played in the sand with Paul, I walked Grant around strapped to my back. He enjoyed sucking his thumb and, as he did so, uttered guttural sounds of 'agoy agoy' extremely contentedly. We heard this to be the beginnings of speech. Paul remarked that Grant sounded as if he would have a 'dark chocolate' voice when he grew up. What a charming thought!

Julian learnt about the problems of having a little brother when Grant swooped in for his first attack, at six months old! Lying on his front in the middle of the bedroom he did a tummy shuffle over to Julian's railway track instructions – instructions that displayed several layouts that he could make. Julian spent many a happy hour in this occupation. We had hazardous tracks that wove their red plastic way around bed legs, under wardrobes and on to the landing where they would pass a little station and return from whence they came. Grant had different ideas for the instructions. Upon reaching them he scrunched them up gleefully and stuffed them into his mouth for tasting and gum hardening. I saw the beginnings of a little devil and a different character from his more serious and 'anxious to please' brother. I looked forward to watching the characters develop in my two small boys.

When Grant was eleven months old we moved house. Our town house in Henley was very large, but the garden small and pokey. The confined close of houses brought traffic noise. We loved Henley but couldn't afford the houses that went with big gardens. Our only choice was to move out towards Reading where property prices were lower. Looking back on our decisions just a few years later we can only feel that our choice of final purchase was made for us from unexplained forces that shape our lives. The hand of a guardian angel, the work of the Lord, who knows? We found the property halfway down a well-occupied bridlepath and next door to a farm. It was a small bungalow with a lovely garden and tremendous views from the large kitchen windows. Cows grazed in the field and pheasants strutted along the hedgerows. The bungalow was much smaller than our town house, but its potential for future development inspired the mind. The garden excited me, there was a lot to do and I found gardening relaxing. Paul saw the potential for a cricket lawn area and in his mind planned his future matches, teaching his small sons the basics of the game, which made me cringe for the poor cows! We could be happy here.

The village of Binfield Heath is a well-spread hamlet then centred on two shops, the Post Office, and a repair garage which used to be the village forge. There was also a public house that lay on the opposite side of the road to the Post Office. The village, was and is, situated between Henley and Reading, and there was an hourly bus service that linked the two. The school that served the area lay at the far end of our lane and was reputed to be one of the best in the district.

We moved in on a cold late-February day in 1976; a small clump of just opening daffodils situated by the front door welcomed our arrival. Our little family was here to put down its roots and create a warm and comfortable home in a safe haven away from traffic and the many hazards of life. How important that was to be; how we needed that protection to stay as a family. How that house and garden cocooned us from the outside and slowly trapped us all into the autistic world.

When Grant's first birthday came around a month after our move, we were aware that apart from 'agoy agoy' at six months he had not gone through the usual speech routines expected. We had not had the 'da da, bab ba' of early sounds and other baby babble. He had said 'all gone' on a few occasions when food had been accidentally knocked on to the floor from his highchair. The next clear words did not come until fifteen months when he said 'gink' for drink, 'keys' and 'mom'. These words lasted for two weeks then disappeared. This did worry me, as he wasn't following the normal pattern of speech development; more importantly, he didn't show much understanding of the spoken word. His physical abilities, however, were progressing. He pulled himself up on the furniture from ten months old and, although he didn't walk until he was sixteen months, he crawled everywhere and climbed higher and higher in an ever fearless way. He had a wonderful ability to be where he shouldn't, doing what he shouldn't most of the time. He would climb and reach for a plant pot until it crashed to the floor, crushing the poor flower to a twisted, broken wreck. While I picked up the mess he would gleefully crawl away to the next mischief, usually something food-orientated such as a biscuit tin which I had thought I had put out of reach.

Grant loved his food and the more mess he got into the better he enjoyed it. He could find food that you didn't know you had and would stuff it with gay abandon into his mouth. When Grant was in the garden no worm was safe. He would eat anything that came near. He preferred his ants uncooked and preferably on a bed of soil with the odd pebble thrown in for crunchiness. Flowers, berries and leaves were tested for their poisonous qualities. Usually Grant or the plants were guarded so closely that thankfully, we never, proved these.

He learnt to unscrew the top off a bottle at ten months old. This is extremely early for this skill, but he had gained the ability from winding musical boxes which delighted him and kept him happy for long spells. Concentration on other toys was non-existent; he was usually too busy looking for mischief. If there was anything he should not get he would find it, spill, eat or break it!

In his first year he would love to look at his image and would gaze for long times into a specially made baby mirror. In his second year he refused to look at himself.

He made overtures to Julian at about sixteen months in the form of rough and tumble games. He would jump on his brother in a wrestle, but Julian did not welcome these activities so Grant gave up. His talents for unscrewing tops and winding toys meant we had to be more vigilant with cleaning products including his own baby cleansers and creams. Food and drink items were also unsafe. It is surprising how much mess a jar of Marmite (a dark brown sandwich spread) can make on a gold-coloured carpet, as can Copydex glue, the remains of which can still be seen today, hidden under a bed, on the carpet now cut down to fit a small bedroom.

Grant always slept neatly covered. Most babies would fall into an exhausted sleep where they fell, be it upside down or whatever. Our little son always would be found tucked under his duvet or blanket with his head at the top of the bed. By his third year he would prefer to hide right under the covers, shutting out the world around him.

In the early months I didn't worry too much as he kept me too busy to have time to think. One day, when Grant was eighteen months old, my mother was staying with us and spoke her thoughts, which brought my underlying worries to the surface. 'I'm wondering whether there is something wrong with Grant,' she said one day in the kitchen as I had just extricated a fine-cut glass goblet from his hand, which he had obtained from the inside of a high cupboard in the living-room.

'What do you mean?' I retorted. 'All children of this age are into everything, some more than others.'

'He wanders aimlessly around the hall and seems to be lost in himself,' she said carefully. 'The items he gets don't have a purpose; he just grabs them and drops them. Also, when Julian was his age he would be looking eagerly for his father coming home, but Grant doesn't even turn to see who it is when he comes through the door.'

My blood froze! She was right and she was putting into words my deepest worries. I had dismissed these concerns and rationalized the reasons for his lack of language and slight strangeness.

Paul's mother, Edna, had also expressed concerns mainly related to his lack of speech. My underlying worry was that he didn't understand. Speech couldn't possibly come if he was unable to comprehend the world around him.

Until Grant had become mobile I had done some agency nursing work. This had mainly been with a lovely lady, Mrs Hughes, who had rheumatoid arthritis. She was a good listener, usually over a bedbath. I decided to call on her after leaving Julian at playgroup, which was next to her house. I told her of my mother's fears and watched her closely to observe her reaction.

'I see Grant as an exaggerated form of Paul,' she said. 'He is often remote and in his own thoughts.'

'I know,' I replied. 'It is part of his charm that made me fall in love with him, so maybe Grant will settle and join our world soon.'

Paul was an accountant, and had passed his exams to become a chartered accountant just four weeks after we had met. He had a great calming influence on me and I found that I was very relaxed in his company. He was tall, fair and gentle. He enjoyed playing rugby and tennis but not too seriously and had a good sense of fun. But he was vague and remote at times and I would often find it hard to talk through a subject because he was still thinking his own thoughts! We married at my home town in Merseyside about one year after meeting at a cricket club dance held locally.

Paul quickly obtained a job in the city with a large firm of accountants and commuted daily. This complemented my lifestyle and career, as being the local district nurse and midwife was demanding with long hours. We had a charming cottage in a quaint part of Henley which went with my job. This gave us the opportunity to save for our own property.

Paul didn't enjoy commuting or working in a large firm, so after two years found fresh employment within industry. This was at a well-known company that had several subsidiaries, one of which made children's clothes – the ones with the ladybird motif [for the older reader]! When our children came along, the factory shop fitted them out nicely with their slightly flawed rejects.

Though I talked to Paul and shared with him my concerns about Grant, I don't think he could appreciate the implications of where these problems might lead.

Now fears had been expressed I began to watch Grant all the time and I worried. I took him to our doctor. 'I am not really sure whether I should be worried, but the grandparents are and perhaps what they are saying is true. I have brought him to you to see what you think. One moment I have definitely decided that there is something wrong and then I think I am worrying unnecessarily.'

My doctor looked at me with a smile and said, 'We always listen to grandparents' opinions; they sometimes see things that mothers and fathers don't.'

We discussed the worries and problems, particularly Grant's lack of speech. He listened sympathetically and looked at Grant and said that he really felt there was nothing to be concerned about. Julian was a bright boy and I was comparing the two children. Grant was obviously developing much more slowly, but after admiring his good looks he told me to go away and reassure the grandparents. I had a lovely child. So I went away and, for a short time, I was somewhat happier.

Grant didn't get any easier. I spent most of my time watching and running after him. He was so active and mischievous. It was the very hot summer of 1976 when temperatures soared to near 100°F and most of the time was spent in the garden. One day I lost sight of him briefly. I searched around but couldn't see him anywhere. About one very long minute later, I heard baby noises and noticed the gate slightly open. There crawling up the stony lane and several yards away was a very happy baby boy looking for an adventure! On reflection, I realize this was the beginning of an obsession to escape, which lasted for several years.

Julian, Grant and I frequently sat inside the playpen on the lawn so that I could read a story to Julian without Grant disappearing. Grant showed interest when shown pictures in books, particularly in this situation where he had no option as he couldn't escape! This was probably a form of 'holding therapy' which I shall discuss later.

Both our children were constantly cuddled and kissed and, as Paul and I were both demonstrative, they probably got a lion's share. Grant liked being kissed but didn't try and give anything back, not even sloppy wet ones! That did not deter us; when he was caught he was cuddled!

Julian, like many children of three or four, was constantly talking. Question after question tumbled out from his inquisitive head and I often felt the need to escape for a few moments' peace. When I took Grant into his room to change his nappy, I found I was doing this in complete silence and had to force myself to say something to Grant. I didn't realize it at the time, but Grant was not giving me the usual signals necessary for a natural response.

I read up my medical books to see what they said about children's speech and how it developed. I homed in on the normal exceptions in order to give a rational explanation and relieve my worries. I knew that speech would only come when he understood what was being said to him. Physically he was so perfect and so much seemed to fit with normal development. Surely if he were retarded his whole development would be impaired. I wondered whether his inappropriate responses were due to deafness. Grant heard the pantry door open if he was at the furthest end of the house, food still being his highest priority in life. Surely he couldn't smell the door opening! He ignored his name, was always running and the word 'no' held no significance for him at all. He dribbled profusely and still posseted (regurgitated small amounts of) his food. His clothes needed changing constantly. The posseting consisted of smelly acidic juices, which made small round deposits that stained and tainted the carpet and furniture. Because of the need for constant vigilance, I usually had to wait until he was in bed to clean up, by which time the damage had been done and the stains were hard to remove. My explanation for this posseting was his hyperactivity and the fact that he spent a lot of time on all fours. His food and drink did not get a chance to digest properly. This was probably a reasonable explanation as he outgrew this problem as soon as he stayed upright, which was soon after his second birthday.

When Grant was twenty months old I found a book at the local book shop called *For the Love of Ann*. I became riveted in this small book, which was written by Ann's father. It was illustrated with pictures of a pretty and very normal looking girl, Ann, who was autistic. So much of Ann's story fitted the picture of Grant. The book told how her father had helped his daughter come out of her autistic cocoon and live a relatively normal life. He approached this in a controversial way, as his methods were to slap her very hard in order to stimulate her senses, which were dulled and affected in peculiar ways (as is the case with autism). It worked for them.

I found I was very emotionally affected by this book. So much applied to Grant, but then there was a lot that didn't. This confused me, but I later learnt that children with autism, although displaying linking similarities, are as different as any other set of individuals. Autism manifests itself in varying degrees of severity resulting in a whole spectrum of often unrelated problems for parents and carers. Ann screamed, shouted and bit. She ignored her parents completely, but did simple tasks such as line up all her toys and count them. Grant was, in contrast, a sunny, happy child, who enjoyed a cuddle and didn't 'play' with any toys at all, not even to line them up. I could never get him to stop long enough to concentrate on a toy let alone play with it.

As a district nurse in Henley, I used to regularly drive past a large building on the outskirts of town, called Smith Hospital. I had heard it was used for the care and, through its associated school, education of children with autism. At the time this meant absolutely nothing to me. Somebody explained that the children had problems with communicating and were very difficult to manage. After reading the book on Ann I started linking the two, but still had very little idea what it was all about. My nursing training had never touched on the subject and I wondered why.

I belonged to a group called 'The National Housewives' Register' which met to provide stimulating interest to women who were frustrated by being constantly tied to house and children. Amazingly, a speaker who came one week worked as a teacher at Smith Hospital School. Her name was Caroline Simmonds. She was bright and cheerful; her very interesting talk included a demonstration of some of the work that the children had produced. Grant at this time was about eighteen months old. She agreed that my son could have a problem, but nobody at this stage, including most doctors and specialists, would be willing to say he might be autistic. It was my first meeting with Caroline. She was to feature strongly throughout Grant's life and play a very significant and helpful part in his progress, education and care.

As time went by, my concerns increased. One day my health visitor called for a routine visit.

'Please watch him for a few minutes,' I implored. 'He still walks around with his hands up like a baby who has just learnt to walk.' Grant was now twenty-two months old and had been walking for six months. 'He still loves to crawl, there is no speech and in many ways he is still like a baby.'

She watched, while he tottered at great speed, hands held aloft, and completely ignored my call of, 'Grant, come here to mummy.'

The health visitor replied, 'He's only a baby, still. Don't worry, you are just comparing him with Julian. He is developing much more slowly, but he'll be fine. We will see you at his two-year-old check, that will be in early April, and the doctor will assess him then.'

Oh dear! Two months to watch and worry about him without support. I already felt that I was becoming rather isolated. Going to someone's house for a cup of coffee was no pleasure as he was into everything. The things that attracted him most were the biscuits and drinks. He didn't just go for them, he grabbed and scattered everything, sending biscuits, coffee and juice flying in all directions. They would be cleared, but it would happen again and again. No wonder we became unwelcome. Julian had reached five and had now started at the local primary school, so thankfully was not totally isolated.

I became very good friends with another Caroline, Caroline Print, the wife of the local vicar, Norman. Julian and Ben (her eldest) had been together at the local playgroup and had now both moved on to the primary school. Caroline started up a 'Mother and Toddler' group in the local church hall, and this was somewhere that I could take Grant. Here he had some space and could run around without too much disruption to others. The toys, however, were ignored. While other mums talked to each other and rescued their little ones from toy tussles, bumps, and so on, I spent the whole time trying to find something that might stimulate or interest Grant. If I wasn't doing that I was frantically retrieving a drink or biscuit from a giggling Grant and returning it to its crying owner!

His hyperactivity was quite amazing. I not only needed eyes in the back of my head but on either side, and a pair looking downward from my bottom would have been useful too! I have never known a child who could get up to so much mischief in such a short time. Paul, one evening, wrote down an account of a small section of my day.

Thirty Minutes in the Life of a Little Boy 5-1-77

9.15 a.m.   Quiet spell. Discovered sitting amongst spilt washing powder in pantry and still emptying the packet ...

9.25 a.m.   Bang heard. Unable to enter his bedroom, as he had knocked over the bedside cabinet on to its side and this was blocking the door. Once in the room and furniture replaced, child lost briefly and found sitting amongst the contents of his nappy bucket, which had been turned out. Talcum powder found sprinkled all over the carpet and himself. Jar of cream found in one hand, the lid of which was in the other ...

9.40 a.m. Crash heard in the kitchen above the noise of Jimmy Young. Julian sent to investigate. Discovered Grant sitting on the kitchen floor rocking in time with the music, mouth crammed full with Christmas pudding ...

In March an appointment was sent from the clinic in Henley for Grant's two-year-old check. My list was long: I had prepared myself for this visit, viewing it with trepidation. I was scared at what the doctor might tell me. Our name was called; clutching my bit of paper in one hand and firmly gripping my wriggling child with the other, we looked for the doctor's room. The doctor was a female who had recently joined the practice. She was pleasant and approachable. I tried to hold my very fidgety son on my lap, while I ran through the long list of what I felt he should be doing by now and wasn't. I told her about his hyperactivity and our worries about his development. She asked what I felt about his hearing. I explained about his love of food and how he heard the pantry door open from afar, and other clues that indicated he was hearing correctly. She asked me other questions and watched Grant who decided, contrarily, to behave quite well! The simple tasks which she asked him to do he did, just to prove that his mother was neurotic. It is amazing how children have that wonderful ability to make you look stupid! We finished the consultation. The doctor felt that a reassessment in six months was all that was needed and that hopefully he would catch up. He was probably just a 'slow developer'. How many times had I heard those words before!

We made our way home. Was I reassured? I didn't want to be told there was something wrong with my child, but on the other hand I still wasn't happy.

Three days later I walked into his bedroom. He had his back

towards the door and he didn't turn when I entered. This was an apt moment to test his hearing. There was a toy telephone behind him in the cot so I dialed some numbers which rang loudly with each turn. He didn't stir! Horrified, I rattled the cot bars, but he still didn't turn! I clapped my hands – no reaction! Walking in front of him into his line of vision Grant's little face lit up. I lifted him from his cot, cuddled and talked to him. My heart ached, my stomach churned. Whatever it was there was something very wrong with our son. I now had the job of convincing my doctor and the health visitor. We needed help.

The next morning I rang through to the doctor who had performed his two-year check-up. I told her of the test I had performed. She agreed we needed to do something now and not wait any longer. She would make an appointment with the audiology unit in Reading and this would be our first step. We now had to wait for the appointment to come through and a few days later it arrived. It was timed for about six weeks hence.

The weeks that followed, while awaiting the appointment, were probably some of the most testing times for me. How I wanted someone who was knowledgeable on childhood development to sit in my house for an hour and watch him as I watched him. Knowing that there was something wrong, but not knowing what, was unbearable. Feeling utterly helpless to speed up anything and watching, watching him and trying to fathom out the nature of the handicap that afflicted this beautiful child. Watching him and constantly studying him from every angle; feeling frightened and alone. I shared these worries with Paul, but he wasn't at home all day feeling so desperately helpless ...

Paul was not sure how to cope with the situation so his way of dealing with it was to cut off from it. He had taken up an old hobby of aviation and got lost in its lure. He was more interested in talking planes than Grant – it was less worrying. He would go out for whole days at the weekend leaving me to struggle with the two boys and the worries of the added psychological concerns of what next and what would happen in the future. When at home he did give Julian a lot of his attention, as we realized that, not surprisingly, he was missing out. Julian loved board games and lots of adult stimulation so we always made sure that he had at least an hour of undivided attention, usually when Grant went to bed.

One week prior to the visit to audiology, a letter arrived delaying the appointment a further six weeks, owing to staff taking holiday leave! It really was too much. Now we knew there was something the matter, the days had been agonizing, and I wanted answers and ways to help. If somebody could tell me his problem and show me what to do, then I could get on with it. I phoned our doctor, with whom I had worked, and knew well.

'Please help,' I implored him. 'I have had this letter, putting back his appointment. It will be three months by the time we see anyone and we know there is a problem. If there is something very wrong with Grant we have to know, as the longer we wait the longer we put off doing anything to help. If he is autistic, we have been told the earlier we begin correct education the better are his chances. We will do anything, go anywhere, pay anything, but somebody must be able to tell us something.' I felt desperate and near to tears.

'Right,' he said slowly. 'I think the quickest way into audiology would be a direct referral from a speech therapist. I will arrange for you to see one at the local hospital on Monday, then you will be referred on as an urgent case.'

The first week in June, Grant two years and two months, found us in the audiology department. The doctor who ran this department was interested in Grant. He found his hearing completely normal. I told him I worried that he might be autistic, but he said that he knew all about autism. In his opinion he wasn't.

'How did he know?' I muttered to myself. 'He hasn't watched him like I have; he doesn't know the problems of my little boy.' I would have loved to have believed him correct.

I thought that would be the end of our visit, but no. We were then directed into a room and told to wait, for we were now to see their speech therapist. This young, but confident woman, brought in a file and started working her way though a series of statutory questions. The sort of questions that I would have so liked to have been asked before.

About halfway through her list she stopped and looked at me. She paused, then quietly said, 'Grant certainly does have a problem!' I didn't know whether to laugh or cry. Somebody at long last had seen what in our hearts we knew. It was official; now somebody might do something to help him and give us some guidance on how to deal with his behaviour. I thanked her profusely and was told that we would now be referred to the paediatrician.

Paul, unfortunately, was unable to make this visit. He had just begun a new job as an accountant in the overseas division of a company called Metal Box, based in Reading. We didn't feel he should take time off so soon for hospital visits. When I told him the news he, like me, felt relief at having someone admit what we knew to be true. It was odd to find relief in being told that your child is handicapped, but it made us realize that we had suspected it for a long time. Now what did life have to offer us? This was quite a challenge that we were taking on but, now that the medical profession had seen the problem, they could give us the right guidance and we would be able to make our little boy better. I would show them it could be done. We would defeat whatever was the matter with him and I would leave no stone unturned.

The latter statement at least was true.

Three

My career as a nurse was now on hold. This didn't concern me as I firmly believed that a mother should be around for her children in pre-school years, if at all possible. I had, however, done a course in family planning when I was pregnant with Julian. In the latter half of the course I felt a label attached to my greatly expanded stomach should read, 'This one was planned!' But needless to say I had to submit to quite a few witty, if not derisive, comments from the girls who attended the clinic! This course would give me options to do some medical work while in the throes of bringing up my family. Not only that, but I had worked in Africa with starving and dying children and I was convinced that many of the world's problems could be solved by teaching and providing good family planning methods.

In Africa I saw women go through childbirth ten to fifteen times in order to end up with two or three children that they could raise to maturity. These women also worked the fields and their reduced strength from repeated pregnancies affected the resulting crop yields. A family planning and education programme could have led to fewer babies and consequently better health, which in turn would give increased crops that would feed and protect her children. An idealistic thought, maybe, but a motivating one, even though I was now a long way from Africa!

When Julian was just two, a vacancy had become available for a nurse on a Monday evening. The clinic was classed as an advisory clinic for young people and I enjoyed the work. The clinic fitted in well with Paul, who worked flexi-time, leaving him available to take over the care of Julian. After Grant's birth I continued with this clinic and also took on an evening hospital session on a Thursday, where contraceptive coils were fitted. This work became invaluable as a form of escape; I returned into the normal world for a few hours a week.

Following the reports from the audiology department, it was not too long before we were seen by the paediatric consultant. He required quite a few tests to be done including several blood analyses, for phenylketonuria, dietary, chemical and chromosomal defects. For these we had to go to a hospital ward for half a day. Some sedation was given and I enjoyed the pleasures of a long cuddle from my sleeping child, recovering from the traumas inflicted. I also had a quiet moment to reflect on him, his vulnerability and his complete reliance on us.

Our next referral was to a doctor who was attached to the paediatric unit on a part-time basis to assess problems similar to Grant's. She asked me lots of questions and gave Grant simple tests to do. He failed miserably at most things. He was not in the mood today to perform in his usual contrary way. She asked me if he held his hands in the air when I removed his clothes before bath or bed.

'Yes,' I replied.

'Are you sure?' she retorted. 'I can't believe he does that.'

'Do you think he might be autistic?' I asked tentatively.

'Oh no,' she said, 'he looks at you not through you, and he cuddles. Your child is mentally retarded and I advise you to move into Berkshire as there are no suitable schools or educational assessment centres in South Oxfordshire.'

That seemed to be just about the end of the interview. We left very dejected. Those words 'mentally retarded', so cruel and harsh, would remain with me forever. The next day I took him for a swim and, as it was easier for me to leave him in his pushchair instead of walking up steps, I pushed him up the grass bank in his chair. An irate groundsman glared at me and bellowed, 'Get that chair off the grass.'

I looked at his glowering face and said very defensively, 'If I take him out I won't be able to manage – he's mentally retarded.'

There! I had said those awful words and they were connected with my son. I think the look on my face must have said everything, as the man looked down at the attractive blond-haired, blue-eyed boy in the chair and said quietly, "Ere, I'll help you, you just have to ask.'

Grant was over two and a half years old and we were well into the autumn when we went back to the paediatrican for our next appointment. He had a friendly, round face with gentle eyes that looked at us over the top of half-moon glasses. Paul was with us this time and we wondered what this appointment held for us. The consultant took a deep breath, then very slowly and carefully said, 'I am very sorry to inform you that Grant is mentally handicapped.'

I wanted to giggle. All that preparation for that speech. Not only had we been trying to tell the professionals that there was a problem for the last nine months, but his colleague (who had assessed Grant) could not have been more direct on the subject! He did say, though, that he was inclined to agree with us that Grant certainly might be autistic. He wanted us to see yet another doctor, this one being a child psychiatrist, Dr O'Gorman – an expert on autism.

'What exactly is autism?' I asked the paediatrician.

'Well,' he said, scratching his chin, 'well, um, ummm, well, actually I think you had better ask Dr O'Gorman. Autism is a very hard condition to describe, and he will be far better able to tell you than me.'

Another doctor, another wait and we were still no further on. Grant was now two years, nine months and his behaviour was getting worse. His abilities, particularly in communication and play, had not progressed at all. He had other noticeable sensory impairments, one of which was an apparent indifference to pain. If he fell or cut himself he didn't cry so I didn't know of an injury until I found it. One day I noticed a dried run of blood down the back of his neck and a large dried blood stain on the back of his shirt. Rooting through his hair I found a deep gash on the top of his scalp. I questioned Julian who told me that Grant had been under the climbing frame when a toy gun had been dropped from the top, straight on to his head! As he didn't cry he presumed that he was all right.

We worried that he would seriously hurt himself without knowing it. He became increasingly fearless and climbed to greater heights daily, but he was very sure footed and hardly ever fell from these escapades. I found him swinging from the top bars of the climbing frame and if he let go he would have fallen about five feet. I ran to him screaming, 'Hold on, hold on, Mummy's coming,' and he did, as he had no fear.

His increasing obsession with escape was demonstrated by climbing on to windowsills, opening window catches and clambering fearlessly through, letting himself down to the ground with great skill. Had we lived in a two-storey house I am sure it would have made no difference, and probably we would have found him sitting, or more likely running, over the roof! [It is not rare to find an autistic child sitting on the top of a house!]

It was about this time that I became pregnant again. We had not used contraception for a long time as we had hoped for another child, although we hadn't deeply thought about it or discussed the consequences, being so preoccupied with our existing family. I was thrilled, but when I thought sensibly about it another baby would be impracticable. How could I extend myself any further to look after a baby *and* watch Grant; as for Julian, he was already being denied the attention he deserved. Paul and I had little time for our own relationship, which had to take a back seat in view of the demands placed on us by our children.

Seven and a half weeks into the pregnancy I was hit by a severe bout of diarrhoea and sickness, which brought on a miscarriage. I was desperately upset as I knew I could never allow a pregnancy to happen again as the consequences were too dire to contemplate.

Paul was relieved that there was not going to be another baby, as he, too, was very concerned at the thought of us trying to cope in our situation. However, he did not have my maternal hormones, which at that moment were going quite crazy! We realized that had the pregnancy continued, our family risked destruction and we were still very much united despite our difficulties which increased daily.

In later years I was often consulted by couples on the wisdom of trying for a third baby when there was already an autistic child in their family. Could they cope? I became very involved with families in similar situations to our own and I was ready to advise, if at all possible. No couple can make a decision without a thorough appraisal of their own situation, bearing in mind present difficulties and those likely to manifest themselves in the future. I think I would advise any reader seeking guidance on family size to look at all the factors influencing the family's capability to stay complete, such as the husband's ability to cope, your own limitations and your childrens' characters and needs. In a 'normal' family, financial considerations although important, are not as crucial as they are here. A handicapped child will receive a state benefit, but that doesn't go very far when you take into account the extra financial demands imposed on the family.

We found our friends gradually deserted us and only the true ones remained. Maybe that sounds harsh, but our isolation was inflicted by being totally wrapped in Grant's difficulties. We couldn't visit people with him, as staying in another house would be out of the question. Babysitters could not cope with Grant's behaviour and I wouldn't risk damage to them, him or the house by leaving him. Anyone not used to Grant would be a nervous wreck within the hour. Friends had to come to us, but the visits were not relaxed and conversation was difficult.

Some people can accept abnormality better than others. This can be desperately hurtful, but this is one of the realities that a parent in this situation has to accept. Our only babysitter was Paul's mother, Edna, who would do everything in her power to help us. We didn't call on her often, but she bravely came for the occasional function at Julian's school where we would let our hair down for a few hours. My sense of freedom increased the enjoyment and I often felt that we were experiencing something that others didn't – a pleasure that surpassed words and for just one evening out!

We were now becoming isolated within our four walls and the fence that surrounded our garden. Grant was active and destructive, though not deliberately. If we did visit people it was impossible to socialize as our attention was focused on the unpredictable behaviour of our child. If they lived in a two-storey house, he became obsessed with going up and down the stairs which were a novelty to him, as we lived in a bungalow.

If a child has no play skills and an attention span of no more than fifteen seconds, he needs constant encouragement if he is to learn the art of play that would be natural for other children. I would try so hard to find something that might interest him. Our walls were adorned with brightly coloured posters, which I used daily to stimulate his interest and encourage words. Occasionally, he would repeat a word or come out with something quite unexpectedly. One day we were carefully looking at a lovely poster on the wall that Paul had brought home from work. It advertised Ladybird childrens' wear, and depicted gnomes and elves working in the forest with lots of cute animals and, of course, ladybirds. Holding Grant in my arms we went to the picture to talk about it. Before I had time to say anything he excitedly and clearly said 'ladybird!'

I would bring out and encourage all manner of bright stimulating toys, but I could not hold his attention. I would crawl round the hall floor pushing a bright red bus and saying 'brum, brum', but before I got to the second 'brum' Grant had gone and I was left playing roads and buses alone!

There was a lady who lived further down our lane who ran a small playgroup. She said Grant should come to her group as she was very good with children and they always did things for her! I told her that Grant was very different and his attention span minute. She was insistent that I should give her a try, so I delivered him to her half an hour after the usual starting time when the other children would be settled in.

When I think about the sight that greeted me on my return I can't help but laugh! She opened the door and chaos reigned. She looked extremely dishevelled and fraught, the children were high and giggly and toys were everywhere. Grant was halfway up the stairs and was just about to descend, probably for the umpteenth time, by sliding down on his tummy. He arrived at the bottom and collapsed in uncontrollable, highly infectious laughter. The other children caught up in Grant's mood rolled around in their chairs giggling happily, their usual controlled morning of activity totally turned upside down. I gathered up my happy child, containing his wild arms and legs against my body, and beat a hasty retreat. Not surprisingly she told me that she would not be able to keep him on at the playgroup!

Three of our friends got together and decided that if they took it in turns to have Grant for two hours each, once a week, it would give me just a little relief. I was so grateful to them, as two hours a week of relief was better than nothing and that time was pure bliss!

Paul was still on flexi-time so he could be home early and ready to support and help. Another wonderful bonus was that his company had a superb leisure centre in the basement of their office. We had the use of their large generously heated pool and pleasant changing rooms and took advantage of this facility as often as we could. Swimming was something we could participate in as a family and there were not many things that fitted this bill. I would take the children after school and on a Saturday morning. Julian could have lessons there and, although he did swim well already, he improved his technique and learnt some horrific forms of diving!

Grant loved the water, and swimming used lots of energy, although his obsession for escaping meant that he was always looking for opportunities to get out. With safety armbands secure, I placed him in the centre of the pool. Then I could swim around him until he reached the edge and return him to the middle, if I caught him in time. Sometimes, however, he got there first and clambered out, running as fast as he could. Often he disappeared into the men's changing rooms and this is where I joined Grant in shutting out the world and everyone else around me in order to retrieve him!

The summer of 1976 was exceptionally hot, and when temperatures soared again in 1977 into the high 80s Fahrenheit, the children spent the days in the garden cooling down in the spray from the hosepipe. Our family holiday was booked at a campsite on Exmoor, chosen for its mixture of lovely countryside and proximity to the beaches. We had a large tent which had an inner lining with zips, so that the worry of losing Grant in the middle of the night under the edges of the tent would not be a problem! The site was large and safe providing a lot of running space and we had soon pitched our tent. With Grant strapped firmly into his pushchair, I arranged my camp kitchen and our sleeping gear, while Paul took Julian to the nearby farm for milk and eggs. Once the tent was prepared I released Grant out of the pushchair to let him run around. He headed straight for the kitchen compartment scattering my beautifully stacked tins and grabbing and scrunching up the sandwiches I had prepared for lunch. Retrieving the mushy remaining crumbs I gave him a sharp smack on his leg which as usual made no difference, as he giggled with glee. I picked him up and took him to the centre of the field and deposited him on to the ground. He leapt to his feet and ran as fast as he could back to the tent to wreak more havoc.

I looked up to the heavens for some solace only to see some extremely black storm clouds gathering! Our beautiful summer of 1977 had decided to terminate with our holiday and oh how it rained! Coping with an extremely active small boy with severe behaviour problems is difficult enough at the best of times, but in a tent in the pouring rain, protected only by canvas that would leak if touched, was practically impossible. We awoke the next morning to damp beds caused by the touched tent sides letting in water. Going out in the car was the best option and this we did, spreading out some of the essential wet things into the back of our estate where the roof sloped and would catch warmth from any sun. But it didn't appear that day or for the next three days and by now we had run out of dry things to wear. We decided that we would have to return home.

That night brought the biggest storm of all and we awoke with the bedding floating in water. As we hated to be defeated and the sky looked brighter, we planned to have the day away from the site then come back and pack up and go home. We had been out about an hour when the sun shone bright and strong! We paddled in the sea, enjoyed the beach and our spirits were quickly lifted. Our clothes in the car dried and we relaxed, feeling warm and happy. We still knew we would have to return home as we had no dry bedding, so mid-afternoon we returned to the campsite to pack.

As we drove on to the field a wonderful picture met our eyes. We had had a visit from a good Samaritan (or two) and our bedding was laid out around the tent resting on groundsheets and chairs. I went from item to item feeling for wetness and exclaiming with delight when none was found. Absolutely everything was bone dry! The people who had performed this kind act had departed the site, but a message had been left on the table secured by a tin of baked beans saying that they hoped that we didn't mind them going into our tent, but as the sun looked set to stay out they thought that our things had a good chance of drying if they spread them out for us. We couldn't even thank them, but that single act restored my faith in humanity.

The late autumn of 1977, Grant just over two and a half, saw our first visit to Dr O'Gorman in Melrose House in Reading. We were ushered into a room until he was ready to see us. This room was very drab but there was a good selection of toys, including a baby bath full of sand. Sitting in this room often made me wonder if we were being watched by two-way mirrors to see if I played correctly with my child. I am sure now that we weren't but, in the past, autism has been put down to faulty bonding with the mother, so I couldn't help feeling that I might be on trial here too!

Before too long we were joined by Susan Wagstaff, who was

Dr O'Gorman's social worker. After a brief introductory chat, I discovered that she was American, very pleasant and quick to put me at ease. Dr O'Gorman came into the room and introduced himself to me and to Grant, who by now was trying desperately hard to escape from the room. I tried holding him on my lap, but to no avail as this was all too threatening and he just wanted out! I had taken the pushchair as it was an important interview and I suggested that it would be easier if he were fastened into it. Dr O'Gorman readily agreed as by now Grant had swept his desk clear of paper clips, pens, etc., and had also grabbed and broken the pearls around my neck so that they danced and bounced merrily over the desk and joined the scattered paper clips on the floor!

'Quite an active little lad!' Dr O'Gorman addressed Grant. 'And a good-looking chap too. Would you like to play with this?' and he offered Grant a little car. Grant looked at it very briefly then dropped it into the mêlée on the floor. It was picked up and passed back to him. This time he twisted it back and forth in his hands and finding the car had a little door that opened and shut he continued to waggle the door to and fro, shutting and opening it and looking at the car quite intently. Dr O'Gorman watched him carefully and at the same time asked me for past history. That was becoming a well-repeated story!

The whole consultation must have lasted about 30 minutes and his conclusions were that Grant, in his opinion, had been through an autistic phase, which can happen to some children but then they come out of it. He felt that Grant was now on his way out and would gradually improve. He felt that understanding and speech would come. He wanted to see us again in six weeks.

As Susan Wagstaff saw us from the premises after listening to our story, she said she felt we were far from being out of the woods yet. She would come and see us at home and assess our needs.

I should have gone home overjoyed, but I didn't. I still felt that Dr O'Gorman hadn't seen Grant as he really was, the way we saw him.

Three weeks later, one cold dark evening in November, an amazing coincidence occurred when someone knocked on our front door. This in itself is a rare occurrence as we are in a remote location, but for that person to be Dr O'Gorman was a surprise to say the least. He had called in his capacity as an assessment officer for people who had applied for a state benefit; just another string to his bow!

He was invited in and given a cup of tea. I could not have been more prepared for a doctor of his standing as I had been experimenting with a large cardboard box by cutting out holes in strategic places. Julian had used this box in a number of different ways and was getting an enormous amount of pleasure from the imaginative games such a simple thing can bring! We had used the holes to encourage Grant to post things but as usual this was not easy despite Julian being under the box and making all manner of interesting noises when something was dropped through the hole onto him.

Dr O'Gorman sat on the settee, slowly drinking his tea, filling out his long form, and watching. I didn't know how much he was watching but he was taking everything in, the lack of play or invention, understanding or speech. He was seeing our little boy as he really was and he was the right person – in fact, the only person in our area that had expert knowledge of autism. So when we made our next visit to Melrose House, Dr O'Gorman apologized profusely, saying that he thought Grant was probably severely autistic.

Now we needed answers!

Four

Henley toy library was set up by Melba Pitt in 1973 and I learnt of its existence through a friend. They operated from the clinic in Henley on a Saturday morning and offered a lending service and, manned by volunteers, gave parents a break for an hour or so to do their shopping. As toys to suit Grant were hard, if not impossible, to find, I felt it was a good opportunity to borrow them to see if we could interest him in anything. There was a long play tunnel made from large rings and plastic, which he enjoyed crawling through. We took it home and both children got fun from it, particularly Julian, who was imaginative, using the tunnel to run from a home-made tent to adjoin other devices, thus extending its capabilities. Grant had no inventive skills and used it only as a means to develop his physical prowess and, as with the toy car, there was no real purpose to his play.

We borrowed jigsaws that had big sections and large knobs to assist lifting the pieces in and out, which altered the picture, changing it to a fresh one that lay underneath. Grant liked clear and well-defined pictures that looked like what they were supposed to represent; for this reason he took to the Ladybird series of children's books. At this stage it was the very simple picture books with single words of 'boy', 'girl', 'dog', 'cat', 'cow', 'flower', etc. We would try to get him to point to the picture and to say the word or sound, and occasionally he would utter something or make a noise that sounded very similar to the word or sound required. Anything he said or pointed to was very rewarding and we would talk about it excitedly for the rest of the day.

Both children liked going to the toy library as siblings were welcomed, giving Julian the opportunity and pleasure of playing with some super toys, which he was allowed to borrow for a week or two. This also gave Julian an invaluable advantage over his friends, which was some compensation for the hardship of living in a handicapped family.

It was here at the toy library that I met Pam Chaplin who worked at Smith Hospital School as an occupational therapist. The voluntary work she did at the toy library was invaluable. She had been observing Grant and was aware of our hospital visits. Therefore she was very interested to hear that we had seen Dr O'Gorman and that he thought Grant to be autistic, which she, too, had felt was the problem as she had worked with these children for many years.

'So what exactly is autism?' I asked her. 'He isn't mentally retarded, is he?'

'Oh, yes, he is,' she told me. 'He is retarded through his autism, as it impairs normal development. If he can't understand and sort out the world around him then he won't be able to learn and he will get progressively behind in comparison with his peers. He ignores the other children and associates mainly with adults which is a common feature with autistic children. You are lucky that you have a good relationship with him. Many autistic children reject their parents completely which makes it extremely hard and hurtful for them. As their behaviour is so erratic and difficult, caring for them is very stressful. I think you are managing marvellously.'

It was good to have her vote of confidence, but I was not happy with what she was telling me.

'Will he get better with lots of help?' I asked.

'No!' she replied bluntly. 'Once autistic they are autistic for life, but Grant could improve quite considerably. It is very hard to tell at his age just how much improvement he will make and what to degree he will be affected.'

I was shocked by her words, but glad she had answered my questions as honestly as she could. That is what we wanted to know, but it still was so undefined. What would he be like at six, ten or twenty? Would he have any sort of independent life or would he always be dependent on us and others for his care?

We searched the libraries for information on autism, but there was little written. The book that I reached into most was written by Dr Lorna Wing, a consultant psychiatrist who had specialized in autism. This gave clear and precise information, but no long-term answers. It appeared that it was a fairly recently defined condition and that little research had yet been done, although work was currently being undertaken at Nottingham University. I found that local health workers had little or nothing to offer, as like me they had had no lectures or discussions within nursing training. Likewise, doctors had only had the subject briefly touched on within their psychiatric tuition, unless they had chosen to specialize in the condition or had worked in Mental Health. My own health visitor admitted she felt helpless, but was happy to deliver my incontinence pads and rubber pants as toilet training was out of the question with Grant; he didn't even know what the word 'toilet' meant, let alone the use of it!

There were a lot of people who tried to help such as the charity MENCAP whose welfare worker came around to see if there was any support she could offer. I had to repeat my story so many times, but ultimately we were on our own to cope as best we could.

How often I reflected on my experiences in Africa. There I had worked as a volunteer in a mission hospital and frequently found myself left to my own devices when the doctors were away making bush visits and I had to do my best whatever the outcome. Often the results were satisfying and I could look upon them as an achievement, but there had been other times when more expert help would have resulted in a better outcome. In our situation I was sure that there must be someone who knew something that could help to break though this awful barrier between us. So many people told me that they felt it must be something small because he looked so normal, and if people saw him only briefly they couldn't see that anything was wrong. You felt that if he fell over and banged his head badly he might knock something back into position, then he would be fine … if only!

Dr O'Gorman's social worker, Susan Wagstaff, offered us the best and most positive help. Just over two miles away on the outskirts of Reading was a hostel, recently opened, to provide respite care to families whose children suffered from severe mental or physical disabilities. The care offered was anything the family needed – be it an hour to cover a dental appointment or two weeks for a complete holiday break. She had put in an application for Grant's needs quite quickly after our second visit to Dr O'Gorman, and arranged for us all to go round to have a look at what Heathcroft had to offer.

Julian was immediately impressed with the vast array of strong, brightly coloured toys, which any child would find exciting. There was a large selection of musical toys and we soon guided Grant, and a willing member of staff, in this direction. As usual Grant was confused and frightened by a new place and ran through the doors that led to the bedroom area and leapt on to a bed and disappeared under a duvet giggling uncontrollably. We later learnt that he wasn't necessarily happy when he laughed, as autistic children's emotions are inappropriate and this giggling could well indicate fear and confusion. In his case this was probably true at times.

We were happy, on the whole, with what we saw of Heathcroft. It was bright, modern and purpose-built, the bedroom area was pleasant but I didn't see how they would manage to keep him in his room as he was awake quite a lot in the night. That, however, would be their problem. I worried for his safety as he was obsessed with escaping. Heathcroft was situated in a road, off a busy main road that still was far too close for comfort. However, I was assured that he would be watched constantly.

They had a large garden with a sloping bank and this was fully enclosed by a fence which looked secure. I don't think the staff believed me when I told them that our son could have been related to Houdini, but it didn't take them long to find out!

Grant, although not yet three, was now fixed up with respite care if and when we needed it. Using it was a different matter as passing over your very small, much loved and protected child into another's care was no easy task, particularly when you feel your child's problems are only fully understood by you. I was watching him 100 per cent of the time he was awake. Would they do that too? He could run very fast and if carers averted their eyes when the front door was open he could be away and on to that main road before they got to him. So initially we didn't take up the facility, except for the occasional couple of hours for an appointment, or for tea. If I did put him in, it was Julian who benefited most as he followed me talking non-stop as if to make up for valuable lost time. I realized at this point that Julian was missing out on his mother's closeness and somehow I had to allow myself to release Grant more to the care of others if I possibly could.

Julian was doing exceptionally well at school and his teachers told us that he was gifted and maybe we should think of sending him to a preparatory school so that he could get more individual attention in a smaller class group, giving him a chance to develop his academic capabilities. This was going to be costly and for us to have been able to afford it I would have had to work more. Apart from the couple of evening clinics I already did, extra clinics would have proved impossible. I couldn't consider doing any night work as we slept little already and I needed as much sleep as I could for the long days. If he were to go to Reading School (our ultimate aim) without first attending a preparatory school in Reading, he would have to board and to both of us this would be out of the question, as our time with him was already far too short.

Our existing financial situation as we were would give us enough to take the children to interesting places where they would both get stimulation such as zoos, swimming pools, and so on. When we could muster enough courage, we could leave Grant in respite care in order to take Julian away on a separate holiday that would be his time alone.

Fortunately, Julian needed little encouragement to work, but he tended to cling to adults such as the teaching staff and rather than play would spend the breaks talking to the teacher on playground duty, possibly seeking the adult attention he was missing at home.

Our village life centred around the primary school and events which were frequent and pleasant. Apart from sports days, parents' evenings, Harvest Festival and the carol service, they had jumble sales, craft fairs, dances and all sorts of other events that caught the imagination and raised valuable funds for the school. It was at one of these activities that I spoke with Julian's current teacher, discussing Julian and how he was doing. I expressed my worries concerning the possibility of having to move him because of Grant's future education. I explained our problem and how we had been told that a move to Berkshire might be necessary as there was nothing suitable in the educational field for Grant in Oxfordshire. The teacher expressed immediate surprise, advising me that only three miles down the road there was a school, recently opened, for children with learning disabilities, and that they had an assessment class which would be ideal for a child such as ours; it was called Bishopswood! What a revelation and a relief that one worry could possibly be over and also that a move might not be necessary.

During our next visit to the toy library I spoke with Melba Pitt and asked what she knew about the school. She was amazed that nobody had told us about it before and explained about Bishopswood, which really did sound very suitable. I told her how much I wanted someone to tell me what I could be doing with Grant to help him. I needed somebody to give me guidance and show me how to increase his practically non-existent attention span, as our days were spent following him around, keeping him from danger and clearing up the mess and confusion he left in his wake. We did nothing positive. Again Melba expressed surprise that nobody had put me in touch with the teacher-counsellor appointed to South Oxfordshire district for this very purpose. Melba even had her telephone number.

'Can I make my own referral?' I asked.

Melba thought for a moment before replying. 'Oh, I am sure that would be permissible and anyway if it isn't, Gill Burnham will tell you how you should go about it, she is a very nice lady.'

First thing Monday morning I phoned and spoke to Gill, a very approachable person, who was only too pleased to arrange a visit. She explained her work as a teacher-counsellor was to visit pre-school children with problems such as ours. She was to aid in their assessment, educational referrals and home teaching. The referral should have been though my own doctor, but she was happy to bridge that gap for me. She arrived in a small car piled high with toys; what a welcome sight! I opened our front door wide as she staggered through with a choice selection of her wares from the car. After going through the usual history appraisal she approached Grant with some of her toys, inviting him to investigate. Grant took one look and disappeared! I retrieved him from the furthest corner of the house and this time she held him on her lap, but briefly. He wriggled and was gone! Gill asked me what interested him so she could get his attention. Grant now was standing on the lounge windowledge, laughing and jumping up and down.

'Does he usually do this?' she asked, leaping to her feet to catch him, expecting him to fall (I knew by now that he wouldn't).

'Oh yes!' I replied. 'I just can't stop him doing anything he wants, as he still seems to have little understanding of the spoken word, and certainly does not respond to, no'. I *long* to teach him but he is just so active that I can never hold his attention for more than about ten seconds, then he is gone. He does like a cuddle, but he now uses this to stop me trying to make him interested in things. I will show him a shape to post in a box, but he just takes one look, throws it on to the floor then wraps his arms around my neck to distract me.'

'What do you do then?' she enquired.

'Well, I firmly remove the arms and try again, but I must confess that sometimes I just love the cuddles!'

She laughed. 'I'm not surprised,' she said. 'You must have your rewards too. Learning is a two-way process and both sides need to be rewarded by a response, be it a smile, the right word or a sweet.

At the moment it is one-sided and you are the one giving all the information that is only returned by a negative reaction. Grant does this by running away. He still wants a response from you but because he does not have the language ability, he uses the only way he knows, which is by doing things that will make you react, whether good or bad. Unfortunately, the things that you find hard to manage make you behave by shouting, scolding or smacking him. He has your attention although it is not the kind of attention that you wish to give him. He knows you enjoy being cuddled and if he does this it will stop you forcing him further into doing things that he doesn't understand.'

Gill lifted Grant to the floor from the windowsill for the umpteenth time (giving him the attention he was seeking!) and said, 'This behaviour has to be tackled. At two and three-quarters it isn't good, if he still does it at six it will be intolerable!'

Gill left me with a few simple toys that I could use to try and encourage play, but she told me not to pester him all the time, just to set aside ten minutes in each hour so that I wouldn't feel constantly pressurized and unrewarded!

Gill arranged to return in three weeks when we would discuss his future school arrangements. Bishopswood school, in her opinion, was a very suitable option for Grant and she was sure of procuring a place for him there when he was three, which would be after Easter, even if it was for just a few hours a week. The school drew attention to its assessment class where Grant's schooling needs would be examined, thus playing a part in determining the course of his future education. So at last we were moving forward, if slowly, and now I didn't feel so alone.

One thing that worried us when autism had first been mooted was that more than one person had said it was important to begin the correct education as soon as possible, preferably geared specifically to autism. We were told that if the correct input was given when the child was two then he would be more likely to improve. Here we were with Grant almost three years old and the only input was from me (and Paul), who felt totally inadequate, and the teacher-counsellor who had visited only once. She had told me some interesting and useful facts, but one and a half hours of teaching in three weeks could hardly count as education!

Five weeks later, Gill had arranged a visit to Bishopswood. Grant was to have a couple of hours in Heathcroft so that we could see around the school and talk to the staff and Head in peace.

A wintery day, shortly before Grant's third birthday, saw Paul and me at the door of the modern, purpose-built school, a stone's throw away from home and situated in a very rural position on a main, but not too busy, country road. Gill introduced us to the headmaster, Mike Hudson, and we were shown around the school including the assessment class where we met Beverley Edney, the class teacher, and Marjorie Blake her class helper. They both made us feel most welcome and introduced us to the children.

One little girl, Claire, was six, smiled a lot and repeatedly clasped her hands together. I don't think I saw Claire do much more than this ever, even when I met her when she was sixteen. Then there was Glynn, who couldn't walk, but they were working on it. His eyes were half shut due to faulty lids and he peered through the slits with his head tilted back. Glynn was the same age as Grant. Sally was four and was, I felt, very similar to Grant in her mannerisms. She was a good-looking little girl who flapped her hands a lot and was always into mischief, ignoring the staff when told to sit down or not to switch the light on and off continuously. I asked whether Sally was autistic and was told that she could be, though no diagnosis had yet been made.

Beverley and Marjorie asked about Grant and made us feel that here was a good place for him to be. I explained his obsession for escaping and advised them that because of this he needed to be watched constantly. They showed me the garden, where there was a small fenced-off area for the younger children. The gate from here had a catch which I was sure he would be able to undo. They assured me that if everyone was happy about his entry to the school the gate would be made suitably secure.

We discussed Grant's needs with Mike, the head of the school, and he convinced us that starting Grant at Bishopswood would be the best option. His condition would be observed and assessed by a multi-disciplinary team and the method of education to be followed would then be decided and monitored. This seemed to be a good arrangement so we agreed to a start date just after Easter and for three mornings a week.

I asked if I could come with him for the first couple of mornings to help settle him in, as it would be a frightening experience for Grant. It would also give me the opportunity to show the staff some of his needs, help me to see how they tackled behavioural problems and hopefully continue their methods at home, giving the necessary continuity. Mike was only too pleased with this arrangement as he liked parental involvement with the school.

We spent Easter with my parents in Birkenhead; it also happened to be Grant's third birthday on Easter Day. My parents had tried to make their house as Grant-proof as possible, putting away all their china, turning cupboards to the wall and putting locks on the upstairs doors so that we could relax as much as possible.

We put him to sleep in a small downstairs room from which we initially removed all the furniture so that there were no dangers. The door already sported a lock which would be essential if we were to sleep without too much worry: when he awoke early he would be up and down the stairs, these being slatted wooden ones that held a host of dangers. The room had a high narrow window at least five foot from the ground and, apart from the bed, little else, as everything had been removed from the room. We settled Grant to sleep that night in his safe cell.

The following day was Easter Day and his first birthday since his diagnosis and our knowledge that he had a handicap for life. I felt my parents would be making sympathetic comments on this fact and I wanted on the surface to ignore it. We had a handicapped child and we had to get on with the problem. We didn't want sympathy as we loved him dearly whatever his afflictions, and probably more so because of them.

Easter Day dawned, with noise from downstairs, then some

thumping sounds. I leapt from my sleep and rushed downstairs to see whatever Grant was doing. Opening the door I gazed into an empty room and my heart stopped beating. Noticing the high window swinging free on its catch, I caught my breath in horror. How had he managed to climb up there, open the window and … then what? Was he in a crumpled heap below the window which reached up higher from the ground on the outside?

Beside myself with worry and clad only in a flimsy nightdress, I ran to the front door, which now shook slightly with the thumping of small fists upon the glass panes. His obvious safety was already an enormous relief even before I found the key and turned the latch. There on the doorstep stood a cold little boy wearing only pyjamas with his feet bare and blue. He looked none the worse for wear! He must have lowered himself from the window and dropped to the ground, not even falling down the step or slope underneath. He looked completely undamaged. My admonitions fell on completely deaf ears as I carried him upstairs to be warmed up by his daddy in our bed, while I broke my heart and faced the frightening realities of this child's problem.

Five

School days began for Grant in early April 1978 and I had the honour of sharing his first two days. It was a precious time because it was a special school with children who all had very individual problems. I am ashamed to say that when I first visited Bishopswood and saw children with varying degrees of learning difficulties, and some looking far from normal, I hated the thought that my son needed to come to such a school. But by the end of my first day there I had learnt differently – these children were so individual and interesting. In my career as a nurse I had found out how to ease a pain or give appropriate comfort or treatment to most parts of the body. These children had an injury to a part of the body not easy to treat, the brain, and the result of this caused them to display behaviour inappropriate for their age.

I watched these special children and I became interested in each child and was happy to be involved with anything I could do to help. It was also lovely to have Grant's care shared with people who had been trained to cope. They immediately suggested they start him on an hourly potty regime, but to put this into operation in a few weeks time when he was used to the school, his teachers and helpers.

The first day went well and he didn't seem any more or less disruptive than usual. Day two also went well and by the third day I felt they knew him well enough for me to leave him in their care. When I collected him on the third day, and his first without me, he was being cuddled by Marjorie and enjoying the moment. They said he had been very active, but loved looking at books and listening to music in between running or trying to escape. Beverley said he was good for keeping her weight down as she had done several laps of the school!

Grant was now displaying more of the classical symptoms of autism, one of which was avoidance of eye contact. You would ask him to look at you and he would do anything but this. Then there were some times when you felt he was gazing at you but if you followed the stare you would find he was looking slightly to the side of your eye, possibly at the reflection he could see there. His hearing was obviously inappropriate as there were noticeable incorrect misinterpretations of sounds.

One evening he was seated on my lap on the hall floor while Julian bounced and punched a very large balloon around him. Suddenly the balloon burst by Grant's side which sent my heart into a flutter. However, Grant did not flinch or even turn his head to the noise. Later, when I had my electrical whisk in operation, he ran screaming from the kitchen and I had to stop what I was doing to find and console him. He had the same reaction to the Hoover and other loud electrical equipment.

Having read more on the subject of autism I learnt that a child might respond better to words softly spoken or even sung. It must have sounded, to the uninitiated, as if I was in the midst of an operatic performance! Grant, however, just looked through me or ran away chuckling. I often felt he was thinking Mum's trying hard, but I am not coming out of me! He would play mischievous games with me. I would ask him to choose his blue toothbrush and he would stare at the toothbrush rack and very deliberately pick out the red brush. 'No! Grant,' I would say, 'the blue brush.' He would then go to the yellow one.

'No! Grant, the blue brush,' I would stress. He would then give himself away by going for the remaining colour that was not blue so by not choosing it I knew he really did know the right answer. This happened too many times for it to be a coincidence.

Once, and once only, when he was two and a half years he watched me clean my teeth and then copied the procedure! After that, teeth cleaning was always a complicated exercise, which must have been uncomfortable for him, as when you tried to get to his back teeth he clamped his jaws firmly shut on the toothbrush! He had a super set of straight white, healthy teeth which never needed a filling; this must have been partly due to the amount of fluoride he swallowed, as he never learnt to spit out!

This isolated display of so-called normality is a recognized feature in the diagnosis of autism. From a parent's standpoint seeing that your child can do something that won't be repeated only adds to the increasing frustration of trying to rear him. School was experiencing the same frustrations, but the staff shared his management with each other and passed the problem back to me at 1.30p.m.

School did, however, have an immediate impact! For one thing it gave me a few hours to take a deep breath or two, and I really needed this as Grant was becoming increasingly active and difficult. School would tie him into his chair for spells just long enough to give him a chance to see that if he did stop there were other things in life apart from running (again a form of 'holding'). They asked me if I was happy about this method as it was a fairly drastic measure. Beverley assured me that they would only have to use it for a short time until he could understand that he could also sit down as well as run! After a period of sitting he was then either taken outside to run around the grounds or the class would have a session in the gym. They found the gym rather hair-raising as he would climb to the top of the wall bars and if they were not quick enough in retrieving him he would crawl fearlessly along the ledge that lay between the wall bars and the ceiling! I shuddered with horror when they told me this, but I had to trust them. The fact that they were so honest with me helped us realize they were doing their best and were very vigilant. I always felt that we had to live one day at a time with Grant as he was so vulnerable to numerous dangers and I thanked God each bedtime for seeing him through another day.

The escaping obsession increased and so did climbing. If you put the two together you have either a lost child or quite a problem!

We were determined to make our house and garden as secure as possible and we were so fortunate to be in the position we were, surrounded by fields on three sides and just an unmade lane on the other side of the gate. My next-door neighbour was amused when I asked her if she minded if I threaded brambles through the top of the fence of our adjoining gardens to deter him from climbing over and thus escaping into the lane through her gate. She had five children with ages ranging from fourteen to a baby. She suggested that we erect a Colditz style tower on the fence and commission the children to stand on guard duty! We laughed but it would have been very useful!

We had a barn gate and very quickly we had attached a large 'Please Shut the Gate' sign in big bold letters, and most people co-operated. However, Grant quickly learnt to climb over it so we had to think of other tactics. Paul fitted fine chicken wire over the bars so that Grant had nothing to latch his feet into. This lasted a day and, thinking he was safe, I left him alone for a couple of minutes which gave him long enough to work out that if he lay on his tummy and put his head on to one side he could slide his whole little body underneath. I came out from the house as the last foot disappeared through the gap and caught him several yards up the lane! I was not going to be beaten so, holding his hand very firmly, I pruned our bramble hedge of its longest stems, then wound and threaded these through the chicken wire so that loops nearly touched the ground along the length of the gate. To nullify any other ideas he may have I then covered the whole gate with threaded brambles. It worked for a few weeks until he found that he could squeeze through the rotting palings on the garden fence!

At a later date, when he had grown somewhat, we replaced the brambles on the gate with a single line of barbed wire; the catch on the gate needed complementing with a second. It was quite amazing how a child who appeared on the surface to understand so little could work out complicated catches, and also know that barbed wire or prickly brambles are to be respected. This was one of the many things that made me utterly convinced that deep down we had a normal little boy in this beautiful shell who peeped out occasionally just to show those close to him that he was there.

It was just when we were feeling desperate about how to cope with keeping him safe, while at the same time allowing him enough space to run off his excessive energy, that our 'guardian angel' stepped in. The company that my husband worked for, Metal Box, had set up a fund to help any of their employees who had relatives with special needs and would pay for any item we needed that might help. We used their donation to surround the whole garden with a five-foot-high chestnut paling fence. We were advised that even an athletic adult would not be able to climb over it as it is very flexible, so now we were completely secure. Only a wooden horse would now help Grant escape the boundaries of our fortress!

How did *I* escape? It wasn't easy and times were few, but I managed in my own way and, if I hadn't, I don't think I could have survived those years. Paul escaped to work daily and his aviation hobby every couple of weeks for a day at the weekend. I loved my garden and found ultimate peace and relaxation there. When I started to receive an allowance for Grant, the first thing I did was to have someone to help with the housework which I resented doing in the small amount of 'time free from Grant'. I would choose any spare moment to dig furiously in the garden and plant up vegetables and flowers enthusiastically. We also had an allotment and every three weeks Paul would give me a complete day to myself at the weekend to do what I wanted. Usually I chose that day at the allotment, where I would take myself off with a can or two of Coca Cola and a chocolate bar and feel completely liberated and high. The caffeine in the two products did nothing compared to the euphoric sense of just doing what I wanted for a day. I am quite convinced the garden was my salvation and an hour with my flowers would work better than any relaxation drug.

Grant's main loves and obsessions were music and books. We would both read to him endlessly as we felt this must be achieving something. He had now graduated to some of the simple Ladybird stories and his early favourites were *Tootles the Taxi*, *The Gingerbread Boy* and *Chicken Licken*. It was hard introducing anything new. If you tried a new book he either ran away or took it from your hand, dropping it to the floor and pushing the original book back at you. I can still repeat verbatim most of Grant's favourite stories, as can Julian and Paul.

Grant appeared to be understanding something when the story was read to him, but we will never know just how much. Some words, a picture, or more often the intonations of a word would set him off into uncontrollable laughter that was so infectious it had us all in hysterics, so you would repeat that word or picture again, until eventually the laughter waned.

Paul would play his guitar to him and he liked to twang the strings, but he had no idea how to treat it with respect, so we couldn't leave him with it. As he had shown an interest in something we decided to try to find an old guitar from a jumble sale to encourage the interest. But, intriguingly, when we did acquire one for him he wasn't interested because he quickly knocked it out of tune. He always preferred Paul's which meant we were continually searching for a suitable place to hide it in order to keep in good condition, but it was quite amazing how he would always find it!

As he loved musical boxes so much, we had acquired a good selection of strong wind-up varieties. Sometimes he would go into his room and wind them all, resulting in a tinkling cacophony of nursery tunes. This purposeful activity, which actually involved some thought, put me on cloud nine.

Grant was incredibly strong for his age, which was apparent from some of the havoc he wreaked daily around the house. He would tip the settee upside down time after time. I tried making him return the upturned items to their right position. Why, I wondered, did he seem to prefer the furniture in any way other than the right one? Perhaps the wrong way up looked the correct way to him.

If he walked past a table or sideboard he would sweep

everything off. Anything that resembled a book would be picked up, examined, then dropped, and daily the whole place resembled a war zone, until he was behind the door of his room when I did a frantic clear up!

We had to empty the house of anything removable, breakable or dangerous to him. One day he climbed behind the television and pushed it over shattering the tube so we had to buy a new one and chain it to the wall! Fortunately, the old one was on its last legs anyway. Every cupboard had to be locked and if it didn't lock it was kept empty, which was easier than continually having to clear things up and sort out the confusion. We lost the door keys frequently, which added enormously to the frustration. Early the following year we had locks fitted to all the doors and above each door was a hook where we left the key, but it was amazing how many times the key to the room had disappeared, just when you were in a hurry. When Grant was a year or two older and taller, the keys would invariably be found in his bed or buried beneath a pile of tatty books!.

Being one step ahead of him was the name of the game and I was determined that he would not get the better of me. Once you felt you had overcome a behaviour that wore you down there was something else he came up with to thoroughly test you again. He climbed over the fireguard and also on to the cooker which he managed to switch on before you could say Jack [Grant] Robinson! On more than one occasion, anxious for his tea, the fish fingers or sausages disappeared from under the grill. He burnt the top of his fingers, but he didn't seem to feel the pain and, on the first occasion, I was unaware he was burnt until I saw the blisters. Subsequently I immersed his hands in cold water just to be sure.

So, apart from school, Grant was by my side all the time. I could not take my eye off him for more than half a minute, and I am not exaggerating this fact. He even came to the toilet with me so that I could lock him in with me to know where he was and what he was doing. Cooking had to be done holding one hand to stop him trying to climb on to the cooker or to pinch or grab the food I was preparing. This situation lasted for three years!!

I suppose it is here that for completeness I should mention our nights to further illustrate the sheer frustration of our lives. Grant didn't sleep much, in fact he didn't sleep properly until he was fifteen! At this time, as at any time of his life, he presented challenges that I was determined to overcome. We started by putting a stairgate across his door. At eighteen months it kept him there, but not for long; he soon clambered over the top.

For a short time we put the two boys together in bunk beds and one of my most treasured memories is the 'um' game they played. This was very significant, because it was one of those 'islets of normality' that remains with me. The 'um' game was Julian saying 'um' from the top bunk and Grant replying with 'um' from the bottom bunk and this wonderful turn-taking went on for some time. Any 'normal' family would take this in their stride, but it is imprinted on my mind as one of the only games they played together.

The shared room didn't last more than a week or two as Grant disturbed Julian too much and would climb up to the top bunk and wake him up.

I hated the idea of locking Grant into his room, but if he realized he couldn't get out he would eventually get into bed. We fixed a chain to the door so that he could peep out and not feel excluded. He was shut into himself enough without doing anything to increase this isolation, but it was still important that Julian had some of our time. We maintained a strict regime and would put him into his room by six-thirty when it was Julian's time, and one or both of us would devote the next hour, at least, to him.

The chain on Grant's door was fine for a short while, but soon started to wear away the door as he opened it back and forth! This usually happened at about 4 a.m. and the reverberating banging and rattling woke us all. Our solution to the problem was to stuff a pillow between the door and wall to help wedge the door, but as far as Grant was concerned this didn't create enough activity and the consequential reactions from his parents. He enjoyed being the centre of attention at this early hour when he was alone. He wasn't one to give in so he lay on the floor and kicked the door as hard as he could. You would think he had hobnailed boots on, not little bare feet. He also banged the door with his sturdy Fisher Price toy radio, which he liked to wind up constantly. 'Hickory Dickory Dock' would play over and over again and the banging on the door drowned the repetitive sounds of the tinkling nursery rhyme! We then decided to have locks fitted on to all the internal doors. We didn't like locking him in because we didn't know what he was doing and with the door open, on the chain, you could hear and analyse his actions. Once the locks were in place we used a baby alarm to hear his actions inside the room. However, he could still drum his feet on the door and apart from thick padding we were at a loss to think of an answer to this problem.

His next ploy for attention was one which I found the hardest. This was smearing. He decided to examine the contents of his nappy either by removing it first and then playing with what he found, or just putting his hands down his nappy and playing with what he brought out. The room would be plastered with excrement in next to no time as his hyperactivity spread it on to the walls, door, window, books, musical toys, the bedding and the carpet. Naturally this was the biggest attention seeking success of all. Mum would scream, cry, rant and rave. Dad, in order to soothe her, would take his stinking child and put him into the bath and shower him with nice warm water. After the main smelly bits had gone Dad would even talk to him nicely while Mum still shouted, now mainly at Dad for talking in a friendly way to him! A good smearing would see him up at least another hour as it took Mum that long to clean up and change his bed. The room was always left smelling strongly of flowery disinfectant and the bed clean with sweetly laundered polycotton sheets. Now having got all the attention he wanted he would go back to bed and sleep often for just an hour or two, which would refresh him enough to start again!

It was suggested that we should use cold water to shower Grant after an episode such as this. I know that for some this can have miraculous affects, but not so for Grant who just shivered and made us feel cruel. However, this new and objectionable behaviour was not going to defeat me so, before he went to school one day, I got Paul and Julian to help me lay him down on to a piece of wallpaper and I drew around him to get the shape of his body. I dropped him off at school then drove into Reading in order to buy some soft, high quality, stretchy towelling material. Finding just the thing required, I bought two lengths in blue and pink stripes. As soon as I could I made them up from the pattern of his shape, leaving just a small slit down the back, which was just large enough to pull over his body. I then fastened the back slit with two or three buttons and loops. He looked rather like Andy Pandy, but it was very effective and solved the problem for a couple of years. The material used was of a quality so high that it took to being washed every other day for two years, and I still use them today as dusters!

Grant was beginning to spend hours awake in the night and I began to recognize each sound for what it was. If it spelt danger I would leap from the bed and storm into his room to try and stop the offending behaviour. There were book shelves in his room that Paul had fixed to the wall. He had positioned them high so that he wouldn't sweep the books to the floor, which was his usual style. The shelves started off at four levels and Grant used them as a ladder, clearing each shelf as he ascended. Paul's solution was to saw off the bottom shelf, but he had to continue this action until after three weeks only the top shelf remained! I think Grant only fell twice in these escapades, but we did try to position the furniture in his room to make landings as soft as possible in the event of a slip!

Our windows were fitted with secondary double-glazing and in front of this in Grant's room was a venetian blind, which was good for keeping out the light in the early hours in the summertime. In the night Grant would part these blinds to see out and they became battered and broken. One night the whole lot came crashing down causing both Paul and me to leap out of bed simultaneously, falling over each other at the door to inspect the damage, and scared of what we would find. Grant looked most unperturbed, but pleased to see us as his work had brought both Mum and Dad to see him and they were making a lot of fuss!

We didn't replace the blinds, but this made the window more accessible and very soon he had mastered the catch on the secondary double-glazing. This time it was an ominous silence after lots of noise that made me stagger from my bed to his room. He'd gone! The window was wide open, but looking through into the garden I saw him happily wandering around and none the worse for wear!

We bought locking devices that fitted over the rim of the double-glazing, but this didn't solve the problem for long as he found extra strength to slide the window and the lock together. Our last resort was to screw the window catch into the wood so that if he did manage the double-glazing then he couldn't get out. This did worry me as I felt it was a trap in the event of fire, but there were many more hazards if we didn't do it.

The next bedroom fiasco was his curtain, as he frequently pulled the whole lot down, including the screws and some plaster! Every day I needed to sort it out from the confusion of books, bedding and toys. One night I had replaced the curtain one time too many for my sanity. There had to be some other way. After deliberating for some time I came across the solution – Velcro! A life-saving substance for parents of children with behaviour problems. In this instance I used a strong glue to fix one long piece of one side of the Velcro to the wall and cut the other side in two and sewed it to each curtain. In the daytime you could attach it at intervals, so that the curtains were separated and let in the light. At night they could be spread across the window. They usually came down each day, but it was little hassle to put them back. Sometimes in the night they would be replaced five or six times as we were forever optimistic that each trip into his room would be the last for the night and he would settle to sleep!

Paul and I became partners in night vigilance and in the morning we would recount the numbers of times we were each up, as we didn't always hear each other go when exhaustion had taken over completely. We made it a rule that our bed was sacred and he was not allowed to come into it until 6.50 a.m. We felt this rule was important for our marriage and also for Grant to learn that he had his own room and we had ours. Grant loved to be in our bed with us, snuggled down in between his Mum and Dad. Possibly he may have settled better there, but Paul and I had so little time together that we had to create a place which, for a few short hours, was ours alone.

The continuous broken nights were very wearing and weren't conducive to us feeling fresh the next day. If we did have a reasonable night then coping with the day was much easier. I worried about Paul's ability to work effectively, as he often came home saying he had not been able to concentrate because he was so tired.

We were both concerned about Julian as lack of sleep would surely affect his school work. We decided to build a bedroom extension at the back of the bungalow that would run off the dining-room, creating two shut doors between him and the hallway. The room could also accommodate its own toilet and basin. This would give us a very small, but pleasant, guest suite overlooking the fields.

It was not the easiest of situations having workmen in the house with Grant around, so we arranged for the extension to be completed during term time. Grant had graduated to full-time schooling very quickly over the year and this helped relieve the increasing stress on the family. While the extension was being built I ensured our evenings were full with shopping, swimming, and so on, so that the men had cleared and gone home before we returned.

The extension proved its worth and Julian enjoyed having a smart new room of his own, although at times I think he was a bit nervous being right at the back of the house and would always insist on the dining-room door being left wide open before he went to sleep. Once he was asleep he was happy for the doors to be shut so that he wouldn't be disturbed. When he got much older, there would be trouble if a door was left open as he enjoyed being secluded from the rest of the family, particularly when he was studying.

In a situation like ours when one child demands so much attention, it is easy to neglect the needs of the others. If the siblings number more than one then they will have each other, but one other child becomes like an only child with tired, fraught parents. Paul and I were very aware of this as was his grandmother, Edna, who gave Julian treats such as taking him to a pantomime or circus so that those treasured childhood pleasures were still experienced, although I was sad that I could not participate in them too.

Paul took Julian away for a few days on one of his extended aviation weekends. Julian came home full of the experience of parascending – although only seven, he had been catapulted into the air and caught before he landed by the outstretched arms of many trainee airmen. I had to smile and accept his new learning adventure.

Six

Visits to Dr O'Gorman were at regular six-week intervals and I found them very helpful. He usually said that I had thought through a behaviour problem myself without his assistance, but there were many things he told me which helped, even if it was only to explain why Grant was behaving in a particularly unacceptable way. It was also good to talk through my problem or situation of the moment, even if there was no immediate solution.

He told me about a new therapy being tried out in America, with some degree of success. It was called 'holding' and he demonstrated on a very surprised Grant what it was all about. Placing Grant on his lap he put his arm behind his back holding the other arm firmly in front. For a brief moment Grant was stunned into submission and looked at Dr O'Gorman in utter surprise, then gathering his senses and strength he kicked his legs furiously, trying hard to wriggle free.

Dr O'Gorman – who was not a young man – wrestled with the flailing arms and legs sending his glasses halfway up his head and making his hair wild and wispy, but he still held on! He then pinned Grant's legs between his own and his arms tightly to him, and Grant couldn't move. But he could shout and cry and this got deafeningly loud. Dr O'Gorman said something like, 'You just hang on and he will quieten down eventually!' Susan Wagstaff and I tried hard not to laugh as they really made quite a picture. He discontinued the holding after about ten minutes and Grant still sobbed. Dr O'Gorman explained that you should keep holding him firmly until the crying subsided and in his submission you could then talk to him and get him to respond and relate much better.

'Holding therapy' became popular as a method of helping our children about six years later, but although a lot of improvement has been seen in some children it was a controversial method and claims of cures were refuted. On reflection we had already used a form of holding when we all sat in the playpen on the lawn, and later, when Beverley tied him to the chair, both achieving good results by way of restriction. The method used later was not entirely what Dr O'Gorman was now advocating. To me, at the time, the doctor's action seemed positive and I decided to give it a try.

My first attempt was in the lounge in an easy chair and we struggled and fought for a good twenty minutes with Grant screaming, kicking and struggling wildly to escape the vice-like and determined grasp that his mother held on him. However, I would not let him go, despite the fight he made to break away, and eventually he fell asleep utterly exhausted and I felt triumphant. Here I was cuddling my child, although asleep, and I had held him in my arms for the longest time since his hospital tests. It was exciting and a challenge and at last something positive that I could do to try to help him. I had brief visions of taking my 'cured' little boy by the hand into the local primary school! I survived on those dreams!

The next day I couldn't wait to try again and after fewer struggles he settled down and actually gave me some eye contact. This was wonderful and very rewarding. How true were the words of Gill, the teacher counsellor, who said we all need rewards to help us carry on. The few moments of eye contact were giving me rewards that were worth more than thousands of pounds.

After a few days of 'holding' in a chair and a realization that at last I was doing something more beneficial than anything I had yet attempted, I knew that I must continue with this technique. Holding him on the chair in the lounge was not the best place as we were disturbed by Julian, the phone, and occasionally somebody at the front door. Also Grant's physical strength was greater than mine at times and in this position he often managed to escape.

I was not happy about the effect on Julian as Grant screamed for a long time until he settled and as our lounge was the central room of our small bungalow it was unfair to shut Julian out of here. When 'holding' came to Britain as a method several years later they advocated that the whole family should be involved. At this stage I felt it better that I do it alone, as when Paul came in we would have our meal and, following that, Grant would be too full and tired to try the struggling, exhausting exercise. Consequently I decided the best place would be on his bed where I could pin him down much better. I soon learnt that keeping his shoes on helped considerably in holding him down, since with his legs between mine, the shoes jammed any attempt to slide them out.

Julian was only too anxious to let me try and help his brother. He was only seven, but had matured beyond his years because of the circumstances and happily manned the phone or the door and told whoever called that I was working with Grant and couldn't be disturbed. I would tell him at what time I would be finished and he would advise a caller to phone back. My ears were always atuned to any problems he may encounter so that I could intervene if necessary.

During this session I would talk to Grant constantly, stroking his head and hair to try and soothe him. If we had a calmer moment I would sing to him a repertoire of nursery rhymes, lullabies and action songs. Action proved difficult, as if I let him go to clap hands, and so on, he would take the opportunity to escape!

I talked to him in song, whispered words and mouthed each syllable carefully, in a conscious effort to help him to understand the spoken word and give meaning to language. We always finished off with a story from a book. His favourites were *The Three Little Pigs* and *The Three Bears*, to which he listened carefully and with enjoyment as if he completely understood what it was all about. I accompanied these stories with lots of physical actions which he loved. I tried to encourage responses such as the 'blowing' of the wolf in *The Three Little Pigs*. We huffed and puffed and blew daily! I would also encourage pointing to things in the pictures, but more often than not I needed to use my hand to guide his finger. Although once I asked him to point to the little dog that appeared on each page of *Tottles the Taxi*, somewhere in the picture, and he pointed to the dog on every page and wherever it was, even if slightly hidden or very small! An exciting breakthrough and a glimmer of the inner Grant.

These sessions helped develop a close bond between us and, for the first time, he began to initiate a cuddle that was affectionate and not with the ulterior motive of trying to stop a learning process. We were also getting occasional eye contact. The sessions usually lasted about forty minutes and I continued with them daily for about a year. Of all the things I did to help Grant this undoubtedly had the best results. I can't remember now what made me discontinue the sessions, but I wish that I hadn't stopped them. I do remember Susan Wagstaff offering to help support me so we could continue, but I declined at the time. I am sure there must have been lots of factors that forced the issue.

Just before Easter 1979, Grant's fourth birthday, we paid another visit to Dr O'Gorman. He had a new idea that he wanted me to try to help calm Grant's hyperactivity. It was to use the amphetamine Ritalin, usually prescribed as a stimulant! He told me that in adults it will stimulate, but in a child given in small doses it usually has the opposite effect. He did warn me though that there was the possibility that it could stimulate him further.

For the first three days Grant was very dulled and I hated the effect it had and stopped it. On the Sunday following Easter he was very hyperactive so I thought I would try the amphetamine tablet again as he had been up for the last two nights and Paul was away. To my horror it speeded him up more! By the time Paul came home I was a physical wreck and the amphetamine tablets were flushed down the toilet, never to be used again. It was strange that medications seemed to have a different effect on Grant than on other people. Later I found out from other parents that their autistic children were also affected differently by drugs and usually seemed to need larger than normal doses for any effect.

When I was on night duty during my nursing days I found it very hard to sleep in the daytime and discovered that if I took a small antihistamine tablet called Phenegan, (produced to counteract allergic reactions), its side-effect would make me drowsy and sleep for at least eight hours, but I would wake up bright and refreshed for the night's work. When I gave Grant one of these it made him sleep for one hour more than normal. Vallergan, a similar drug also had little, if any effect on him.

That Easter holiday break was not all bad news; during a family outing to a local bird park we noticed that Grant was showing small signs of understanding and interest in his surroundings. This was a noticeable advance. He still needed his pushchair mainly to control him and we had acquired a large buggy, provided by our social services department following an application through our family doctor. When we were in a safe area such as the bird park he could be let out to run. We found on this occasion he was happy to walk around with us, pushing his buggy and holding on to it when asked. I had started using reins to encourage him to walk as much as possible as it used up his energy and this might help a night's sleep! The buggy was an absolute boon – we could not have managed without it. Grant was a big four year old, so the large version was necessary.

Early in 1979 I heard there was to be a meeting in Oxford at which Dr Lorna Wing was to talk on autism. After reading her book, which clarified the subject so well, her talk was not one to be missed. The meeting was to be held in 'The Friends' Meeting House', a hall used by the Quakers in central Oxford. It had been arranged by a group of parents of autistic children in the hope of bringing together others with similar problems. Ultimately they hoped that by a combined fundraising effort, a group home could be set up that would cater for families needing long term care for their autistic youngsters.

As expected the talk was fascinating because Dr. Wing talked as clearly as she wrote, explaining – in relatively simple terms – the complex subject of autism. Those who had little knowledge of the condition now had a much clearer picture. The meeting was well attended and I noted that amongst the audience was Dr O'Gorman.

At the talk a parent made a speech to describe the lack of specialist provision for autistic adults in our area once education had finished. There were numerous parents in the audience who had to send their children hundreds of miles to care homes suitably adapted to the many and varied needs of the autistic. They hoped people would sign up that night offering their help and involvement with the project. Many, along with myself, committed signatures to their list, though at this moment my young child seemed such a long way off needing adult provision. It was great to be with others who shared the same problems. I just wished we could have more opportunities to meet up to give each other support.

It was some months later that we received a letter to tell us of a coffee-morning arranged locally to meet others in our area who had autistic children. This was held in the house of Tom and Anne Taylor who had a twelve-year-old autistic son, Paul. There was a group of about fourteen mothers who met that day. Dinah Moss had a stepson, Anthony, in an autistic unit at Raby in the Wirral, near Liverpool. It was she who had co-ordinated the meeting. She had singled me out quite early when I suggested that one of the best things about the gathering was that we were meeting up with others in a similar situation. The next day she called me to see if I would be interested in being the Reading area co-ordinator for the proposed new group to be known as Oxford and Mid Counties Autistic Society [OMSAC]. I was a little reluctant at first as free time was limited, but she came back to me the next day. Dinah asked if I could do it if Anne Taylor helped me, as Anne already had said she would be willing. I agreed and an inaugural meeting of OMSAC was held at which I was duly co-opted on to the committee.

Anne and I got together and arranged local group meetings and we met every four to six weeks, finding it very therapeutic to talk. We discussed all the horrendous things our children did and laughed hysterically at some of their appalling antics. We could share our problems knowing we were not alone. Those with older children would give advice to the members with younger children on how to cope with a particular problem. The child who had progressed the most would be the yardstick against which we would base our hopes for our own children.

The group listened and heard and comprehended the problem, without giving you that look, as an outsider would do, that made you feel desperately sorry for yourself. We had all either been there or were going through it. There was always some aspect of behaviour in someone else's child that you were glad you were spared.

We began holding fund-raising events: coffee-mornings, sales and box shakes. Our most successful achievement was a dance held in Reading. Members had influence in different fields and our combined expertize helped to ensure we had minimal overheads. Between us we served a superb buffet and acquired from various sources an ample selection of raffle prizes. We pre-sold books of tickets before the event and these contributed 100 per cent profit. The local newspapers were contacted and a journalist from the *Reading Evening Post*, Rosalind Renshaw, was interested in our cause. She wrote a whole page article, entitled 'The Childhood of Grant Robinson' which showed how much empathy she had with us. She was the mother of two young children of similar age to our own and could see only too clearly how different our life was from hers.

Rosalind chose our family because I had called at the *Evening Post* one afternoon to make arrangements to see the journalist who had kindly offered to highlight the dance and was caught unawares by her asking to do an article on Grant while I was there! The whole event raised over £1,800 and led to an increased awareness of autism in the area. It also cemented a comradeship between us as parents.

The dance was the beginning of the fund-raising activities. I began talking to groups such as Rotary, Lions, Rotaract and Round Table and this led us into all sorts of fund-raising functions. An annual event, which we all enjoyed, was the Caversham Water Carnival held on the banks of the river Thames. The Caversham branch of the Round Table chose us to be their main charity for the year and we were invited to have a stall in a prime position. We chose to run a tombola bottle stall but felt to make it successful we must have excellent bottles to draw the crowds. Before attending an Oxford meeting of OMSAC I sent advance notice for bottles so that together with our own local members we had accumulated a vast quantity. With our quality bottles to draw the custom we were constantly patronized – in fact there were times when the queues for tickets stretched for many yards resulting in an impressive total of takings!

One year we decided to hold a 'Strawberry Fayre' and we even dressed in red and white. We asked members to make or provide anything to do with strawberries including strawberry cordial, which we sold cheaply to draw the children with their parents to our stall. However, despite it being June, because we were in Britain, when four o'clock turned British minds to thoughts of tea and scones (with strawberry jam, of course), the true British weather stepped in and it rained! Everyone else went home and so did we with stacks of delicious strawberry tarts, scones and enough cakes to feed to our families for the next week! No profit was made that year.

But it was lovely to see the families together with dads and children calling to the public to 'come and buy'. Picnics were munched on the grass at the back of our ladened stall. One parent would take two autistic children around the carnival holding two hands very firmly, giving another parent a short break and a chance to relax.

Julian always enjoyed participating in these functions and one year spent a very happy hour or so creating a large ball-throwing game. He stuck a hundred plastic drinking cups on to transportable cardboard sheets and colour-marked the cups which he coded on to a chalkboard. The cup with the black sticky paper marker won £1, and cups marked with different colours took winnings down to 10p on the many red marked cups. He charged 10p for three ping-pong balls which you had to throw from behind a line into a cup. He had tried and tested the game at home and was satisfied that it was not too easy, but that prizes could nevertheless be won. However, once the game was set up at the Water Carnival, Donna, the able autistic daughter of one of our members, decided she would like to try and she gave Julian her 10p. Much to Julian's horror she aimed two of her ping-pong balls straight into the £1 cup. Delighted with her win she carried on playing and winning until I had to tactfully intervene by pointing out to her mother that our profits were rapidly disappearing before the Carnival had even begun. Donna was demonstrating an exaggerated skill that some autistic people can display. Julian did make a profit from his game as very few people won the star prize apart from Donna. Unfortunately, she pestered her mother all afternoon as it was hard for her to understand the reasons why she was not allowed to continue to win.

Donna was around fourteen when we first started running our stalls. She enjoyed counting the money at the end of the function and usually she would not let anyone else intervene. Her unfaltering accuracy was incredible. So long as there were no complications, such as somebody asking for change, she managed very well. Her mother or father would supervise and step in if she had a problem.

Autism can affect a person in varying degrees of severity. The most severely affected can be so bad that in order to receive any stimulation from the world they resort to self-mutilation, biting and hitting themselves or even banging their heads against a wall, often resulting in the need to wear a protective headwear. This can cause relentless and lasting damage to the body and usually these children will need long-term care and protection.

At the other end of the scale are those who are quite able and are deemed to be suffering from 'Asperger syndrome' where the problems are mainly in empathising with others and the inability to form meaningful relationships due to an acutely impaired understanding of social customs. These people are left anxious, confused and isolated from society. Educationally they can be functioning normally or above average.

In between these extremes lie the rest who, depending on their care and education, can and often do, make considerable but slow improvements, some more than others, depending on the amount of structuring and input they receive. The general behaviour of the group who lie in the moderate band is also variable as some will display many characteristics that are inappropriate for their age or situation. Classic autistic behaviours will be seen, but these will differ from child to child as each has his own personality.

Within our support group our members had children with different degrees of severity, but sharing many common features. The film *Rainman* demonstrates this beautifully. I believe Dustin Hoffman, before making the film, lived for some months with a family who had an autistic son and he studied his behaviour. He had also done other research so that he could imitate their mannerisms correctly. The resulting film was excellent and our autistic group could relate to the features portrayed whatever the severity of their child. *Rainman* in the film was an autistic savant, which means that he had exaggerated talents. There are very few autistics who have these exceptional abilities, but those who have can sometimes perform headline-making feats inexplicable to normal human understanding, such as the ability to paint, from a mere glance, a complicated building in the minutest detail, and get it right, or being able to quote correctly the day of the week for a given date centuries back, or repeat a piano concerto from one hearing, complete with any mistakes the pianist may have made! Yet he or she may be unable to tie their shoelaces or cross the road.

Dustin Hoffman not only managed to demonstrate this sort of behaviour in the movie, but also portrayed brilliantly many of the other idiosyncrasies of our children. Humour can be seen in some of the bizarre things that our children do and it helps parents if they can see this and laugh. The film sensitively highlighted the humour, which added to the cleverness of the production.

Lorna Wing lists the features that make up the essential diagnostic criteria and these are:

1   Impairment of social interaction
2   Impairment of social communication
3   Impairment of imagination
4   Repetitive stereotyped activities.

According to Dr Wing,[1] recent research has shown that the first three criteria always lead to the fourth, the repetitive pattern of activities, because of a missing or damaged function of the brain that almost certainly starts to malfunction during development. Research is currently being undertaken to establish the precise region of the brain that is affected. As the basic impairments vary in their severity, so the learning disability varies. It is estimated that 50 per cent of all people with autism will have severe learning difficulties, with a further 25 per cent mild learning difficulties. There can be associated handicaps such as other brain damage, sensory impairments and epilepsy; the latter is present in a third of all people with classic autism, often not showing itself until puberty or adolescence. Autism effects more males than females by a ratio of four to one.

A study by Wing and Gould in 1979[2] and Gillberg in 1986 showed that the occurrence of children with the basic impairments occurred in 21 in every 10,000 children. A recent study by Ehlers and Gillberg[3] in 1993 on children with average or high ability suggests that Asperger syndrome can occur in as many as 36 in 10,000.

[1]*Autistic Spectrum Disorders*, Lorna Wing, 1995. Available from the National Autistic Society.
[2]Wing L and Gould J, Severe impairments of social interaction and associated abnormalities in children: epidemiology and classification. *Journal of Autism and Developmental Disorders*, 9 (1979), 11–29.
[3]Ehlers S and Gillberg, C, The epidemilogy of Asperger Syndrome, a population study. Journal of Child Psychology and Psychiatry, 34, (1993), 1327–1350.

Looking at these facts, we put Grant into the severe range and he had most of the features that would have been defined by Kanner [1943] as classic autism. We have seen how Grant has displayed his impairments in social interaction, social communication and imagination, the latter through his inability to play. Now I would like to explain how he demonstrated the fourth feature, 'repetitive stereotyped activities': he certainly had many of these. He would go through phases which would frustrate us as we tried to control those of his actions that were anti-social and we found there was little that we could do to stop these behaviours. Just as we began tearing our hair out he would stop the mannerism and begin something else. The following are examples:

- jumping up and down which indicated excitement or pleasure;
- hand flapping or clapping which usually indicated frustration or fear;
- picking his cheek which would lead to a very sore face;
- a complete obsession with the pantry even when he had just eaten well;
- an obsession with the Ladybird series of books and an ability to 'flick' the pages over with the book held in one hand, leaving the pages tattered and torn after one day;
- an obsession with brushes of any type – he became obsessed with the texture;
- an obsession with carpet sweepers and, at a later stage, vacuum cleaners and the greenhouse, which in his early years caused acute fear;
- great pleasure in music led to an obsessive interest in records, guitars and music boxes.
- a love of cars, in which he liked to just sit.

A fortunate obsession was a neighbour's house in which he would always be found on the rare occasions that he managed to escape.

Seven

Grant's first year at Bishopswood school saw him achieve many little goals that helped him and relieved me. The staff there very gradually increased his attention span, enabling him to sit longer and dispense with the need to be tied to his chair. The potty regime they introduced did have a little success but owing more to good timing than any realization on Grant's part of what he should do and when.

He stayed with Beverley's class for the first year, becoming full-time after Christmas. Easter 1979 saw several new children needing assessment places. Mike felt he should split the class rather than have one large group. Marjorie Blake was to have five children, including Grant; Beverley Edney the new intakes.

Grant performed well for Marjorie as he liked her approach, which was firm but motherly. As I have already described, our visit to the bird park during the Easter break of 1979 was our first glimmer of improvement in Grant. We felt for the first time that what we were saying was not falling on completely deaf ears. Marjorie had him carrying things for her, such as a moderately filled washing basket or the class register. She even entrusted him with milk bottles, which she let him carry from the staff room fridge to the classroom, but, as a precaution, she walked closely by his side. Unfortunately, her trust was not completely founded and the milk bill increased dramatically so this exercise was stopped!

He was regularly sat on the loo and praised with much applause if he performed, which pleased him. He still had many accidents, although the idea was beginning to dawn. I tried to follow the same routine at home, but at this stage I was not as successful. Yet I would not go back to using nappies, however many pairs of underpants and trousers we went through because I felt we would never achieve success unless we made a continued effort. I still put him into nappies at night to give us the best chance of a continuous night's sleep.

Horse riding was introduced at Bishopswood and, after an initial battle to get him to wear a riding hat, he enjoyed the new experience and would sit for short, though ever increasing lengths of time, on top of the horse before fidgeting and leaving the saddle. We managed to keep up his interest in horseriding after school, at a later age taking him to a Riding for the Disabled group which he enjoyed if the weather was good. After the first year he received an award for the pupil who achieved the most. This accolade was for learning to stay sitting in the saddle and keeping his hat in place! But we were as proud of his honour as would be the parent of any child receiving an award for achievement. As far as we were concerned he could have won the Grand National!

He was encouraged with jigsaw puzzles, but still preferred and coped best with the chunky ones that had clear pictures and a knob to negotiate each puzzle piece. They would also try him with painting, using bright colours and a thick brush, but it was very hard to prevent him putting the brush into his mouth; I could detect a painting session from his colourful teeth and hair!

At home I made up check lists of stimulative routines and ensured that I covered each item daily – the more input he was given and the number of times a task was repeated had a direct bearing on its success. I stuck the lists on to the kitchen cupboards and marked each task with a tick when done.

The list consisted of the following: ice round mouth, lick something sticky, forty-minute holding therapy, read one book, play record, blowing, game with Julian, game with daddy, try with fork, swimming, use potty.

I found this list proved to be particularly useful in the long summer holiday when I could just glance at my list and see the next thing to do. It also highlighted his and my achievements of the day which I needed as a boost to my flagging spirit when I worried that I had not done enough with him to aid his progress.

The first two items on the list were suggestions from the speech therapist who wanted to try and make Grant more aware of his mouth. We used blowing for this purpose too. He still dribbled, sometimes quite profusely, and his clothes became dirty, stained and wet. He needed more awareness of his mouth if he was to find sounds. He had learnt how to suck one evening in one of those special moments when he watched Julian with great interest suck his milk through a straw while he used a cup with a spout. Despite the spout he still dribbled his milk down the front of his bib. Noticing the interest I gave him a straw and put it into his cup. I put my head close to his and with another straw demonstrated the act of sucking. He tried hard, but it was accidentally, breathing in and out over the straw, that he briefly breathed in with his lips closed and received some fluid! This skill must have been agreeable to him as he never let it go. After that we rarely left the house without a straw as it made him much more socially acceptable.

School had also introduced Grant to a sign language system called Paget-Gorman, where signing represented words. Signing also proved difficult to understand as with autism all forms of language and communication are affected. Grant did pick up the sign for 'please' and found it a small way of communicating that he wanted something. It also stopped him having to try and use other signs as 'please' covered enough of his needs without having to try much harder. At a later stage in his schooling the Paget-Gorman sign language was changed to Makaton, which is more widely used and signing 'please' was not allowed. I was worried about adding more confusion into his life, but he had learnt so little of the Paget language it hardly made a difference. He did manage to learn the sign for 'drink', 'biscuit', 'car' and 'home' which were the things dearest to his heart!

Words did come occasionally and often unexpectedly. He would say 'drink' or even 'coke' when desperately thirsty, or take you by the hand to the kitchen to indicate that he wished to eat or drink, then you had to do the rest. If he wasn't well at school he would cry and sometimes whimper 'mum-mum'.

If asked specifically to say a word he would sometimes try and say something that sounded vaguely like the word requested. Speech usually came when he was in an extra active, alert mood. This mood would be associated with more difficult behaviour problems which was a shame as it was lovely to hear words.

When he went into a slower duller phase, then the speech and alertness went too. These phases tended to go in roughly six-week cycles. We would see Dr O'Gorman six-weekly and I noticed that I would be recounting terrible difficulties, bad behaviours, broken nights and complete exhaustion one session then the next would be better as everything would be calmer and easier.

One day when I was fetching Grant from school, Marjorie exclaimed, 'Aren't you thrilled he is saying so many words? This must be the beginnings of speech.'

Having experienced this before, I couldn't get excited as our hopes with language development had been dashed too many times and I felt it would probably disappear, which it did when he went back into a quieter phase.

In the November of his fourth year there was a conference on autism organized by the National Autistic Society and held at an abbey near Watford. Paul felt he could manage for a couple of days with the aid of Heathcroft. We felt it important that I try to seek out as much new information as possible and make contacts that may help Grant in the future.

What freedom!! Two whole days to escape and two nights' sleep!

It was a very enjoyable weekend and I met some very interesting people who worked in autism. The subject had now taken over my whole being and anything that I could learn that might help with our approach to Grant's care was becoming my sole aim in life. I was still sure our little boy was there deep down.

Surely somebody here with expert knowledge and experience on the subject would hold some answers that could provide a key to unlock the door and set him free. I listened intently to all that was said and came to the conclusion that autism was a condition that was still a puzzle. People were fascinated by it because it held so many mysteries that needed solving. They had little idea as yet of its causes; as for any solutions they only had new forms of schooling (or old methods revamped) and little else. They could tell you a lot about how the children presented, but so could I!

We had small workshops where they found my experiences useful to enhance their presentation. I didn't mind this but I wasn't gaining anything, only sharing with professionals a wealth of practical skills achieved through the necessity of self-preservation!

A plenary session at the end of the conference and a question from the audience raised my hopes about new help. The question was, 'What would the speakers do to encourage motivation?' The answer I took home came from Dr Elizabeth Newson, who works at Nottingham University on research into child development and autism. She said, 'A camera!' She went on to say, 'If you have a Polaroid camera and take a picture when the child does something useful you straight away have an illustration of that action and can talk about it and relive the experience. Autistic children often relate to pictures better than reality so if the two can be interlinked then this can encourage motivation.'

I went home and bought a camera!

Grant got used to having his photo taken and, as he had no social worries, the odd situations where his mother took his picture made no difference to him! The Polaroid camera was unfortunately not the answer as the photos were too small so I requested an easy automatic camera for my birthday in February. I had the photos developed quickly and produced albums that were small enough for him to hold, but were toughened with cardboard and Sellotape so that they were durable. They depicted all our outings and everyday events such as swimming, shopping, the library, school activities such as eating his dinner and clearing his plate to the hatch, the gym with the wall bars, etc. We had shots of him helping me to stir (and taste) the custard, seated at the table, on the swing and going to Heathcroft. Whatever we did, I took a picture for discussion.

I became very autistic myself as I photographed him taking tins from a shelf in Waitrose to put into the trolley, or at the checkout. Quite often during these photographic sessions he ran, and I had to leave my shopping, and occasionally my bag, to chase frantically after him down the aisles, often knocking people to one side to lunge at him in true rugby fashion before he reached the door. My best method of controlling him was to grab his hair which would bring him to an abrupt halt and I would return him to our photographic venue to continue as if nothing had happened. It was no wonder that so many people appeared to know us around Henley!

The photographs did help and I used this method of communicating with him throughout his life. It helped to explain many situations such as school changes and holidays. On a few occasions he would spontaneously show me pictures which made me realize he knew what they represented.

I always used shopping as an activity although sometimes it was rather tortuous. Buying food is a lifelong necessity and has to be done with regularity. For an autistic child anything that is done on a regular structured basis makes life more orderly and therefore less confusing and frightening. If the task is introduced early enough and frequently, it will become something to which the child can adjust and hopefully enjoy.

The parent will need considerable patience in order to cope with the attitude of the public, particularly elderly ladies, who may view your child's behaviour as the result of bad upbringing. Things your child does can appear so appalling when taken at face value, that the parent is often viewed as someone who cannot handle his or her offspring, and this may provoke comments such as 'that child needs to have a good smack' or 'parents don't know how to bring up their children these days'.

It is hurtful to hear these comments, but as autistic children look so normal it is easy for outspoken people to confuse the issue. If people know there is a problem they are normally understanding and are sympathetic. For this reason, and to help me to grab hold of something, I used a child harness and reigns on Grant until he was about six years old.

(Recently the Berkshire autistic group (see Advice and Information section at the back of the book) have made sweatshirts, T-shirts and sew-on labels that say, 'Please be patient, I am autistic' and their popularity is ample proof of their need.)

My supermarket incidents were numerous, as we always shopped together. Many were the times he pinched something tasty from a passing trolley. He would sink his teeth into the contents, crushing packets of biscuits, or would open with amazing dexterity a passing can of beer and begin drinking the contents with most of it ending down his front or on the floor. I muttered embarrassed apologies but also became engrossed in cleaning-up Grant.

One day in a supermarket in Reading, I was waiting at the cashout holding Grant tightly by one hand and my basket of shopping in the other. An elderly lady in front had a basket of shopping and on the top were some warm doughnuts, probably bought for herself and her husband to have with a cup of tea on her return from shopping. They had been cooked on the newly opened bakery section and the smell of steaming new bread and hot cakes was mouthwatering. Grant obviously thought so too as with a quick swipe of the one free hand a warm jammy doughnut was taken from the bag and stuffed into his mouth, sugar and red jam trickling from the corners.

I looked at him with horror as did the elderly lady who could not believe her eyes to see this child, who should know better, eating her treat. I apologized profusely and explained simply that he was mentally handicapped. She looked at the now extremely sticky, jam and sugar coated Grant, who was oblivious to any fuss, and said warmly, 'Oh, is he? Do have the other one!'

On one dreadful occasion I lost Grant while shopping. It was in a large department store and I had stopped to look at a garden fork.

I took my eyes and hand off him for seconds then looked down and he had gone. Panic stricken, I mobilized everyone around me into action! I grabbed at the people nearest to me and gabbled at them. 'Please can you help, my little boy has run off. He has blonde hair and a camel coat. He doesn't understand language or dangers so please can you man the main doors, stop him and hold him tightly.'

I made sure the doors were covered then spoke frantically to two assistants who dashed off to look. Five minutes later one came running up to me to say he had been found – could I come and get him. He was on the first floor wriggling and giggling with pleasure on one of the beds. How he had got up there I shall never know – did he take the escalator, stairs or lift?

As I have illustrated, shopping, particularly in large stores and supermarkets, can become a source of extreme difficulty and frustration. I learnt through the years that supermarket staff are only too pleased to help if they are asked. Our children look so normal that we are not picked out as a category that is in need of assistance. A word with a supervisor on the way round to request help with packing shopping at the checkout is all that is needed. If the child is particularly difficult that day they may happily loan an assistant to help with the whole shopping expedition. Helpful service is often worth a letter of thanks as it motivates shops to see the need.

An embarrassment which increased as Grant grew taller came from his enjoyment in touching people. He would hold his hand out so that it trailed and knocked against every one in his path which resulted in many turned heads to see who or what had hit them in the legs. As he grew the part of the body he touched moved higher – hence my embarrassment!

Once a young man turned and looked at me with a smirk on his face and I realized with horror that he thought it was me, causing Grant and me to make a very hasty get-a-way!

The autistic son of a group member had a obsession about people crossing their legs and if he saw them seated or standing with their legs crossed he would, given the chance, make a great effort to uncross them. One day his mother was in the bank when she let go of his hand to sign a cheque and to her mortification he was on his hands and knees uncrossing the legs of all the businessmen waiting their turn for the cashier!

There are many embarrassing autistic situations, most being linked to lack of social awareness. The need for tactile stimulation in some autistics can often lead to unusual obsessions with things such as the feel of stockings (on the limb!), fur coats or hairy legs. Even the unimaginative can appreciate the embarrassment this could give the parent caught off-guard!

Within the Autistic Society we were discussing new methods, theories and fads of the moment which stemmed from educational, psychological and nutritional research. Several people had discussed the latest on diet factors influencing hyperactivity in children sensitive to additives in food. The diet they were suggesting followed that devised by paediatrician and allergist Dr Ben Feingold in America who had written a book, *Why Your Child is Hyperactive*. In it he explains his hypothesis on the affects of chemical additives on some children.

I obtained details of the diet from the chairwoman of the Hyperactive Children's Support Group and they included shopping lists and other details which were helpful. I felt I must try the diet on Grant as we had nothing to lose and everything to gain. So off I went to Sainsbury's supermarket, this time unaccompanied, as I needed to study ingredients on packets. That would have been out of the question with either of the children with me. At that time Sainsbury's and Marks & Spencer department store were the best shops for additive free products.

The support group stressed label reading for colour and flavour additions. Forbidden additives were monosodium glutamate, nitrate vanillin and anything with artificial colouring or flavouring. Fruits and vegetables that contained salicylates were forbidden as these could also cause problems and a list of these was included.

There were a lot of things to choose from that Grant could eat but the worry was when he grabbed and ate other things that were not necessarily food such as plants, anybody's drink, and worst of all he could be affected by chlorine in the swimming-pool, from which he drank great quantities of water. To give up swimming would be unthinkable, as it provided much stimulation and exercise and filled many spare hours. I really needed something to clamp his mouth shut in the pool!

Despite these difficulties we embarked on the Feingold diet and I found it necessary to add a column to my list on the kitchen cupboard for the extras that might have been swallowed and any noted changes in his behaviour. After four weeks I had not seen any noticeable alterations and the numbers of added extras on my list was high so I stopped being fanatical about it. I did, however, continue buying additive-free food for all the family as this could only benefit us all.

Christmas 1979 was a memorable one for me as that year Grant showed the most interest in his presents. Up to then Christmas had been a non-event and any eager anticipation of interest from Grant in carefully chosen presents proved ill-founded because of his total disinterest. This year, however, we had obtained the old guitar and some new musical boxes. My parents were staying with us and sleeping in Julian's bedroom suite. Grant first picked up his new guitar and took it into their room to show his grandparents. He then came back and got his musical box and took it to show them. He was now starting to display a lot of good signs that were encouraging for his future.

Sadly, after Christmas, he had a setback that upset and confused him. There was a fresh reorganization at school and Grant was to have a new teacher. Marjorie had only been a stand-in as she wasn't teacher-trained although her abilities with these children were as good as anyone who had full qualifications. Grant's new teacher didn't understand him and couldn't cope with his running. It was a vicious circle with one provoking the other and Grant's behaviour becoming progressively worse, which spilled over at home. During a visit to Dr O'Gorman I confided to him my pessimistic view of the current situation and he could see that I was not coping and getting very tired and run down.

'I think you have had enough,' he said. 'It is time we thought about putting him into residential care; you can't go on like this. Think about it and talk it through with your husband, and Susan will come and see you at home. I think we could probably find a place for him at Smith Hospital in Henley.'

I took Grant back to school and before I got there I cried bitterly that it was all coming to this when we had begun to break through to him. On returning him to his class I told his teacher what had been said.

'I quite agree,' she said with a look of relief. 'He is such a difficult young man, and so strong. Nobody could manage him for long. I have worked with handicapped children for years in Borocourt hospital and he would be well cared for there or at Smith Hospital.'

I went home in deep despair. We loved our son so dearly – how could we possibly give him up to an institutionalized hospital existence? I told Paul when he came home and we forlornly discussed what we should do. We knew his behaviour had gone downhill since he had changed class and not had Marjorie, with whom he had responded so well.

'Why don't you go into school and discuss this with Mike,' suggested Paul. 'If I looked after him more we could manage.'

I brooded about it for hours. How could Paul look after him much more? We already shared the night and he had to have his sleep in order to work and be our breadwinner. Julian needed us too; if he took him more at the weekends then Julian would miss out.

I agonized over the situation until the solution came. We had never made the most of using Heathcroft, our respite care home. I left him now for the occasional night so they did know his ways; maybe I should use them more. Although it was a super place and the staff very caring and friendly, I did find it hard to take him there as we had only to set off in the direction of Heathcroft and he would begin screaming and holding me tightly around the neck. Once home I would call them back, to be told that it hadn't taken him long to settle to a story and the sound of a few musical boxes. If Heathcroft took Grant for a whole weekend once a month then we could sleep and do things with Julian that were impossible when Grant was with us. Maybe he could stay a night or two more at other times, to make life a little easier.

Having sorted this out in my mind I went to sleep and told Paul of my thoughts in the morning. He visibly brightened at the prospect of keeping Grant at home, and thought it could work.

I spoke to Mike at school and we discussed our ideas. Mike left it with me to speak with Susan Wagstaff, Dr O'Gorman's social worker colleague, as soon as possible to see if Heathcroft would be happy with this arrangement. Mike said that there would have to be another reorganization in school as Grant's current teacher was not able to cope with him.

The utter despair of the day before was already evaporating with our new plans. Susan made arrangements with Heathcroft who were only too pleased to accommodate him fully into their system. He had already won the hearts of several of their staff and I was told that they were just waiting for me to let go. They could see it coming as they knew the difficulties and didn't know how we had managed to hold on for as long as we had.

Mike Hudson made new classroom arrangements and Marjorie was to be the helper to Pauline Grady, a new teacher, starting the next term. This arrangement was to last very satisfactorily for the following two years. Pauline was excellent and quickly got the measure of Grant, particularly having Marjorie's help.

After about two months he felt secure again and small but new steps forward were made.

Eight

Paul came home one evening early in 1980 to say Metal Box wished him to consider a move. They felt, if he was to further his career, he needed wider experience and this he could get by being an assistant to a factory accountant at one of their manufacturing locations. We would have to move. What did I think?

I remember my internal reaction was one of horror. We had got our safe spot and Grant was beginning to settle at the school that was just up the road. In the other direction was Heathcroft which we so desperately needed to keep us all together, and the chances of finding all those conditions elsewhere were negligible. But it was Paul's career and the ultimate decision must be his.

I think he had already made up his mind, and I am sure my face must have confirmed his own thoughts. I voiced my feelings carefully about Grant's position. Julian could resettle anywhere as I am sure could Paul and I, but uprooting Grant could possibly tip him away from us forever. Paul said he had thought that too and he was happy to turn it down, particularly as it would have been only a lateral move, not a promotion. They had said that there would be some internal posts being advertised and it wasn't long before he heard that there was an accountant's job available in a company subsidiary in Henley. Paul applied for this position and got it. We couldn't believe our luck as it was even nearer home than before and it offered the kind of work he much preferred. With it being a division of Metal Box we still had use of their swimming facilities which I found so invaluable.

Our respective families often let us know they wished to help us, but felt at a loss to know how. My parents were a long way away in Birkenhead and, whereas we had seen them frequently before Grant was born, there were now so many difficulties that the times we could visit were infrequent. They would usually come to us in the summer holidays to break up the endless number of days that needed filling. Most frustratingly Grant played up much more when they visited, to try and get more attention, as most normal children probably would. However, this would then show him up in a more depressing light. My parents wanted, like all parents, a happy and peaceful life for their children and, knowing this, I tried to hide some of Grant's misdemeanours, as the ones they did see were enough for them to endure! Had they been nearer they would have assisted the way Edna did, by sitting for the boys so we could have an occasional evening out, or by doing a pile of ironing or entertaining Julian.

Julian was eight or nine when I put him on the train at Reading, under the care of the guard, and my father met him at Liverpool. He enjoyed a week of undivided attention; deservedly and predictably he was thoroughly spoiled!

Both sets of parents helped us financially as the need arose. When Grant was four I had had a succession of old banger cars that frequently let us down. The local bus service was reasonable, but coping with Grant, pushchairs and shopping became increasingly difficult. Somebody suggested that I apply to the Joseph Rowntree Family Fund who aim to help families with a handicapped child by providing financial assistance for the purchase of anything that would make life easier, such as, a washing machine or tumbledryer. I wondered whether they might be able to help with financing towards another old car. Grant was extremely good in a car as, not only did he enjoy the rides, but he had something different to see, and it was the key to a whole new range of educational and entertainment possibilities. When he was strapped in he wasn't getting into any mischief. I sent off the application and heard from them the following week. They would arrange for someone to visit to assess us very shortly.

When Grant was around it was usually impossible to talk to anyone, but it was holiday time and their representative said she would like to see him anyway. When she was due to arrive I went around the house locking all the doors so that there were as few distractions as possible. The only door that didn't lock was the toilet, but there was little in there that he could do to cause harm. A pleasant middle-aged lady arrived at 2 p.m., as arranged, and with all the doors locked, a pile of Ladybird books, several music boxes and a clean, spruce and normal looking little boy, it made my tales of woe look like a well-fabricated story to get some easy money! But after fifteen minutes Grant became bored and he began wandering from locked door to locked door trying hard to get somewhere, so that he could wreak a little havoc. He just didn't know how to distract us and focus attention on himself. Then he found it! I heard a bit of a noise, but being lost in the questions from the long form, I didn't investigate. Into the lounge came Grant, staggering under the weight of the ceramic top to the loo cistern! I secretly congratulated him as the following week a cheque arrived accompanied by a letter explaining that it was not what they usually did, but in the circumstances they understood our need and would make an exception! My parents heard of this and also contributed a sum so that I could acquire a reasonable car that we hoped would be reliable.

In the summer, when Grant was three, we were invited by Stella, Paul's sister, to stay with her, her husband and son Richard in their house in a village in Luxembourg. They knew all the problems and felt they could overcome them. We decided to combine this stay with a week's camping in the Vosges mountains in France.

This holiday proved reasonably successful, helped by hot, dry weather in the Vosges, although while we were in Luxembourg poor Grant was quite ill with tonsillitis.

Stella had ensured that his room was completely safe. The main light was from a roof window that was utterly impossible to reach even with Grant's climbing skills. There was also another window that had heavy wooden shutters on the outside much like other continental houses. There was a lock on his bedroom door and she had cleared anything unnecessary; all that was left was the bed and a few appropriate toys. It is unbelievable that anything could go wrong in this situation, but it did. In front of the window was a radiator of the older cast iron style (the kind that resembles a fully extended concertina). The metal ridges on the top were thinning and somewhat sharp. In the early hours of the morning Grant had awoken and tried to make his escape. Finding the door shut he looked for the window and had climbed up on to the radiator to try and reach the window catch, only to cut two toes quite deeply on the ridges. He walked around the room, kicked the door and then climbed in and out of bed. Not realizing what was happening we didn't go to him until the noises were persistent and likely to wake the rest of the house. When we opened the door it looked as if there had been a murder as there was blood everywhere. The walls washed clean easily, as did the sheets and the woodwork, but the carpet where the blood had dried was another story (the enzyme-dissolving solvents of today were not available then). We felt very embarrassed about the situation although they tried to reassure us that the fault was theirs for having a sharp radiator and not realizing its potential danger.

The attack of tonsillitis made Grant lethargic and kept me at the house, but it gave Paul time with Julian and his cousin Richard. They drove out to the hills of picturesque east Luxembourg and spent an exciting hour careering down a purpose-built bob-sleigh track .

Our camping in the Vosges was a success for all the family. The sun smiled on us and skies stayed clear and blue. We ate outdoors in the minimum of clothes, usually just bathing suits, thus reducing the washing load drastically. Any dirty clothes could wait until our return and didn't risk becoming mouldy.

The following year, 1979, we camped again, this time in Cornwall, but by Grant's sixth year we chose just to go out for days, as the preparation for, and the clearing up after, a camping expedition had become too much trouble. Coping with the long summer holidays was becoming quite a nightmare.

The year Grant was seven we hired a caravan owned by the Hampshire Autistic Society on the Isle of White. We saw the advertisement in the magazine produced by the National Autistic Society and applied for a week in August. We didn't look forward to it as most of our holidays so far had been difficult, but it turned out to be a great success.

The caravan was old, but clean, sturdy and autistic proof. It was one of two in the middle of a large field in a very pleasant part of the island and on farmland which was off the road. There was a strong farm gate with a tight fastener that even I found difficult to undo. Here Grant found freedom with a whole field to run in and his family around him all the time, his security was assured. He was relaxed and very happy as were we all, as our peace of mind depended on Grant.

Following this success, Paul's parents bought us a good second-hand caravan and this was worth its weight in gold for our family holidays for the next ten years. We joined The Caravan Club which provides small sites all over Britain and we found that these were the best for Grant, particularly when small. We would choose a site that was well off a main road and had no known dangers such as deep water. We would explain our problems with the site owners who would fill us in with exact details of the surrounding area so that we could assess its suitability. Only five caravans were allowed on these sites which meant Grant had only four vans in which he could disappear or invite himself to breakfast!

Until this very useful acquisition our family holidays had centred around our family-sized tent. I always looked forward to us all going away, but found the holidays so frustrating when camping because of havoc wreaked, especially the food and drink that inevitably got spilt. Coping with wet washing had been a nightmare, but the warmth and protection of the caravan made it much easier.

Here Paul and I would take it in turns to sleep with Grant in a zipped-up inner tent in the awning, thus ensuring sleep on alternate nights. If it rained we could stay dry and warm, without the worry of leaking from the, inevitably touched, tent walls. Our caravan took us to places all over England and France and, as long as we chose our sights with care, gave us reasonable holidays.

During 1980 when Grant was five and with his new teacher, Pauline Grady, Grant's and our life had gradually calmed down again. He was happy to see the return of Marjorie to his life and soon struck up a good rapport with the new teacher who had a quiet but firm approach and insisted on his completing a task. She also believed in the importance of the parents' role in the child's development and made regular visits to our home to liaise with me. This support was invaluable as it enabled us to make progressive steps. Heathcroft was invaluable too, allowing us a weekend each month to ourselves, to rest and prepare for the weeks ahead. I often worried about leaving Grant, particularly if there were members of staff on duty who were new to the job and were not attuned to his uncanny ability to know when someone had averted their eyes, giving him ample opportunity to disappear, be it to the kitchen, (when a plate of food was handy), or to an open door. One day I had taken him to Heathcroft while I shopped in Reading. Before I left him, a member of staff confessed that the nuns who lived next door had asked her who was the attractive little boy they often saw in their grounds scooping leaves from their wheelbarrow? I was horrified, thinking that if he managed to climb over into their garden without being seen, where else could he go? Obviously somebody had not been supervising him.

I went round the shops bothered and concerned at what I had been told. Coincidentally I bumped into one of the original members of staff at Heathcroft who was particularly good with him. I told her why I was so worried and she immediately reassured me.

'Please don't worry any more,' she said. 'I think I know where he could be getting through. I'm on duty this evening so I will see to it and also thoroughly check all our other boundaries. I'll also make sure every member of staff knows of this. It won't happen again, I assure you.'

I trusted this girl as she had always been very honest about his care, telling me when he was difficult or good, happy or sad. I knew she was genuinely concerned for his welfare. The next time I visited I was told with a laugh that the nuns would miss him as he would not have the chance to call again! They had also changed their door handles to doubles, one of which was very high. Apart from having to be tall to reach the second handle you also needed two hands to work the two together.

I became more involved with the school, helping regularly with swimming and becoming a parent governor. Watching and participating in school activities helped me to collaborate in Grant's care and teaching. This was also helpful with my next two methods of therapy.

The first of these was another diet. I had spoken to a doctor who lived locally and worked in London as an allergist. He believed the causes of many conditions lay in our allergic reactions to certain substances in the food we ate. He had devised a diet that eliminated every food that had ever been known to cause allergy problems. Reactions can be in the form of a rash, hyperactivity, behavioural problems, mental or physical conditions. The list of foods that Grant was allowed to eat was very limited and not very tasty. They were as follows: sago flour, kosher margarine, carrots, cabbage, rhubarb, lamb, pure pineapple juice and all food cooked in bottled mineral water. This diet had to be strictly followed for three weeks then a new food could be introduced at the rate of one a week, noting any reactions. Any that caused a problem would need to be immediately stopped and a few days allowed to elapse before introducing another one.

Putting any child on to a drastic diet such as this would be difficult even if the child understood why it was necessary. We didn't know if Grant understood anything, but I explained it to him simply as if he could, and we began the regime.

I made him carrot cakes from the soya flour, margarine and grated carrot. Beautiful lamb joints provided him with copious meat and the fat and juices supplied dripping to spread on to his carrot cakes for breakfast. Meat juices, fat and sago flour would make up a gravy. However, he could not have sugar or seasoning to make his food more palatable. Stewed rhubarb without sugar is very sharp! Julian, Paul and I agonized at breakfast as we watched him eat a bowl of stewed unsweetened rhubarb and found it impossible to eat ourselves. Grant ate it all up as if he knew we were trying to help him, his face grimacing only slightly at the sour fruit. I had to send a packed lunch into school, which included carrot cakes, raw carrots and chunks of lamb.

We managed to continue the diet for three weeks, but this was with great difficulty. Having to prepare his food separately was hard when Grant was around. Our food was temptingly close and had to be denied him. A microwave oven would have helped as a meal could have been prepared in advance and made during school time. However, they were not widely available then.

We monitored, by way of a graph, alterations in behaviour or sleep patterns. We were told to expect a possible deterioration in his behaviour until his body had eliminated all the damaging toxins and this could take a week or two. We managed to follow the diet closely, and took great care to ensure that nothing else, bar the allowed substances, entered his system. However the graph went up and down. There was no noticeable deterioration or improvement after the stipulated time for toxin clearance. After three weeks I decided to introduce my first new food substance and this was wheat flour in the form of bread. Four days later he developed a rash all over his body and was generally under the weather, with a slight temperature. The rash, I hoped, would prove wheat flour to be an allergen. Unfortunately, we were to prove little as, when his temperature rose, I examined him for swollen glands and found the typical bobbly chain down the back of his neck, which indicate the rubella virus. I took him to see the doctor who had helped me start him on the diet and he too felt the rash was probably German measles. As the incubation time is around twenty-one days the diet and graph would have been completely thrown by the incubating virus! He did suggest that I give him a massive dose of sugar to see what his reaction would be. Sugar is often a common cause of hyperactivity and Grant had been free from sugars for three weeks. A sudden introduction would cause acute hyperactivity if he was allergic to the substance. We braced ourselves as we indulged him in sugary drinks and sweets but there was no significant change in his behaviour. The diet was discontinued, but I did feel we had given it a good try and proved that sugar at least was not a problem.

Personally I feel that, although difficult, diets are something to be tried as there are some children who can have severe allergy problems to food substances. The allergies can cause behaviour problems akin to autism and these might be controlled by eliminating the offending foods. Hyperactivity is one symptom that arises if there is an allergen in the diet and knowing which substances cause the problems can only improve the life of the whole family. There is nothing to lose from trying, apart from your sanity for a few weeks!

We had another attempt at allergy diets when Grant was eleven and again there were no noticeable changes. I asked my family doctor if I could be referred to a new, local allergist. This time the list was different for his elimination diet, the meat being turkey and the flour, rice flour as well as rice itself. The fruit allowed was bananas. There was no fat in the diet, but I managed a little from the cooking of my very free range, once happy turkeys, in which the whole family could participate. Grant enjoyed and freely indulged in the bananas. At the age of eleven he was calmer, making the whole process easier, but despite this it made no improvements to concentration or other aspects of the condition.

I was constantly searching for anything new, spoken or written on the subject. I subscribed to Autism Research papers from America, where all leading authorities in the world submitted their latest data of studies. There was a wealth of new ideas but nothing really positive. The Institute for Brain Damaged Children based in Somerset, England sent me, on request, evidence of their work. There was no information as to how they succeeded with autistic children and whether their extreme methods of 'patterning' the children would help or disturb them. These procedures consisted of gathering together many volunteers who then put the child through hours of 'patterns' that simulated its early physical development as a baby, thus re-educating a damaged or under-developed brain. The 'experts' were still not sure what was happening within the autistic brain, so how could anyone know if this method would help or hinder? I decided to put a letter in the UK National Autistic Society's quarterly news bulletin *Communication* asking if anyone had used this treatment before and, if so, what effect it had had on their child. I received three letters from parents, two of whom said that it had been disturbing and detrimental to their child's behaviour and this remedial therapy should be discouraged for autistic children. The third said they had tried it with little effect, but they had felt the constant one-to-one attention and perseverance with a task had probably led to their child being more aware of its surroundings. Weighing up these facts I decided this method was unsuitable for Grant, or for that matter the majority of autistic children for whom socializing is so difficult. A constant succession of different people coming and going would, in all likelihood, be very frightening and disturbing and could have a severe detrimental effect. On the other hand, bearing in mind the parent who had expressed that the continuous attention had helped and that I had definitely broken through to Grant with the 'holding on the bed', I now had to think how I could give him more of my undivided time. I had also recently read *To Love is to be Happy With* by Barry Neil Kaufman, who claimed to have cured his severely autistic son spending hours and hours with him in an enclosed environment and joining the child in 'his world'. He did this by copying his son's obsessive habits such as spinning tops, plates, and other things that isolated him. Accepting him as he was enabling him to join our world when he could. (This method is now known as 'The Option Method'.)

This book had made me very discontented. When I thought someone was doing something to improve his child's condition, I wanted to do it too and this book was advocating something almost impossible for most families. To begin with, you have to create a room that has no distractions and is not used by the rest of the family. The Kaufmans used a bathroom. (I presume they had a separate toilet and everyone had washed early!) Working by yourself day after day in an enclosed space would be difficult enough, but who would shop, cook, collect from school and so on?

I wondered if I could compromise by giving Grant concentrated time when it wouldn't interfere with the rest of the family. I discussed it with Pauline at school and asked what she felt about me bringing him home when he had had his lunch and thus allowing two and a half hours of very structured 'him and me' time. Pauline liked the idea and said she would support whatever I had in mind.

So I set to work to draw up structured afternoons with specific schemes in mind. I would try and link up with his obsessions which I knew to be the only possible way to gain any motivation. At the time these were food, books and music. He enjoyed tactile stimulation so I had gathered suitable material together. I tried to link my programme to what we would do after I had picked up Julian.

We had a 'car' day. As we came home from school I would talk constantly about the car. I sat him on my lap in the drive and held his hands on the wheel and pretended to drive, putting his hand to the gears, etc. He enjoyed this, but his attention span was still only limited. We would then go into the house and into our small dining-room, which had already been prepared for my work with him. I would continue the car theme with a selection of small toy vehicles, which we would push around a play mat with a road design. We would sort out vehicles by type and see if Grant could pass me the correct one. If he managed to choose correctly he was rewarded with raisins. Some days he would do quite well, but on other days he couldn't or wouldn't even give me a car when requested and would often sweep them all to the floor. While on the car theme we would read a book on cars, try and draw cars and attempt a jigsaw with a vehicular picture. We finished the day with a drive to somewhere like a bus depot, where we could continue this input.

Other themes would be food. I would use jigsaws and books on the subject, food textures and smells, sucking and blowing, and our day would finish by baking something. The cooking would start well, but I kept losing him and would have to rescue him so many times that there used to be more flour on him and me than there was in the cake!

Music was a third theme and working a tape-recorder and playing all kinds of musical instruments formed part of this session. I encouraged eye contact and words, and again used raisins and nuts as rewards, but speech, as such, only came occasionally and clear words were rare.

I enjoyed these very positive sessions and Pauline felt his behaviour and understanding had improved with the intense input I was giving him. She also found him much more calm and settled. We kept up these sessions for several months until schedules at school changed and Grant would have missed out on interesting and beneficial activities, such as swimming, by coming home. I still, however, continued to work with him for at least an hour after school.

Grant was with Pauline for two years, between the age of five and seven. The classroom helpers were Marjorie Blake, and Sylvia Oakley who succeeded Marjorie, working with Pauline towards the end of this time. She then transferred to his next teacher, Carol Bonas, thus providing some continuity for him. Pauline was good for Grant and it was a happy classroom group. Grant's classmates, Glynn, Sally and Claire, had stayed with Grant and were joined by Tammy and Sarah. Grant's sixth birthday on a lovely, warm, sunny, spring day brought the whole of the little group to our house to share it with Grant. He usually preferred to disappear into his bedroom, given half the chance, but was happy to reappear for the party tea which would be unlocked from the kitchen halfway through their stay.

Pauline became a very good support to our family and our liaison and co-ordination with Grant's care helped him feel increasingly secure in his confused world. He was learning the use of the toilet and would now usually take himself, making accidents less frequent. If he felt insecure then wetting would become a problem even if he had just been.

Grant was using occasional words daily, but they were not clearly pronounced. You would have to know him well to detect what was said. The words spoken were mostly to a prompt. Regularly used words heard were 'hello, bye-bye, biscuit, drink, yoghurt, mummy, gaggy (Daddy), Gulian (Julian)'. He used other words and phrases on occasions and sometimes these would be clearly said, but that was fairly rare. He always confused people with his comprehension as he gave contradictory indications. He enjoyed stories appropriate for his age, such as 'Mog' books and 'Topsy and Tim', and could pick them out from a large pile. But he would get confused with a simple request, for example, when told to get his coat he would take down his trousers! His play was still almost non-existent and almost everything he did resulted from the input of somebody else. He loved rough and tumble games particularly with Paul who spent a lot of time throwing him around, wheeling him in the wheel-barrow or tickling him into helpless laughter. Paul, as promised, was spending much more time with him and taking him out for some time every weekend. He found some trips difficult due to missing toileting signals, but nevertheless got increasing pleasure from his difficult charge. I would send them off with two spare pairs of pants and trousers, a wet flannel, books galore and musical boxes. It was giving Paul the chance to learn much more about the complicated workings of his younger son and the beauty of the little person locked within. At home Julian and I had time to talk or just be more relaxed.

Nine

Paul had a burning desire to visit America and now Grant, at six, was staying happily at Heathcroft for nights we thought we could consider having a longer special holiday. We knew it would be a wonderful opportunity for the three of us, but hated the idea of leaving Grant for so long, and excluding him from this exciting family break during which we planned to visit Disneyland.

The staff at school were adamant that we should not even consider taking Grant as, for one thing, he would not cope with the long journey and change of hours. They also felt that a two-week break would do us the world of good and recharge our batteries.

We booked our trip to California from where, after seeing the usual Los Angeles attractions, we would then drive to the Grand Canyon, Las Vegas, Yosemite and Zion National Parks. We planned to take a Greyhound bus overnight to Oregon, where Paul's relations lived, and stay with them for two or three days before returning to our car, travelling on to San Fransisco, our final port of call before returning home.

The planning of that exciting trip helped us through the difficult winter. I worried about leaving Grant, so decided to try and ease him into it by getting him used to the idea, if possible. We would attempt to accomplish this with photographs. We hoped this way he would realize that we had not deserted him and that we were coming back. I compiled an album consisting of pictures of him getting into the taxi at school and getting out at

Heathcroft, as well as pictures of his room at Heathcroft, the toys, the garden and its array of playcraft such as the slide, swings and other large, interesting, physical equipment which he enjoyed. I took photos of him with the telephone in his hand so that I could try to make him understand that we would speak to him that way. Unfortunately, through the winter months until late April he was desperately unhappy when I took him into Heathcroft, which made us increasingly uneasy about leaving him. He usually settled, but it could take some time. We were to leave in mid May. However, it wasn't until early May when the sun came out and Heathcroft opened up its doors to their garden with its many pleasures, that Grant decided it was not such a bad place after all!

Thankfully, we left for holiday reasonably reassured that all would be well. I had told Paul that, if I was to make this trip, I must be allowed to ring Grant at Heathcroft at least every third day: I am not sure what I would have done if they had told me he was unhappy.

Our holiday was a great success and Grant coped with our absence extremely well. The staff went through my book with him at least twice a day. He demanded and received lots of attention being read to and cuddled lavishly, as they knew that was the best way to keep him really happy.

Julian wallowed in two and a half weeks of undivided parental attention. He loved every moment as we all did, but it really was a physically exhausting trip as we wanted to pack as much into our time as we possibly could. We *did* that area of America as well as any American could *do* England! The whole holiday went smoothly and by phoning Heathcroft many times we were assured that Grant was happy enough without us. When we saw the effect a holiday without Grant had on Julian we perceived the necessity to keep one week (at least) a year free to have a break away with him alone. We kept to this until Julian, at sixteen, preferred to make his own plans.

Two people came into Grant's life during the year he was six – Anne Tucknott and Claire Arthan. Anne answered an advert I placed in the local Post Office for help in the house during the summer holidays. My previous help had moved on and I had managed without for a few weeks. However, in the holiday time I needed assistance with simple things like making the bed and washing up which often had to be left undone until after Grant had gone to bed, and I hated that. Once a bed was made the door to that room had to be locked or else he would leap into the bed and it would need doing again!

We were never unduly surprised at the items we found in our bed! More often than not there was a book or two, a prickly hairbrush and a musical box that had become lost under the pillow and would ding into your ear when you put your head there. It was not uncommon to stick to a piece of honeyed bread, not to mention Bovril (beef spread) sandwiches, his favourite, which made an awful stain. We often shared our bed with half-eaten cooking apples which had been plucked under-ripe from the many apple trees in the garden.

Anne had not done this type of work before, but when I explained what I needed she was happy to give it a go. She came in every morning and helped sort out the confusion. She became very proud at the speed she could replace the pieces of the inset jigsaw puzzles that usually lay in a mixed confusion on Grant's bedroom floor. One day she declared that she would be a very rich woman if she had a penny for each curled book she had picked up, straightened and neatly replaced on to his shelves.

Grant was nearly always pleased to see Anne arrive, not entirely unconnected with the fact that on numerous occasions she brought treats of sweets for the boys and a cream cake for me. If she thought I was having a difficult time I was sure to get a consolation cake the next day! Grant often managed an ''Ello Anne' or 'Bye Anne' or 'Thank you, Anne' when asked. Anne soon became very fond of him and continued to help when the summer holidays ended, staying with us for the next fourteen years. We could not have done without her.

Claire came in the summer holidays for a week when Grant was six. She was on secondment to Bishopswood school from the

Nursery Nurse training college in Reading and was looking for a family she could help for a week, as part of her training. She was introduced to me at a school function and I welcomed her offer with delight. I picked her up from college daily and she helped with my day, thus easing the difficulties. It increased her interest in autism and she later produced excellent project work on the subject.

In these early stages she couldn't believe some of the methods we used to deal with Grant's autistic behaviour. This is a completely different methodology from that learnt at Nursery Training for a normal child, so Claire was appalled at my reaction to a certain incident one day.

Binfield Heath holds an annual village 'Show' in August and it makes the day more enjoyable if you can enter something. As I had Claire to help, I thought I would try and produce a fruit cake for my entry. I removed a very successful effort from the oven and was delighted to see that it had not split on top, as usual, and the fruit looked to be evenly distributed. I placed it on a rack to cool and went into the garden to do some weeding. Grant was sitting quietly with a book in my car so Claire grabbed a fork and began to help with the garden. I was habitually aware of Grant's every movement, so I looked up to check the car and found it empty. I knew where he would be and ran frantically to the kitchen to discover my worst fears were confirmed. There Grant stood, mouth crammed and crumbs flying. The smooth topped, even fruited cake now resembled Mount Vesuvius. I calmly asked Claire to take him out of my sight while I cleared up. Later Claire expressed her disbelief that I had not admonished him in any way. I had to explain to her that by doing so I would have further encouraged his naughtiness by rewarding his bad behaviour. He did not understand that what he had done was wrong and neither did he understand social gestures. Shouting, smacking or sending him to his room was not a punishment. However, this is an extremely difficult rule to adhere to and much will depend on the offence and the mood of the moment. A few sleepless nights would guarantee a less patient approach!

This was Claire's introduction to his life. It was the start of a wonderful relationship, not just for me but for Claire who felt that she and Grant had become friends. She saw him through many traumas and became the only person apart from Paul's mother, Edna, and later Julian, to whom we could entrust his care.

Claire worked for a time at Heathcroft and if Grant was staying she would be the one caring for Grant, which pleased me. The Heathcroft bugs always hit Grant if Claire was on duty, and she had the awful job of caring for a child who could not tell you when he was about to be sick!

Occasionally she would take Grant to her house in Reading for the night to enable us to get a good sleep and this would mean that her night would be disturbed, but she was happy to help.

When Grant was much older, Claire took Grant and me up to her parents' farm in Shropshire where she gave him freedom on the safe parts of the farm. She showed him how to climb on to the top of the huge grain hoppers and gain sensual pleasure from sifting the sunwarmed grain through his fingers. He lay in the sun on hay blocks, while the family helped with the harvesting, and he watched with interest the cows being directed into the barn to be milked.

This additional help with Grant made life somewhat easier. Without the extreme tensions in me, to which I felt Grant was finely attuned, he began to have a few calmer moments and this was pure bliss.

We encouraged him to walk more and more, although sometimes he was very reluctant. The large buggy was still very useful in situations such as shopping, where you needed to be unrestricted, but we were using it less.

During the year Grant was six he had quite a few tantrums, although nothing like the scale that many autistic children suffer. His tantrums were due to the frustration of being forced to perform a task such as putting on clothes or having to walk somewhere that he didn't want to go. The reason his tantrums were not too bad may have had something to do with an almost total lack of awareness of his surroundings. He was also quite happy to do nothing.

Many autistic children have extremely bad tantrums that can last into adulthood and can prove very difficult and embarrassing for parents and carers. The frustration in me was overwhelming. Keeping Grant occupied was a full-time task. If he did nothing, although happier this way, he was not learning and so became destructive, though not deliberately so, tearing books, rolling around in my car until he knocked the mirror off or sitting in the middle of a freshly seeded row of vegetables sifting the soil and seeds between his fingers. He would walk around the garden picking off the small unripened apples or leaves of any nearby plant and eat them which, could have a disastrous effect on his bowels! It was therefore easier to take him out, but that meant chores at home had to be left undone.

Improvements became apparent and it was now possible for me to frantically peel my potatoes in four minutes knowing that was the maximum time I could allow him to wander the garden before I had to find him and direct his activity to something else!

Through our regional social services department I acquired a large tricycle that would suit his needs up to adulthood. This service, I believe, is no longer available in this area. To obtain the tricycle I was interviewed at Oxford by a departmental doctor, who asked me all the usual questions. He then went on to tell me that he thought I should put Grant into a home and forget about him. I shuddered at what he was saying and glared at him. All I wanted was a tricycle to give Grant another interest in life and not a lecture on how to get rid of him. He realized his words were falling on deaf ears so signed the appropriate paper to release a tricycle for our needs and we went on to the next department to measure Grant and arrange delivery.

An autistic child lacks motivation and trying to get him to pedal his tricycle clearly demonstrated this aspect of his condition. Although there are many advantages in living in an unmade lane, now there was also a disadvantage. Riding a tricycle by an unmotivated child was more difficult than on a smooth surface. He liked the idea but would put no effort into trying to push the pedals around. The lane had stones and potholes which stopped any propulsion that we had obtained. I would go along the lane bent double holding his foot to the pedal and shouting, '*Push*'. As soon as I let go he stopped. I would push his body and sometimes we would go for long stretches, but if I removed my hand he stopped.

Buying treats from the local shops was an incentive to use the tricycle and we would park it and go in to buy sweets or chocolate before returning home. However, it was me who had put in 95 per cent of the effort of our journey!

Grant did enjoy swimming and I worked constantly to help him swim unaided. Water presented another peril as his lack of awareness and understanding made rivers, ponds and swimming-pools a source of danger. If it was a hot day he would have happily jumped off the top of a bridge or walked into a river to cool himself down!

We still made twice weekly visits to Paul's company's pool and gradually I reduced the air in Grant's armbands. Using his obsession to escape as an incentive, I would hold him in increasing distances from the edge of the pool, until with the armbands completely deflated, he made it unaided to the edge. By the time he was six he was swimming with confidence. However, an autistic child is not competitive, so only swims for himself. Grant saw no reason to swim to a certain point unless he wanted to get out or saw food or drink, which did happen as larger pools, especially, would often sport a pool-side café. Grant would not swim unless he was out of his depth, as he would otherwise put his feet to the bottom. When Grant had learnt to swim unaided I would take him into the deep end, where he would swim well. This was a somewhat risky pursuit and if there was an attendant I would ask him/her to keep an eye on us. When I became more confident of his abilities I let him swim down the pool and on a few occasions he would achieve a length. As he got older his speed, thanks to his great strength, greatly exceeded mine, although he had no specific stroke and teaching him such would be an impossibility.

It was difficult to get him into the swimming-pool as, like most people find, the initial shock of the cool water was not pleasurable.

In order to get him into the water I would take him to the deep end and push him in! The next few moments were unnerving as he would do one of two things. Sometimes he would swim under the surface until his breath would not hold out. This was alarming as, through lack of understanding, he might take a breath under water. Alternatively he would twizzle around and around, often disappearing beneath the surface for heart-stopping moments only to appear and twizzle again! However, he never did take a breath under the water or do anything to panic himself or worry me about his safety.

His swimming always delighted us as he was doing something that many people couldn't. His abilities proved to be life-saving. One day at a friend's house in the winter, he disappeared into the garden where they had a swimming-pool. Having an autistic son themselves they told me not to worry as their son only ever walked by the edge. But not trusting Grant's fearlessness I went to seek him and found him gasping with the cold as he frantically swam, fully clothed, to the edge of their near frozen swimming-pool! I hauled him out, none the worse for his very cold experience.

As I've mentioned, Grant was completely obsessed with Ladybird books and uncannily aware of where he could find them, be it on a shelf, deep down in a box at a car boot sale or on a rack in a shop. There were many times when he would drag me into shops that I hadn't been in before, and sometimes even into shops in a different area. I would be taken to a shelf where there would be Ladybird books. It was as if he had a sixth sense. He would usually go for the book of the moment and take it from the shelf and it would then be difficult to get him to part with it. I would buy him a new book, trying to introduce new ones that might broaden his interest. It was always hard to introduce the next story and he would tolerate a page or two before snatching the book from my hand, whence it would be tossed to the floor, returning to his old familiar book of the moment.

Paul was the one to read the most to him, while I was preparing a meal or doing some other chore. We found that new material was best introduced when Grant was feeling sleepy, as this made him calmer and more receptive. Paul loved these moments of cuddling and reading and it was on more than one occasion that I came into the lounge to find them both asleep!

We both read so much that we knew stories off by heart and would have favourites. Paul, to relieve the boredom, would start reading in different accents, the Newcastle 'Geordie' voice being a favourite!

Grant did have a time when he would look for or choose a different Ladybird book until he eventually ran out of new titles in the younger age group. When we became concerned that there was little new suitable reading material for him, *Postman Pat*, *Thomas the Tank Engine* and *Fireman Sam* came out in the same size as the Ladybird books.

Grant also enjoyed listening to music and this helped to lull him off to sleep. So it was with much satisfaction that we learnt that Fisher Price, whose toys are almost unbreakable, had brought out a cassette-player. This gave Grant endless pleasure and was used for several years to entertain him in the middle of the night in the hope that it would calm him and eventually send him off to sleep.

Ladybird brought out cassettes to go with their stories and this brought a new pleasure for Grant and some relief for us. Grant appeared to understand these stories as if we were reading them to him and this would then keep him happy for some time, listening to his favourite tales.

More and more children's books were produced on tape, but he would only listen to tape of a story he knew well. He was put off by some stories which were read in a monotonous voice or an irritating middle-class, old-fashioned accent. Eventually we built up a vast selection.

Grant seemed to need less and less sleep and we could keep him happy with the tapes, but as he couldn't or wouldn't operate the simple controls, we had to leap from our bed at fifteen minute intervals to turn over a cassette! Even though we would take it in turns, it only meant thirty minutes of unbroken sleep. So it was at this point I decided to record stories on to the longest-playing cassette we could buy, which was ninety minutes. This then gave us each an hour and a half's unbroken sleep before our turn was reached!

These story tapes were a source of much interest and pleasure for him and thereafter we never went anywhere without them. We found them extremely useful on holiday as he would sit happily for long stretches at a time in our caravan listening to a story and watching us play a family game, the tapes would keep him settled in the car if we made a long journey, playing them on the car's stereo system.

When Grant reached seven, we wondered if we could interest him in some of these stories on video. The television did not hold his attention at all, but I had noticed the programme 'Words and Pictures' had simple stories, and if I recorded these we might be able to gain his interest. Paul and I went out and bought a video using Grant's attendance allowance money. We felt that if we achieved our goal then what could be more appropriate!

Within the next week or so 'Words and Pictures' had the perfect animated story of 'The Three Little Pigs'. It was an amazing stroke of luck as this was one of his favourite tales. We had to choose Grant's sleepy, calmer moments to hold his interest and it took several attempts at watching to concentrate any attention. Then he became hooked and now I had gained another fifteen minutes of time for myself, allowing me to do normal household chores or use the phone!

From 'The Three Little Pigs' I slowly chose programmes I thought he might manage. 'Words and Pictures' had very suitable material and I recorded many bits and pieces from here. I also recorded 'Chigley', 'Trumpton', and 'Camberwick Green' and these were played over and over with much glee, and then came the introduction of Postman Pat! He quickly became a firm favourite and remained so throughout his life. If only the writers and producers of this story for television knew the pleasure it gave to a very handicapped boy and his parents (and to many others in similar situations) they would be extremely proud of their achievements.

It did not take many months before we had built up three long videos of selected interest giving hours more of contentment for everyone.

Television was something we could rarely watch, but now if we wished to see a programme we would set up a small black and white television on one side of the room, and while viewing our own programme, Grant could watch his own videos. Our ears became selective at cutting Postman Pat's dulcet tones out from that of a good film or a football commentary!

Our video became a lifesaver! What he learnt from it we shall never know. One thing we did see – if he was really desperate he would work the video controls and like many other autistic children had great pleasure in watching his programme running backwards and was very adept at pressing the rewind control button.

These abilities were only seen when he was extremely motivated. He would also turn the key if left in the pantry door when he required food, which was most of the time! We fitted a window-type lock to the pantry door to which we kept keys attached to cotton reels to aid discovery when they disappeared. It was not unusual to find one in the sand pit or, on one occasion, down the loo!

Grant, now seven, aided by the good schooling in the competent hands of Pauline Grady, was becoming more happy and contented. He still, however, refused to learn, and resisted most teaching. His self-help skills of washing, dressing, teeth cleaning and toileting needed lots of help and, even with constant encouragement, he made few strides forward. Mealtimes were still a nightmare. He was so messy and keeping him at the table was almost impossible; once he had finished he would leave – using his uncanny strength to get past us. We sat him on a bench at the back of the table, Paul and I seated either side, but he would dive from his place or eat food from my plate if I got up to serve. His ability to know when eyes were briefly averted was nothing short of amazing. My greatest skill was to complete a drink. Not liking my drinks too hot I had to find a hiding place, but usually I forgot the drink or the secret corner I had hidden the cup for safety. Disgusting cold remains would be found days later in all sorts of peculiar places!

All manner of frustrations made up our family life, and daily we dealt with each one as it came along. Sometimes I collapsed in tears and tantrums feeling the inability to cope or carry on, but our family was close and we pulled together, the placidness of Paul and Julian counteracting my reactions and dutifully putting us all on course again to continue the battle.

Ten

Hurt and sadness play a large part in bringing up these special children. Emotions are many and deep. As with most parents and children a bonding of deep love and affection is formed and, as the handicap is not immediately apparent, hopes and dreams are built for the future.

In our experience a severe handicap such as autism did not change our love for our child, except to strengthen it, despite sometimes feeling desperate. Having to part with a child for the sake of health and sanity produces a tumult of mixed feelings: guilt at handing him over to someone else for periods of time, but also the recognition that it is necessary for the family. Supporting professionals could never understand these heart-rending emotions unless they have been there. Families need help at this time more than any other.

At first when I passed Grant over for care at Heathcroft I felt sick with the pain of having to leave him with someone else. I soon learnt, however, that as the time without him was usually short, it was important to recharge my batteries and give myself to Paul and Julian who needed me too.

I would come home and clear the house of dropped books and jigsaws. Then, having moved away all reminders, I tried not to think about him and make the most of the break. If I had made this decision to pass him to others for care then I had to trust them. It was as if I was on an emotional switchback. I had to learn to turn off my emotions when I left him, which made me feel cold and remote from my true self.

Paul and I believed that Grant gave us something extra in life that others did not have. It made materialistic things unimportant and taught us priorities. We felt that although Julian often had to take a back seat he was gaining more life skills than he would ever learn from others who did not have such a problem within their family. We saw people as they really were and our eyes were opened to the world.

Mothers, in particular, have to keep on their feet despite illnesses and afflictions. A handicapped child, such as ours, has no understanding for a parent's headache, stomach ache, broken leg, and so on, and will still need caring for as usual. The idea of hiding under the duvet for week or two to recover was a fantasy. I worried about how, if I did break a limb, we could possibly manage. I began to have stress-related medical problems such as dizziness, stomach pains, migraines and the occasional panic attack. I could no longer leap from the bed in the middle of the night, but had to change my levels slowly.

My tears flowed freely most mornings as I dressed to face a new day, usually in a blurr of sleeplessness.

One day on a visit to my doctor for something fairly trivial I asked for a few Valium tranquillizing tablets, for those really bad moments when the panic took over. He could not understand all our problems and there was little point in explaining. The story was too long and what could he do anyway!

He gave me twelve tablets only and I stored these on top of my very high wardrobe unit, where it would be impossible for Grant to reach them; it was even difficult for me. This would then ensure that my necessity was dire before I climbed for their rescue! Several years later I threw away the remaining five tablets and their dusty container. Knowing that they were there was enough of a support to see me through.

Susan Wagstaff (Dr O'Gorman's social worker) still visited regularly and expected a call if I was low, but when in this state I couldn't ring. I was afraid her solution would be further respite care, which was not what I wanted or needed.

We lived life from day to day and I would thank God when we

arrived at the end of a weekend. They were long and difficult, the winter ones were the worst, as when the nights drew in and darkness fell by four in the afternoon, then we were trapped inside trying to keep a child happy with occupations he resisted.

When Grant reached seven I fell into my first state of bereavement, which lasted many months. I felt I had not cracked his shell despite trying all I could. According to the books I had read, if language had not developed by the magical age of seven, then the chance of it ever developing was remote. His speech was still only the occasional word, usually said unclearly and forced out of him. When I looked back and compared his abilities in different fields with what he could now achieve, he had made only a few tiny steps forward. I did not know where to go from here for help and I suppose I felt that I had failed him.

At times I felt so desperate that I even thought of phoning the Samaritans' helpline. But I didn't, as I understood the service to be for suicidal people, not just for someone screaming inside for help that wasn't there. I have since learnt that the Samaritans do consider themselves a phone support for people in situations such as mine and often being able to lift the receiver and talk to someone who doesn't know you at the other end, can ease some of the stress.

It took me two years to realize that I needed to accept Grant as he was and not as we had hoped him to be. I think Paul accepted this anyway and much earlier than I did, so when I finally reached this point one aspect of my emotions was appeased. I stopped making such strong demands on Grant, which made him more relaxed.

But, having said this, my ears and eyes were still open to any new methods or therapies that might help, but now I was less optimistic that anything would produce a miracle.

I had read there was a mega-vitamin therapy based on huge doses of vitamin B6 and magnesium. Several studies have shown B6 to help normalize brainwaves and urine chemistry, in addition to improving behaviour. Magnesium aids the body's processes to do this. They suggested the benefits include decreased hyperactivity and irritability, improved attention, improved sleeping patterns, increased learning interest and increased use of sounds or language. They reported no significant adverse effects and suggested it offered some help in 50 per cent of autistic people. What was I waiting for?!

I bought my vitamins after acquiring information on the correct doses. I didn't let the school know what I was giving him but started my trial dose one sunny morning. When I went to pick him up they asked,

'What on earth did you give him for breakfast this morning?'

'Why?' I asked eagerly. Had I cracked it at last?

'He was uncontrollable!' I was told. Then I confessed to the vitamins.

'Please don't give him any more,' they implored, we couldn't take another morning like that!'

So that was the end of my vitamin trials, unless I heard that there were fantastic results. Since it is now known that very large doses of B6 can be harmful, I am glad Grant's adverse reaction didn't let me continue.

Grant, at seven, had left Pauline Grady and moved on with the classroom assistant, Sylvia Oakley. We were concerned about this move. Pauline had made significant strides with Grant and he was much more contented. At lunchtime he went out into the enclosed school grounds and actually climbed on to some of the large recreation equipment with some element of proper play in his use of these interesting play items. He sat on and tried to pedal a tricycle, which, on their playground, was easier than our lane. These actions were all unassisted so this was a significant stride.

However, in other things he was coming to a full stop and Pauline felt he should move forward with his contemporaries, which meant leaving the comfortable confines of Bishopswood school and joining the class in the integrated system at the local primary school. 'Integrated' here meant having their own classroom, but joining the primary school for assembly, lunch and break times. They used the schools facilities such as their gym and swimming-pool. Their classroom was unfortunately on the 'open plan' system so their room opened into the gym.

Grant needed space but he also needed the security of four walls and a door (preferably locked) so that his obsession for escaping could be properly controlled while in a 'work' situation, thus allowing him to concentrate on what he was supposed to be doing. He enjoyed the gym sessions immensely so escaping from any learning situation became his prime motivation, causing disruption to the other children in the class.

The theory of integration is good in many respects, but it doesn't always work as it depends on the child. Autistic children are particularly vulnerable to adverse effects. Their needs are very special because of their fears and their inability to socialize. Grant was completely oblivious to others around him, particularly his peer age group, though he would respond to some adults and was particularly happy with girls in their mid to late teens who showed interest in him, and there were several of these who came into school for work experience. At lunch and break times the children would come in from the primary school and take a child under their wing. One very nice little girl of about eight or nine took a liking to Grant and tried to befriend him. Grant, with his inability to play or socialize, spent the time either trying to get back into the classroom or running away towards the gate, whereupon the supervising staff had to retrieve him. This relationship was so unsatisfactory to his befriender that, although persevering for several days, she lost interest.

Carol Bonas, Grant's new class teacher, found Grant difficult and disruptive and asked for a case conference to be held to rethink and replan his schooling. Carol was an excellent teacher, but the move and the integration system, with less security had disturbed Grant. He needed much more individual attention and worked best one to one. If he was taught within a group he could not cope. He would find the situation frightening and would therefore jump up, leave the group and run at great speed to the gym where it was being used by the primary school children. This was not good for their integrated system!

A case conference was held and Grant's needs assessed by the many people involved in Grant's care and education. We had often wondered whether he should be attending Smith Hospital school as a day pupil but we had always been put off it by staff at Bishopswood as 'their setting was so much better and Smith children were so disturbed and needed locking in'.

The hospital side did not have the best of reputations as it housed some of the worst affected children. Their rooms tended to be bare and uninteresting and they screamed a lot. However, it was the schooling we were interested in investigating. He might have more continuity of staff that were more likely to be finely attuned to his problems, being specialized in the teaching and care of autistic children. It was suggested that we went along to look at Smith, but also that I spend a full day at Bishopswood, observing Grant in his current situation. If we were happier for him to remain as he was, then an application for extra welfare hours would have to be made so that Grant could have some individual attention, improving teaching for the other pupils.

The head teacher at Smith Hospital School was Caroline Simmonds, the speaker at The National Housewives' group to whom I had first spoken six years previously concerning my worries about the possibility of Grant being autistic. I had met up with her on several occasions as she came along to OMSAC committee meetings in Oxford and we found that we shared the common experience of doing Voluntary Service Overseas (VSO). We had looked at properties together as executive members of that committee, for the group was now ready to obtain a property to set up as an adult community. I phoned Caroline to ask if I could visit her school and she was only too pleased to show me around.

The school was situated at the end of a busy, wide, four-lane carriageway, a mile outside Henley. The outer security of the hospital and school had to be extremely tight as some of these children, like Grant, had escaping obsessions, and one child in the past had been killed on the road.

Once inside there was a friendly hubbub interspersed with the occasional scream of a passing pupil. There was a general air of happiness, friendliness and joviality. The building, however, was old, the children very disturbed, and everywhere was locked, so the general atmosphere of freedom seen at Bishopswood was not there. A child was led past me screaming, her head enclosed in a crash helmet, biting her hand and swaying from side to side. They had a high proportion of very difficult children who had been sent from many parts of the country because there was nothing suitable in their own district and they needed much supervised care and teaching.

A few days later I went to the Bishopswood class at Sonning Common and spent several hours with them following their day. I caught Grant in a receptive mood enjoying a gym class in which he was responding well to just oral directions. He walked along a bench unaided and joined hands in a circle with just the minimum of encouragement. I was impressed! It was lovely to see him in this near normal setting. Removing him to such a disturbed group in an old building, and countless locked doors, did not seem right.

Paul and I discussed the visits, but from what I explained to Paul we both agreed that it would be best to leave him in his current setting. I was now Chairman of the Governing body so had to put a case forward to receive an extra welfare helper for my own son. This would also benefit the other pupils in Grant's class. I was told by the Oxford authorities that to gain a welfare helper would mean removing an existing one from another child in another part of the county, as there was no money in the budget to provide helpers otherwise. Where have we heard that before? Statements such as these do nothing to help parents tormented by difficult decisions affecting their child's life!

Grant got his welfare helper for ten hours a week. She worked on an individual basis with him in the morning and supervised him in the playground at lunchtimes and break.

The classroom situation was better, but at break times he felt hounded. She would spend her time running after him to stop him disappearing out of the school gate or preventing him sneaking back into the building to his classroom. Grant loved being warm and comfortable as it increased his sense of security so, if it was cold outside, he would prefer to be in and would do everything in his power to achieve this aim. If he managed to outmanoeuvre his carer he would probably be found seated, with his back against a radiator, looking at a Ladybird book!

So he continued through the next year, and there were many difficulties. The situation was not satisfactory and we discussed it with anyone who would listen or who had any knowledge of the subject.

One option was the Chinnor Unit (a separate autistic unit attached to a primary school), situated about eighteen miles away in Oxfordshire. They had a system of partial integration. Their philosophy was to introduce the child to a mainstream class accompanied by his or her own helper, choosing class levels and subjects according to ability. This was an excellent system, but Grant was not sufficiently advanced for this school and their methods, so it was eliminated as an option.

Parents with non-verbal children usually wish them to be educated alongside verbal children, in the hope that they will copy them. If the child is severely autistic then he or she will not have the ability to copy; therefore it is more important that he or she gets the structured education that the specialized autistic school offers from staff who understand his or her unique problems.

The more able autistic child can present different problems associated with confused language. Education within the non-specific autistic group in a special school setting can often lead to the autistic child picking up wrong or bad language or another child's peculiar mannerisms. The correct assessment of educational needs can make a very significant and vast difference to the child's prognosis and development.

In our experience the necessity of observing a school closely before making any decisions is absolutely vital. We learnt that in choosing a school, having somebody accompanying, who has experience with children with autism, will help in a more objective decision. Essential points to cover include the following.

- Class sizes, teacher:pupil ratio and the ambiance of the school

– do the staff look happy and friendly, and are they talking to
the *non-verbal* children?

- The building – are there lots of interesting things on the walls,
  children's works of art and other evidence that the pupils have
  been fully occupied?
- Do they have plenty of rooms to cover different activities – a
  gym, swimming-pool, art room and large play area with good
  and safe equipment?
- How much does the school liaise with parents to ensure their
  important work continues at home?

It is a good idea to make a list of the priorities required to meet
the child's needs. It is highly unlikely that the school will meet all
expectations, but if marked out of ten and it achieves over seven,
then it will probably be highly suitable and hard to better.

We looked at schools and tried to assess them by these methods.
We knew that we had to consider a change for Grant. After a year
of searching and thinking and seeing the unsuitability of his
present position we spoke to Tim Williams, a clinical psychologist
who had come along to some of our parent support meetings and
had seen and assessed Grant at home. Dr O'Gorman had now
retired and our help and support had come from school, but there
were many home problems that needed the expertise of somebody
of Tim's calibre. Following this visit he went to view Grant at
Bishopswood. He watched how he fitted into their classroom
routines and then advised us that in his opinion he would be much
better at Smith Hospital School. We were extremely grateful for
his help, as this kind of decision is so momentous and, although
the final choice must be made ultimately by the parents, their
emotional involvement sometimes clouds the issue. This change of
school did not happen until Grant reached the summer following
his tenth birthday. It proved beyond doubt to be the best move we
could have made.

I tried to mix Grant into normal settings as much as I could. A
lot depended on his mood. If he was very hyperactive and restless
I found that it was difficult to cope with his strength so we had to

rely on the garden or a local walk. If, however, he was in a more manageable mood I would encourage him into any normal activity I could devise.

I would take him to our local church. He had been taught to sit in assemblies at school so we could often get through a whole service with the help of books and raisins! I would have to position myself with care so that he was hemmed into a pew. Sometimes I would leave the church looking wild and fraught, with little gained from the service. However, I would not let him beat my objective of the day. This paid off as he gradually became calmer in church, loving to gaze at the stained glass windows in a relaxed moment, or at the coffee cups if there were refreshments afterwards!

A successful activity was attending the local 'youth club'. The 'youth' started at about four years and ended at sixteen or seventeen. It was held at a local church hall and if I was feeling very energetic I would walk him there and back. Sometimes I would walk and Paul would pick us up. Grant could not usually cope with more than an hour, but it was a very satisfying way of spending a Friday evening and it was what the 'normal' children of the district did. They had a bar that sold soft drinks and sweets and I would make Grant pass over his money in return for some of the goodies. The children accepted him and some even tried to help him. There was lots of loud music, dancing and lights so he was getting the same stimulation as the local children and also exercise to help make him sleep. He liked to run outside and would run around and around the building. I became quite fit trying to keep up with him and stop him disappearing through the holes in the hedge on the side that led on to the road; we completed many laps in an evening! We went to the youth club intermittently for many years and despite his strange behaviour, he was accepted by the local children.

When there was a skating craze I bought him skates so that he could enjoy the same fun as the others. As the grounds had a lot of concrete, it was a good place to use them. Gary Howland had set up and run the club along with Martin Strong and anyone who he could cajole into helping. Gary would often grab Grant's arm and help him skate around the grounds at much more interesting speeds than I could achieve on my own. Gary and his wife Jan became good and supportive friends who would always patronize our fund-raising events usually by bringing half the village!

The library, shopping, swimming at a variety of pools as well as at Metal Box, taking him out to pub meals, McDonalds and Burger King provided 'normal' interests. Dining out was still problematical as when he finished, which was always very quickly, he wanted to leave the table and didn't understand that we were still eating. It was then hard to complete our own meal as it was a battle to keep him in position.

Several interesting episodes had occurred in the last few years that need to be mentioned to illustrate the idiosyncrasies of the autistic brain. One such event occurred in the Electricity Board showroom in Henley. Grant and I made a visit to look at new cookers and obtained a few of their brochures. I held Grant's hand firmly as I discussed the pros and cons of the latest models. Grant clutched on to his Ladybird book of the moment and flicked over the pages deftly with one hand, studying the pictures intently. Having all I required from the shop I made to leave saying, 'Come on', to Grant.

The friendly assistants looked over the counter and said brightly, 'Good-bye', looking directly at him.

I dropped Grant's hand and put my arm protectively around him and said, 'He can't talk.'

From my side a bright, loud voice piped up, 'I can!'

Trying to hide my utter surprise and delight, I casually said, 'Okay, if you can talk say good-bye.'

'Bye,' he said.

Completely floored I left the shop with the assistants laughing behind me. I wonder what they made of it. I walked down Henley's Reading Road as if on air, overjoyed and elated with the wonder of his spontaneous speech, yet puzzled by what was going on inside him. I chatted away to him hoping that he was going to continue to use language, but nothing else was said; he had re-entered his shell.

There was another incident similar to this that I warmly recall and treasure. I had taken him for a visit to the library, which he liked as I would find books that would appeal to him to such an extent that he couldn't put them down. They would then have to be ordered from the bookshop, as constant thumbing tended to leave them in a poor state of repair. I was often left with the job of patching up a book before return. On this occasion it was his ninth birthday and I had joined them at school for a party. At the library was a very nice lady with a clear voice who showed an interest in Grant and usually spoke to him. This day was no exception and she said brightly and loudly, 'Hello, Grant. What have you been doing with yourself?'

I said encouragingly, 'Go on Grant, tell her what day it is.'

She addressed him clearly, saying, 'What day is it then Grant?'

'My birthday,' he mumbled.

She obviously understood him as she said, 'Oh! It's your birthday, how nice. How old are you?'

'Nine,' he replied.

'Nine!' she said. 'You are growing fast.'

This was the first and only conversation of his life.

Eleven

OMSAC had now changed its name to MIDCAS which stood for Mid Counties Autistic Society. The society had gone from strength to strength because of the energy and expertise of some of its members and a large number of willing and enthusiastic fundraisers.

The society had managed to procure a home in Gloucestershire, called Stroud Court. It was a stately old building set in lovely grounds next door to the home of Princess Anne. It had huge development potential and came with houses in the grounds that could be used for staff and for the benefit of the more able autistic residents, helping them to become more independent.

We were thrilled that we were able to acquire, set up and open a home so soon after founding the Society. We had appointed an excellent principal in John Mortlock, who was well trained in autism and had run an adult autistic unit in the Wirral prior to taking up this appointment.

The Reading group had sent out working parties to help get the property in order before the opening and had enjoyed picnicking on the lawn when all the hard work was done.

Several members' children were awarded places at the unit after a struggle with their local Social Services to fund the specialist 'out of county' placement.

When the residents had been gradually moved into their new accommodation and were beginning to settle, an official opening was arranged. Princess Anne seemed the obvious person whom we should first approach to honour us and make our occasion memorable. She was not only our neighbour but had shown previous interest and opened the unit that John Mortlock had run on the Wirral. She was asked in the usual official way, but said she would be happy to open the home in an unofficial capacity, keeping protocol and security to a minimum.

It was a beautiful, bright, cloudless June day in 1983 when many of our support group made their way from Reading to the delightful countryside of Gloucestershire. Members of the executive committee were to meet Princess Anne in small informal groups and Paul and I were in one of these.

It was a lovely and happy event. The work put in by so many, to give a secure future to young people who couldn't cope for themselves and needed supervision for life, was now being rewarded. To see the austistic residents in this delightful setting and going about their daily tasks was pure pleasure.

Paul and I were impressed by the interest shown by the Princess and enjoyed our informal 'chat' during which we exchanged the problems of bringing up children with strong minds of their own, whether autistic or what we would class as normal!

I looked upon this special event as an inspiration to us. If we hadn't got Grant we wouldn't have had the pleasure of seeing this project launched and come to an exciting fruition. We had had many pleasurable fund-raising events that had brought with them fun and friendship as well as the preparation of the home, and now the opening.

The Henley Regatta brought Traylen's Fun Fair to the riverside. The Henley branch of the Round Table, along with the fair owners, organized an afternoon prior to the start of the regatta especially for children and adults with special needs. They provided free rides on the fairground equipment. As I was not too happy on these I would collect Julian from school and return to the fair and he would take Grant on the rides. The dodgem cars were the favourite and with the chance to have repeated turns Grant began really to enjoy himself. They were given free candy floss, a balloon and maybe a badge. It made a lovely afternoon for both children, but Julian was the one who could tell me that it was exciting. Siblings of the severely handicapped deserve these treats as much as their brother or sister. Julian appreciated that he was very lucky to have had so many free rides, and that this was only because he had a brother like Grant!

When Grant was eight and Julian eleven we met up with Jean Denham. Jean had a daughter called Zoë who was ten and severely autistic and went to Smith Hospital School, and a son called Neil who was sixteen. Jean and I had shared our difficulties having met through the Autistic Society and our support meetings. We quickly became friends as our children were very alike and we shared similar problems. Zoë wasn't silent, however, like Grant. On the contrary, she talked constantly, but mainly to herself. She would chatter away repeating herself over and over again. This incessant meaningless chatter would be just as frustrating to Jean as the 'loud' silence that we got from Grant. Sometimes Zoë would pick up a phrase of somebody's conversation and then keep repeating it. School had been very amused one day when she repeatedly uttered, 'David, you're not going to the pub again!' David is Jean's husband and not that regular a drinker! He was a stalwart supporter of the school and chairman of their school governors!

Zoë was very pretty and, like Grant, loved Ladybird books. Jean and I thought it would be beneficial to get together in the school holidays and share outings. We felt this would be good support for each other and it proved to be so. The two children did some outrageous things and being able to share a laugh about them relieved the tensions considerably.

One day we had the children running free as the area was safe. Suddenly Grant saw a large sandpit ahead and ran at great speed towards it. In it was a large and cleverly made sandcastle which the proud creator, a small boy, was admiring. I saw with horror Grant reach it and dive straight on top. Zoë had run in the opposite direction, to a lady on a seat. She sat on the lap of the surprised lady and entwined her fingers through her hair and none too gently. Jean and I reached our children and extricated them, apologizing profusely. We then slunk away until when sufficiently out of earshot we laughed hysterically at their awful antics.

We had one lovely long day out at Butlins, Bognor Regis. We took Julian and Neil who, despite the large age gap, shared the day's pleasures together. They went boating and on rides and both were super at helping their handicapped siblings. Later Neil said to his mother that he had really enjoyed the day and how helpful it was to meet a family who shared a similar problem. He could chat to Julian and see that he wasn't the only boy who had such a difficult sister or brother. I wished Neil had been that bit younger, as he was at the age when he would no longer be going out with his mother in the holidays and therefore wouldn't be there to accompany Julian.

At Christmas we asked them over to join in with the festivities as our house was as autistic proof as theirs and our toys very similar. Christmas was another difficult time, but it helped to share it with a like-minded family.

Zoë had epilepsy and frequently had fits. She had been epileptic for some time although recently they had been less controlled as she was coming up to adolescence. She was on increasing medication that was difficult to regulate. Following a seizure she slept soundly for a couple of hours.

On the second Christmas of our friendship, Zoë had had a fit earlier that morning and was consequently a bit sleepy and less difficult. She had gone into Grant's bedroom to look at some books and musical boxes. Quite amazingly, Grant had stayed with her, sitting on the bed and, like her, looking at books or winding the music. This companionship is something rarely seen in autistic children as they just do their own thing. I had never seen it with Grant except in relationships with some adults and then he was asking, in his own way, for something from them, such as a story or a cuddle. This Christmas I saw something akin to a friendship with someone who enjoyed the same things as he did.

Zoë left Grant's room after a short while and returned to sit on her father's lap for a cuddle and went to sleep. Grant followed her into the lounge and took hold of her hand as he wanted her to come back to his room. Unfortunately this is where the liaison ended as Zoë was too sleepy to respond, even if her autism allowed her to. When they came to leave we asked Grant to say goodbye to Zoë. Instead of forcing a word he put his arm around Zoë and gave her a hug.

We went on many trips together in the school holidays and this was over a period of two and a half years. Then Zoë started having some awful accidents.

The first happened early one morning while Jean and David were still in bed. Zoë was wandering in and out of their room chattering ten to the dozen about nothing. Like Grant she rolled around with nothing to occupy her. There were some clothes draped over the banister rail and Zoë rolled around these until Jean and David heard an almighty thud and realized almost immediately that she must have gone right over the top. They dreaded what they might see, imagining that they would find her dead or unconscious on the floor below. It went through Jean's mind that she might have broken her back and how could such an already handicapped person cope with such an affliction? They reached the banister rail together and peered over. There was Zoë staggering to her feet and only dazed from her sudden and appalling trip to the bottom!

The second incident happened a few months or so later. This time she fell against the glass-panelled front door, crashing through the glass and severing the artery in her wrist. Jean found her among the splinters, covered in bright red blood which was pumping out of her. Fortunately Jean had recently attended a first aid course following Zoë's last accident, as she was painfully aware of the need to know how to cope with emergencies such as this. She called for help from her sister who, fortunately, was staying with Jean and David at the time and, grabbing a towel to firmly bind the wrist, applied direct pressure to the artery, and elevated Zoë's arm. They drove themselves quickly to hospital where Zoë had to have micro-surgery. Jean's quick reactions and knowledge gained from the first aid course saved Zoë's life.

The third accident was, tragically, Zoë's last. An epileptic fit on the top of the stairs caused a fall that left Zoë with severe head injuries. She died in hospital several days later, only after Jean and David had been told that there was no hope and they had bravely submitted her organs for transplantation. These organs saved the lives of four children; two who received kidney transplants and two who were thereby able to benefit from the use of two free dialysis machines, previously allocated to the donees.

Paul and I were deeply impressed at such a momentous decision taken amid such tragic circumstances. A decision like this, in the past, had saved my life after a long search was made for a free machine following my kidney failure at Julian's birth.

I think I told Grant that Zoë had died, but maybe I didn't. Would he have known what I was saying? Who knows? But in his own way he asked me about it a year later. He had one of his photo albums in his hand and he kept stopping at one picture. It was a picture of him and Zoë together enjoying a picnic. I hadn't registered that he was looking at anything specific. We were waiting for Paul and Julian to return to the car and, while doing so, he pulled my arm as he wished me to get into the back of the car with him. It wasn't often he made such an obvious move to get my attention so I clambered into the back. He thrust his photo album at me and looked into my face. At this age (eleven) this was still fairly unusual and I realized he wanted to know something. He looked at the picture of Zoë then back at me. In his own way he was asking where she had gone. So I said as simply as possible that she had died and gone to Heaven where Jesus would look after her and she would be happy.

Grant never looked at that picture again.

Jean and David had an apartment in Ibiza and about a year after our meeting up they kindly lent it to us for a week. Paul and I needed a complete break away, a chance to be alone, to be husband and wife and have a little time for each other. Grant was nine and Julian twelve. Grant would stay at Heathcroft and Julian with his Nana and Granpa. Making arrangements, packing three separate suitcases and finally arriving at the airport was no easy feat and I was beginning to wonder if it was all worth it. I had a severe migraine on the flight out and felt far from well.

The apartment was in Santa Eulalia in a quiet part of the island. It was spring and everywhere was just getting ready to open. As never before, we understood the meaning of the word *mañana*. Wherever we went or whatever we wanted the answer was always 'next week'!

It didn't matter. It was pleasantly warm and there were spring flowers in profusion, yellow and white marguerites grew wild on every bit of waste land, and geraniums of many colours brightened doorsteps and windowsills. There was a relaxed feel about the place. We found ourselves good restaurants and sat in street cafés sipping something, usually alcoholic, and mopping up the warm sunshine.

By mid-week I was feeling completely relaxed and healthy. We saw ourselves as a couple again and talked to each other! Not about the children or how I had coped with all that Grant had thrown at me through the day, but about the old town of Ibiza and the interesting people and things we had seen and done. We laughed together and went for long walks from one beach to another.

The therapeutic value of that holiday was immense. We came to the end of that week realizing that we had a life and each other. The return journey was so different from the outward flight. We had slept, relaxed and loved. My head was clear, my heart light and I was ready to continue the battle!

We hadn't forgotten the boys completely. Everyone had contact numbers so we could be reached easily. We knew they were in good hands. We had one night at home before we picked up Grant from Heathcroft the next day. The contrast of the holiday with our life at home was so marked I thought I would not be able to cope with going back to it. I was very depressed for a day until I started to readjust.

The holiday was all the better because of our problems, but it showed up the unremitting difficulties and I wondered sometimes how long we could physically stand up to them.

★   ★   ★

Grant changed schools to Smith Hospital School in July 1985. The changeover was done gradually over a few weeks and with this careful planning it worked well.

His teacher was to be Mereta Hawkins. She had a very firm approach with the children and I watched her methods when I spent the first morning in school with Grant. She guided him to a table and said to him, 'Sit down Grant.' Grant sat! I am sure had she told me in the same way I too would have sat down quickly! I liked her approach and I felt confident of her teaching skills. Caroline Simmonds had assured me she was an excellent teacher.

What was immediately apparent about this school and impressed us greatly was that all the staff worked together and weekly meetings kept them all informed as to every pupil in the school and his or her immediate teaching needs. This meant that if that child was learning a skill or striving to overcome a behaviour problem then all the staff would know it and the approach would be the same from everyone. The child then knew where he or she stood, and was more secure.

The locked doors resulted in increased security as the children knew that escaping was not an option and they would get on with the task in hand. This was particularly noticeable in the playground, which had been such a problem in Grant's previous situation. He did get some pleasure from the equipment in the playground once he found that, after several weeks searching, there was no escape route. I am sure this security helped him to settle quickly. His obsession for escaping from anywhere started to diminish; it was as if he forgot it. Feeling safe and knowing what his parameters were made him less frightened.

When Grant had been at the school for some months we noticed that although the gate had been accidentally left open (a rare occurrence), Grant had not gone, but was walking around some distant part of the garden.

Grant learnt to use the new Makaton sign language, using it most comfortably with the person who had taught him. At an evening function in which parents, staff and children participated, I asked

Grant if he wanted the toilet, using the sign as well as the word, but got no response. His teacher at that moment walked through and said, 'All right, Grant, I will take you.' I stared at her open mouthed. She laughed and said that as she had walked into the room Grant had looked at her and signed 'toilet'!

Grant had just over two years at Smith and, of all his schooling, his learning and behaviour progressed here, better than anywhere. Unfortunately, this superb school was to close, as the majority of the pupils were funded by other local authorities. Most were residential in the hospital side of Smith which was run by West Berkshire Area Health Authority and was a financial millstone. The school, however, was run by Oxfordshire Education Authority and received day as well as residential children. There would be insufficient pupils to keep the school going and, despite our efforts to convince the authority of the specialist expertise that would be lost, its future was in doubt. Berkshire and Oxfordshire had to sort it out on an executive level and when that happened the whole establishment fell victim to the rationing of limited resources and, as so often seems to happen, our vulnerable children were the losers.

So, after two years, we had to consider suitable schools again. This time I had the help of Caroline Simmonds and using my 'points out of ten' system, we reconsidered schools seen, and looked at others. Now we were having to look further afield knowing that there was nothing suitable locally. Eventually we settled on 'Hope Lodge' in Portswood, Southampton, and here Grant would have to board on a weekly basis. We hated the idea, but had no option.

Everyone tried hard to improve Grant's eating habits, which varied from reasonable to appalling, depending on which was the mood swing of the moment. Nobody worked harder on this than Pam Chaplin who was employed at Smith as an occupational therapist and had been working there for years. It was Pam who first explained autism to me at the Toy Library in Henley. She was anxious to help Grant and dedicated her lunch hour to improving his eating habits.

She also had very firm, heart-rending methods that worked. She would remove his food if he didn't follow the correct eating plan. He had to lay his place, wash his hands and dry them properly before being allowed to sit at the table. She had him using a knife and fork and taught him to cut soft food with his knife. He had to clear his plate before he got a pudding and wash up the dishes afterwards! He worked well for her but, despite following all the rules, in the home situation it was hard to get a similar outcome. Paul never allowed me to restrict his pudding if he left the table. Grant knew that his dad would always see that he got his pud, making teaching impossible in this area!

It was during those early months at Smith that we decided that it was time to try to get him dry at night. He always took himself to the toilet at home in the daytime, so how could we encourage him to go at night? We did have many dry nights as he would thump on his bedroom door and we would always take him there first before encouraging sleep. As we didn't want to miss his need to use the loo, we would take him many times during the night when he was awake, which we didn't feel was good for his bladder control. If wanting to use the toilet was keeping him awake, maybe if we left his door open he would take himself, use it and go back to bed and to sleep. We decided to leave off the incontinence pad and see what happened.

It was the highlight of the night or week if he did use the toilet and got back into bed. It didn't happen very often and most nights he would bounce into our bed soaking wet before we had woken sufficently to point him in the right direction!

We put a Porta-Potti from our caravan in his room, showed him what it was for and then locked him in again. He tipped it up and spilt it! We tried locking all the other doors in the house including our bedroom door so that he had the run of the hall and the bathroom. We would then lie awake wondering what he was doing. We had one real disaster. One night he used the toilet to open his bowels, but then proceeded to play down the loo and the ensuing mess was nothing short of a calamity!

Our final and best solution was to take him to the toilet just before we settled; we were even brave enough to wake him for this and usually he returned to sleep. When he was asleep we opened his door so that he had the opportunity to use the loo if he was so inclined later on in the night. We then had to lock the door and ignore the thumps. A dry incontinence pad in the morning was rewarded by lots of praise and cuddles. I could never imagine that we would ever achieve a dry bed and a normal pair of unprotected pyjamas. But we did, eventually!

Twelve

Having accepted that Grant was autistic for life, I was now looking into the future and wondering what I could do that would increase my own well-being. When Grant was eight I was still in a state akin to bereavement and didn't like feeling that way. It was up to me to try and improve matters so I investigated what to do.

I had always hoped that after the initial years of child-rearing I would get back to nursing perhaps taking on a part-time sister's post either in general nursing or midwifery. Midwives were desperately needed in the town of Reading and they were willing to accept them on a 'bank' scheme, allowing very flexible hours and offering updating for midwives as an incentive to come back into the service. I sought an interview with midwifery personnel to see how much updating was necessary to make me safe to practice. I had now been out of midwifery for ten years and in the meantime there had been many alterations and improvements in the technical side of the profession. These would need to be learnt. Delivering a baby is a skill, like typing or playing the piano, that once learnt is always with you, so I didn't expect to need more than three months to retrain. I hoped that they would take account of my needs as a trainee. This, however, was not to be and, despite my unusual family circumstances, there was little understanding or willingness to accommodate my special requirements, and retraining was therefore out of the question.

I had a wonderful colleague in Molly Fenton, with whom I worked on a Thursday evening in the Family Planning Clinic and she was very sympathetic to our circumstances. We worked well together, enjoying many a laugh which we hoped rubbed off on our patients, who often remarked on the bright, happy atmosphere of the clinic. At the end of the evening we always had a long chat that was almost like a counselling session for me. I went home feeling better for our discussions.

She heard that the post of Domiciliary Family Planning Sister was becoming available. This work was for just a few hours a week and involved calling on women who had failed to turn up at clinics and on those whose circumstances were known to be such that coming to the clinic would not be easy. These included many social, mental and physical conditions and often required considerable patience to cover the care required. Paul often wondered how on earth I could take on such a challenge for such small reward. Molly rightly said that it could be very flexible and would therefore fit in with me and the children.

I considered the job and went out with the nurse who held the post at the time. I saw the work as a challenge and full of interest so I applied and, following an interview, was offered the position. The hours put in varied, but ranged from four to ten per week. I had to be ready to go out in an emergency, however, many of these 'emergencies' were false alarms. One day I discovered that I had been blamed by a young irresponsible seventeen-year-old girl who had got pregnant for the third time because 'the nurse what brings 'er pills was late', (and this was untrue as she had either mislaid the pills or the dog had eaten them!) This girl had phoned me on two occasions in unsociable hours having run out of her pills. Even emergency contraception allows seventy-two hours following unprotected intercourse.

I did go out one Sunday morning to a poor girl who was frantic with worry as lying in the bath that morning she had discovered pubic lice! I made a 'skin creeping' visit to confirm it and direct her with a note to her nearest Sunday pharmacist.

A large proportion of my visits were to girls whose mental ability was such that taking a pill on a daily basis was not an option to prevent a pregnancy. These girls were often the ones whose ability to raise children was far from ideal and poor parenting and abuse was rife. They needed a lot of support and the ultimate decision on another child was theirs alone. I hoped that with counselling and direction I might help to influence the planning of the pregnancies so that the baby came when the girl and her family could give it the love and support it deserved.

There were many failures and frustrations, but also the satisfaction of achievement. If a girl I had seen at her home finally made a clinic appointment then I felt I had succeeded with my ultimate aim.

My knowledge of children with learning disabilities was such that I was asked to teach contraception to these groups in accordance with the ability of the group and this could often be wide. Demonstrating the use of a condom on the end of a broom handle sometimes made me wonder what they would do with a condom should the need arise! This work made me feel more useful in society and helped to give me a purpose. It represented another side to life of which many people are unaware. These are people who are victims of their own upbringing. They seek the love they were denied as a child by producing children, usually in the wrong circumstances, who they then abuse as they were abused. Drugs in the form of cigarettes, alcohol, soft and even hard drugs are used as a form of escapism from some of their awful life experiences.

In my work I became not just a person to dish out the condoms and the giver of contraceptive injections, but also a befriender to some of these folk who sometimes confided in me the pathetic difficulties controlling their sad lives.

Our life was hard and complicated, but we had love and a nice home in the country where we could walk in the countryside and work out our stresses. I would not have wished to swap with them. Maybe they would not have wanted to swap with me, but this work had provided a new perspective of what we had. I could face our life in a new light.

I did believe Grant had been given to us for a reason. When times were bad and I prayed for help, it came. It was during one of these difficult times that a hand reached out again and guided me through another year.

Caroline Print and her husband Norman came for dinner with us one Saturday evening. Caroline and Norman were good friends who had stayed close through the problematic years. They had shared a drink or two at Christmas despite having to watch it constantly in the knowledge that it would disappear in one swig if Grant got within grabbing distance! The same vigilance was necessary for crisps and nuts, many of which finished up in fragments on the floor. The Christmas robin did well from the contents of our sweeper!

Norman was our local vicar, and over dinner on this night he asked me, 'Wendy, do you have a favourite hymn?'

Surprised at this question, which silenced my other guests as they waited to hear my reply, I immediately said, 'Oh yes, it's "Lord of all Hopefulness, Lord of all Joy". It was our wedding hymn. I have always looked upon it as a prayer and I believe we are in the second verse at the moment.'

He then said, 'The churches in this area of the Thames Valley have been approached by BBC television as they wish to do a "Songs of Praise" programme from the area, focused on Goring and the river. We have all been asked to submit names of suitable people to be interviewed for the programme and I have been thinking of putting your name forward. Are you willing to let me do that?'

Just to be asked was an honour and a boost to my flagging soul. He explained that many names could be submitted, but only five would be chosen to be filmed. He knew how interested I was in promoting the cause of autistic people and showing the world what the condition was about so that more people would understand the problems that isolated them. If I were to be chosen I would be asked to name a hymn that I would to be like to be sung on the programme. I agreed to allow Norman to enter my name and it was only two weeks later that I received a phone call from the BBC to arrange a time for an interviewer to call.

A very pleasant young woman called Hilary arrived and questioned me on Grant, the family and my religious attitudes. We then had an interesting chat on her work as a BBC interviewer. She explained that twenty people had been chosen for initial interview and they would let me know within a couple of weeks if we were to be among the five to be finally chosen for the programme.

A short time later a letter arrived from Hilary to say she hoped I wouldn't be too horrified, but I had been picked to appear on 'Songs of Praise'. The programme would be filmed by the river at Goring and Streatley with local church choirs, participants and members of the public attending, and this would take place in July. I would be filmed at home probably in early spring just before the programme was to go out at Easter.

The filming by the river was a lovely occasion. It took place over two days, recording on Saturday from the Goring side of the river, and on Sunday from Streatley. The weather was typically British with one minute the sun shining brightly and the next everyone running frantically for cover as the heavens opened. It must have been a producer's nightmare, but it made for a lot of hilarity. I went without the family as Paul needed to look after Grant, who would have been far too restless. Julian had seen David Attenborough's 'Life on Earth' so now thought we all 'evolved' without God, and nothing could sway him from that opinion! To attend hymn singing where he would be seen by his friends was far too embarrassing!

On Saturday I sang among the crowd although my hymn was not sung then. However, we had to make ourselves known to the camera men so they could locate us, which evoked many funny comments from the male choir behind me such as, 'Do you think she is on now? I had better open my mouth wide and look as if I'm having a good time!' or 'Shall I wave to mother now?'

On the Sunday I was placed in a very prominent position so that when my hymn was sung the cameras could find me easily. A few members of our autistic support group joined me and we sang our hymns heartily. During my special hymn I looked up to find the camera directly on me and immediately became so self-conscious that I did not know where to look. At the end of the hymn the producer on the microphone announced for the hundreds to hear. 'I'm afraid we will have to sing it all over again as that take was spoilt.' At least it was only me who knew who had ruined it. Next time I didn't even dare peep to see if the camera was on me.

I was excited at the thought of the forthcoming interview. A turn of events a week earlier was to influence what I said on that day and give it even more significance. In the early hours of a cold March morning, just a few weeks before Grant's eleventh birthday, I crept out to the bathroom. From another room I heard the most awful noises, it was as if someone was struggling to breathe, their breath rasping through a closed throat.

'Is that you breathing like that?' I called panic-stricken to Paul. He, waking from sleep, but taking in what I had said, denied it, and then again more strongly as he heard the frightening noises too. I dashed to Grant's room, as by now it was obvious the noise came from there, and switched on the light. He lay flat on his back, his eyes shut and mouth slightly open. He was very pale and his chest heaved up and down with the effort of dragging the air though congested airways. My immediate thought was that he was dying. Then my 'nurse in an emergency' took over and I became calm and did what all nurses would do – took his pulse! This was strong, but rapid and I realized almost instantly that he was having an epileptic fit and that what I had reported as statistics in autistic children when I gave my talks was now a reality with our own child. I put him into the recovery position and turned to revive Paul, who, leaping from bed so quickly, then seeing his beloved son in this state, had almost passed out and was sitting with his head between his legs!

Once Paul had recovered and Grant's breathing had changed to that of a sleeping child, we returned to our bed to discuss the happening. Maybe it would be just a one off. He was approaching puberty and this was a time when a young autistic person was reputedly prone to the onset of epilepsy. But why couldn't we have been spared this problem?

In the morning I rang our doctor who advised me to send Grant into school as usual. He, too, suggested hopefully that it might be Grant's only fit and that we shouldn't do anything yet. A second fit would warrant investigation.

Grant was calmer and sleepier than usual but otherwise none the worse for his experience. We sent him into school with full details of the fit, but they were used to it as there were several pupils in the school who were epileptic. It was a Tuesday and the day I normally went out to my patients so I set off as usual. I stopped on the way for petrol. It was there it hit me, just as I was about to drive off. I started to tremble, then the tears came and I felt devastated. I couldn't go into work like this. Who could I talk to? Who would understand? Then I remembered Heathcroft and they were not far away. They had many children with epilepsy and they knew Grant well. I made my way there and was instantly directed to sit down in their office as I walked tearfully through the door. I was handed a box of tissues and somebody was sent to get me tea, and that was even before I had told them what had happened! By this time I was laughing at their kindness and efficiency and could talk calmly through the events of the night which, as I suspected, got their full sympathy, understanding and support. Several of the girls on duty were upset as they couldn't believe Grant could be beset with yet another injustice in his life.

About a week later it happened again. It happened in the early hours as before and this time he gave a warning 'whoop' followed by a full grande mal attack. Medication and investigations began.

Grant's epilepsy hit our little family like a bomb. Discovering he was autistic was a gradual procedure to which we adjusted slowly. He had enough problems without epilepsy to complicate his life further. We had just started entrusting him to Julian's care who at fourteen was level-headed and capable, and it allowed Paul and me to attend the occasional meeting together which was a touch of luxury! Now, until we knew how much the epilepsy would affect him, we couldn't leave him at all.

The dangers already awaiting around every corner were now

multiplied and of course we couldn't help but think of Zoë and how she had lost her life to the condition.

We considered his few enjoyments in life, particularly his swimming and horse riding and desperately hoped they would not be affected. I had become much more relaxed with him in the pool as I knew his moves, however peculiar ... but now, what if he had a fit under water? Paul didn't have the knowledge I had on coping with a seizure, and he loved to walk with him many miles along beautiful, quiet walks, but the possibility of a fit was going to make him very wary. So at this moment we saw it all in shades of black and as a huge setback to any of the progress he had made.

Sleep for Paul and me was now further disturbed as we both now only slept lightly whether Grant was sleeping or not, just in case we missed a warning sign.

The weekend following his first seizure was Mothering Sunday and I felt that I must go with him to church on that day. He was fairly calm so there was a good chance he would be able to stay for most of the service. We have two churches in our parish and I was pleased to see the service that day was at the smaller church, where children were more accepted by the parishioners. We were warmly welcomed and, feeling as I did, I needed the comfort they offered, particularly with it being Mothering Sunday. Then when the collection was made, Yvonne Chase, who was a mainstay of that church and had lots to do with the children, came and took Grant, and with some difficulty helped him take up the offering to the altar. I saw that scene in a blur. That moment was so memorable and spiritually uplifting and that I used the occasion to illustrate the church, and its relevance to our lives, during the interview for 'Songs of Praise', just over a week later. This clip was used in a three minute slot from an hour's interview.

Filming on the day was interesting. Seven people arrived at nine in the morning and stayed until five or six in the evening! They wanted shots of the whole family, so Paul came home early to coincide with Julian leaving school. They filmed us all in the garden playing with Grant on his energy-releasing trampoline, and many other shots of us all together in action! The team went for lunch at a local pub so that I had plenty of time to collect Grant from school and smarten him up. They then filmed what would be our normal activities, and Grant's autism meant he was fairly oblivious to the camera. I sat on the floor with him, watching his video, and set up a teaching or activity situation to show the lack of motivation and concentration. True to form he was as contrary as ever, threading beads with great alacrity, just because the cameras were focused on him. This skill usually took a great deal of persuasion and commanded only brief interest! I wondered whether a permanent camera would be a good idea for future motivation!

The producer rang me a few days later to say that they had enough material to make a full documentary and it had been very hard to whittle it down to the three minutes required.

The final programme filmed at Easter was one in which we were proud to play a part. I hoped that from our participation we had put autism a little more on to the map.

Thirteen

Paramount among the concerns in children such as ours, who have an inability to communicate, is illness. They can have a relatively insignificant problem, such as toothache or a sore throat, which worries them and affects their behaviour. On the other hand, they could have something really serious such as a grumbling appendix, a sprain, fracture or the prelude to an epileptic fit that could have serious consequences.

I would like to offer helpful solutions to this problem, but I have to say there is little I learnt from our experiences except that as parents you must be attuned to their every sign and signal. I found Grant indicated a sore throat with bad breath, dribbling, fingers down his throat and swollen glands under his lower jaw. That was an easy one!

Often autistics will show behavioural signs because of fear, confusion, or change of scene, or make an action that will produce signals that could be confused with illness such as moaning, hitting their head or a severe tantrum.

One of many examples with Grant happened while at Bishopswood. When he was four he developed a severe limp and a visit to casualty and X-rays revealed little apart from some problem around his hips, possibly a strain. He had two episodes of this so it was worrying when the school taxi-driver passed him over to me outside the village shop saying, 'I have been told to tell you that Grant developed a severe limp following the gym class, last lesson this afternoon.' As the last instance of limping had been a good year previously, my heart sank as I envisaged having to take him to the doctor, which was not an easy task. I drove him home and then proceeded to undress him in order to make my careful examination. I first pulled down his trousers, thinking of his hip problem, pressed bones and wriggled him round noting any wincing, which was not apparent. I then proceeded to examine his knees bending them back and forth, and the same with his ankles. Having seen nothing yet that indicated a problem I removed his shoes to look at his feet. Out from his left shoe fell a drawing pin! This, of course, is an exceptional happening, but as carers you carry the guilt for causing the distress.

How many times in our lives can we remember having to stop when walking to remove a stone, or sand from a shoe? Or wince as a new pair of shoes rubs a sore place or even a blister? People who care for the non-communicators have to literally put themselves into the shoes of their charges!

Are they too hot, or are they feeling chilly, or is it what we ourselves are feeling? How many times do we feel differently from one another about the temperature?

Grant would put anything into his mouth and our awareness of this habit was heightened when sitting on a pebbly beach. On one pleasantly warm day in Dorset, Grant lay on the beach, calmer now at ten, soaking up the sunshine. The smooth pebbles were good to feel and he let them drop though his fingers and clatter back on to the beach. Every so often one was popped into his mouth and I would push his head forward with one hand and flick my finger from the other hand into his mouth to hook out the pebbles of varying sizes. I watched him like a hawk as he had been known to swallow them. On this occasion I felt I had retrieved them all.

That night in the caravan he was exceptionally restless and appeared to be in some pain. The next day was the end of our break and we returned home. The following day I noticed stones in the toilet and fished out ten pebbles that had come through Grant, one of which was frighteningly large!

Even when he hadn't tried to block himself up with stones he became very constipated, mainly because he didn't make an effort over anything. Unless his bowel was completely full and he experienced a real urge, he would make no effort on the toilet. He could go for a week or ten days then would fill and often block the pan! There were some bad times when his stomach would become very distended. We would give him three or more Weetabix breakfast biscuits with bran and rhubarb. He had dried prunes, fresh prunes, beans and lentils, porridge oats and oranges galore. Nothing seemed to make any difference and we were sensibly advised not to give laxatives, as started in one so young could lead to later problems. Different types of laxatives have varying effects on people and the discomfort and pain from griping could be worse than the constipation which, on the whole, didn't seem to bother him.

When Grant was eleven I was not happy about him. I knew something was wrong, but couldn't put my finger on it. Maybe it had something to do with the fact that he wasn't eating much or trying to get into the pantry! He was sleeping much more and still looking tired in the daytime. He was losing weight and his trousers needed tighter elastic to hold them up. After two weeks of being none the wiser I took him to see our doctor and explained our worries. He could only go by what I had to tell him and as he would to a mother with a baby, had to ask for my observations. He tested heart and lungs, looked in his mouth as much as he could and examined his ears. He laid him on the couch and felt his tummy and found nothing abnormal. I directed him to small swollen glands that I had felt in his groins and asked whether it might be glandular fever, even though he was rather young for the virus, which on the whole tends to affect older adolescents. He took a blood test and two weeks later phoned us confirming the condition. This was a relief as it explained a lot about his behaviour.

Mothers, on the whole, are attuned to the needs of their children. Lack of communication increases that sensitivity. As many aspects of their development are still at baby level, the mother's natural instincts are acute. When the child starts to show independence this natural sensitivity is usually eroded. Involved fathers can learn to have this perceptiveness too, as can good sensitive carers. Whether the mother retains these abilities depends on the relationship she has built up with her child. In some cases of autism this will have been severely checked because of the problems brought about by the child's condition and its attendant frustrations.

I was under Grant's skin. I felt that my sensitivity to his actions was extremely acute. Initial holding techniques had renewed and strengthened the natural maternal bonding. In many ways he had not left babyhood even though physically he was extremely fit, strong and agile.

As Grant became older and Paul had more and more of a part to play in his life and care, he too became sensitive to his actions, as did Julian to a lesser degree.

Grant was amazingly good at having blood tests and the necessary brain scans for his epilepsy. I usually made it clear to a receptionist that he did not have the ability to sit to wait for an appointment so I was usually given the first slot of the day. As parents we must make clear our needs if we have a problem like this as most receptionists will be accommodating. If we should meet up with a problem, a letter to the consultant or head of the department explaining the difficulties will usually solve it. Hospitals and surgeries now need to prove themselves as understanding and efficient and will be anxious to please.

Grant's scan showed electrical brain activity that indicated epilepsy and his medication was given in accordance.

He took his medicine initially in liquid form which was easy for him to manage and very palatable so we had few problems in that direction, until one night when he had been on the drug for about eight months. He had never attempted to touch the bottle so I had left it ready on the mantelpiece for Claire Arthan to give to him just before bedtime. Paul and I had hardly been out alone socially since Grant had begun his epilepsy, but this wintery night, in early December, was Paul's company's annual Christmas event. Julian was in the Air Training Corps and going to his first evening dress dinner held at a local college, and looked dashing in his father's DJ.

Grant's seizures were far from under control and until they were we felt we must never be far away. This night we had asked Claire to sit for us as we knew she was competent. She had now worked for some time at Heathcroft and was well used to coping with children during seizures; in any case Grant's fits usually happened as he came out of sleep in the early hours of the morning. Claire had now completed her social work training and, fortunately for us, still lived near. We left them together, Grant cuddling close to Claire while she indulged him in a chapter or two of his latest favourite story.

Our evening was to be at the Lakeside Country Club in Camberley, where we would have dinner and be entertained by a well-known cabaret act. We met at Paul's office in Henley and were taken by coach to our destination. We were just finishing our coffee and waiting for the cabaret to begin when an official of the club came to our table and asked for us by name. She said that there had been a phone call from our sitter Claire to ask us to ring the children's ward at the Royal Berkshire Hospital. The message said not to panic as it was nothing too serious.

Frantically we rang the hospital! We spoke to Claire who told us that she had gone to answer the telephone, leaving Grant in the lounge. The phone call was a wrong number! When she went back to Grant he was lying flat on his back on the fireside rug swigging his bottle of medicine, at least half had gone! He thought it a huge joke as he was trying to get her attention for leaving him in the middle of a story and of course he succeeded with much more attention than he bargained for. Claire rang the ambulance and then telephoned her boyfriend, whom she had asked to come to be around for Julian's return.

Grant enjoyed his ride to hospital, but was not too keen on the emetic medicine which caused sickness to help overcome the overdose. Claire handled it all efficiently, but waited with trepidation for our return, knowing that our evening had been ruined.

We felt trapped as we were such a long way from Reading and without our own transport. Returning to our table we explained

our predicament and a couple who had not used the coach kindly
offered to leave early and run us home. Claire had assured us that
there was no hurry as Grant had brought up the offending
medicine, but would have to remain in hospital for observation
and she was happy to stay until we returned.

We left after the cabaret, of which I remember little! The return
journey seemed endless, but we called home first to see Julian and
grab some comfortable clothes before I sped off in my car,
knowing I would be there for the night. Paul followed close
behind so we arrived at our destination together.

On reaching the ward we soon found the bed, where sat a
forlorn Claire by the side of wan, but cheeky faced Grant who had
that look as if to say, 'I've got Claire's full attention, I've brought
you both back and I've had an exciting ride in an ambulance too!'
Hopefully we reassured Claire that in no way was it her fault as it
was I who had unwisely trusted Grant with his medicine bottle
and we praised her for what she did for both boys. Paul ran her
home and I made myself as comfortable as I could on a couple of
chairs by his side and watched the activities of the night-time in
the children's ward. The trauma of the night's events or the
reduced medication levels in his body caused Grant to have two
epileptic fits in succession. Despite these, he awoke at seven,
fidgety and active and, being in a foreign situation, he wanted out!

The night staff were excellent and very supportive, but the day
staff did not understand or show any willingness to learn. I was
frowned on as a mother who could not control her child.
Breakfast was distributed slowly and when Grant was not given
food quickly enough he made a grab to pinch it, and succeeded. I
tried to explain, but it was on deaf ears. Once I had managed to
acquire food for him we were shown to a day room with toys and
told that the doctors would be around at ten when Grant would
probably (and thankfully for them) be discharged. Grant was a
frightened, lively, hyperactive, large eleven-year-old child who
could not be distracted into any play and, in this situation, wasn't
even interested in a story. Two hours seems an eternity. The
doctors came to do their round and we were asked to return to

the bed. As this was at the furthest end of the ward the doctors took at least half an hour to reach us. In that time Grant had leapt from the bed and run down the ward on a few occasions, only to be frowned on by the nurses and the retinue of doctors.

Eventually we were released and we walked the corridors to freedom. It was on occasions such as these that I shared something of what Grant was experiencing all the time. To him the world was full of strangers who uttered meaningless sounds that confused and frightened him and made him want to run from them. Once Grant sat in the safe confines of my little car holding a well-thumbed and curled Ladybird book, all was well in his world, and he became calm and relaxed, happy to be driven home.

Needless to say we learnt that where dangers were concerned we couldn't trust him and never again was his medication left within his reach. We bought a strong, second-hand wooden cabinet fitted with a small padlock and sited it high on a shelf inside the locked pantry.

The lack of knowledge of the nurses on the ward worried me for the sake of other autistic children and their parents faced with a hospital visit. Already I was a regular speaker on the Berkshire Health Visitor's training course and used our own experiences as a means of identifying the early problems of parents along with some teaching on the features of autism. One day I was discussing my experiences of the hospital visit with a nursing tutor and she asked me if I would be included on their curriculum of paediatric training. I was only too happy to oblige. I explained the problems of autism to the nurses and tried to make them more aware of how they might feel in this very frightening situation.

Grant's epilepsy took two to three years before it seemed to come under control and several changes of medication were made until a final satisfactory cocktail of drugs suited his needs and a fit became a rare occurrence.

At eleven Grant's schooling was settled and in term time all was well. The holidays were a different story. Most families with children with severe behaviour problems will face an approaching long school holiday with trepidation. The three week breaks at Christmas and Easter are long enough, but a six or seven week break in the summer can fill a parent with sheer panic. Some schools are coming round to staggered holidays so that the break is no longer than three weeks, but even that can be enough to stretch a family to breaking point. We were no exception to this and often at the end of the long summer holiday I would find myself near to a nervous breakdown.

In order to try to avoid getting to this state I tried to plan these weeks well in advance and yet another chart would appear behind my kitchen cupboard, this time covering the whole of the six or seven weeks with suitable occupations. The planning had to begin as early as March, when a letter would be sent from Heathcroft asking for requests for holidays for the year. Working this out with the family was a mammoth task. Julian now had his Air Cadet weeks away ambushing 'the enemy' on suitably designated areas in Surrey, or learning how to survive the nights and days sleeping in bivouacs and eating from dried food packs. Paul, too, had his weekends away tied up with his aviation interests. He also had work deadlines in his financial field which limited the dates we could take away. After pestering them both and, lots of arguing and deliberating, we finally managed to fix our holiday date alone with Julian. I found it easier to take all my holiday allowed from my domiciliary nursing in one go during the school summer break. I worked some clinics at a local surgery practice and these had to be taken into the equation of when I should book Grant into Heathcroft. Having these dates sorted I would then balance the rest of the time so that I never had more than two days without a Heathcroft break or the support of Paul, be it at the weekend, or scattered days among the weeks.

My next plan was to make a list of all the activities that we could do, ones to include both boys and ones that would be more suitable for Grant alone when Julian was happily occupied with other things. The list would be as follows: swimming, horse riding, theme park, ice skating, Burger King, flower gardens, fishing, zoo, tri-skating, tricycle, shopping centre, train ride, day at the coast, day at Butlins holiday centre.

I would then list local events that might be suitable and watch the Henley and Reading newspapers for anything which would possibly stimulate or interest him.

I would arrange to double up if at all possible with someone with a similar problem, but this was less easy after Zoë's death as most of the people I knew had much older children who were usually settled in care and didn't have the long summer break. By planning this way I made my way much more successfully through each week and even enjoyed and looked forward to our days. Employing Anne Tucknott to come in daily and sort out the house left me free to cope with Grant and his problems and helped us into an easier exit for our days out.

It was just before the summer holidays of 1985 that I heard of Camp Mohawk – a group of scouts who held a camp in the woods in nearby Wargrave, who were looking for autistic boys between the ages of nine and thirteen to look after in the summer holidays! Up to now I had hardly spoken to anyone who had even heard of autism let alone seek our children in order to care for them! I found out more and drove up to the camp to make inquiries. It was tucked away up narrow roads and muddy tracks and after some searching I discovered the huts and Roy Howgate (known as Skip by his scouts) who made me welcome with a cup of strong tea. He explained to me about the camp which had been running for some twelve years. Primarily, it was a camp for children from one of East London's dockland boroughs and run on the lines of a scout camp. They had the use of a large area of forest land and here they had built a wooden barn to complement the large sleeping tents.

In 1976 they were 'found' by the father of a boy who resided in a mental institution in a not too distant town. The father was anxious that his son should be able to enjoy a near normal a life as possible, in spite of having to live permanently in hospital. As a leading member of the League of Friends, he had organized the fundraising and purchase of some camping equipment.

This led to four years of very happy camping between combined groups of the deprived, but able-bodied children, from the East End and the mentally handicapped children from the hospital. But after four years the hospital had almost completely dropped out of the scheme, having developed their own facilities. The camps continued, but handicapped children were selected from all over the South of England.

One day a parent pleaded for them to take a profoundly handicapped boy who had had meningitis as a baby and was now epileptic and doubly incontinent. They took on the task, which opened a new door to the care offered. They then concentrated on opening the camp to children who needed the most care and, by chance, found that this also gave a break to parents who were often over-stretched by the demands made on them. Mostly they felt they were giving these children a chance to find some freedom among children of their own age.

They allocated two boys to each handicapped child so that the care and responsibility was shared. Roy watched over all the boys with an eagle eye and an infinite sensitivity and he supervised all of them with strict kindness.

The camp was not to start until the end of the following week and Roy suggested that I come to the camp with Grant to see it in action and watch how the boys cared for their charges.

I did have reservations – quite natural ones which Roy recognized and could only address by inviting me to stay until I was happy. The first was the age of the boys given this responsible task and the second, their ability to watch over their charges consistently, knowing from my own experience how much unremitting patience and staying power is needed while supervising our children. I found it hard to believe that boys of this age could be expected to keep up their vigil with children who gave little in return.

My second worry was a regular one: Grant's ability to escape at the blink of an eyelid. Roy talked about Grant staying overnight which I had not even contemplated. If they slept in large tents without inbuilt ground sheets then Grant could escape in the early hours of the morning, either through the entrance or under the canvas before anyone was awake.

The following week I returned with Grant and it was my first chance to see them all in action. Roy sat in the middle and, although talking to me, it was as if he had antennae picking up waves to every boy and his charge. Our conversation would be interrupted to call out a direction, admonishing or warning 'his troop'. He did have the help of Mike, an older scout, and Roy's son, Graham. They helped with the administration, supervising and the cooking.

We had no sooner arrived when Grant was taken from me so that they could give him a second breakfast, to which he had no objection. He would be happy to leave the safety of his mother for food and any place was 'in' if they fed him well.

I was then shown around the camp and the huts with all the facilities they had built fitted with safety and alarm systems, which were quite sophisticated. They were even linked to the ambulance service! They had intercom and alarm systems so that if the boys went out into the woods they could be contacted, and make contact, at all times.

If Grant were to sleep overnight then he would sleep in a small inside room and his carer would sleep in the same room with him. They would have an alarm system connected to Roy's room so that in the event of any problem he could be alerted immediately.

I was beginning to contemplate the idea of leaving him, as they did seem to be very organized. Sometime later Roy sent me home for a few hours, giving me their mobile number so I could call to check all was well, which of course it was. When I returned, Grant was eating and I was told he had been eating most of the time and needless to say was very happy! His young charges said that they had been running after him in between his dining sessions and were exhausted, but were eager to know when he was coming again as they liked looking after him and *please* could he stay for the night?

Later that week I left him again for a few hours and the following week I left him overnight. Roy told me, when I collected him the next day, that the care his two young charges of eleven and twelve had shown had been highly commendable.

Steven Sharland, aged twelve, had been allocated Grant and he had been with him for the day. Steven was a sensible lad and Roy didn't doubt his abilities, but was surprised when Grant's toileting signals were missed, resulting in a disgusting mess for Steven to clean up, and he couldn't cope. Roy was in a dilemma as to whom he could now give the responsibility. There was one lad called Marc Taylor, who so far had only made himself unpopular with the other scouts because of home-induced problems within his personality. He stepped forward and requested to look after Grant. Roy questioned his ability, 'Are you *sure* you will watch him all the time and particularly around 5 a.m., which is the time Grant could have a fit?' Marc was very insistent that he was up to the job.

Ten minutes later Roy went to check on Marc and was impressed to find Grant happily lying in a bath, well scrubbed, and the mess in the room almost completely cleared and washed clean.

The next morning Roy called early and found Marc and Grant were asleep. Waking Marc he questioned him carefully. 'Was everything all right, Marc?'

'Yes, Skip,' Marc replied sleepily.

' Are you sure that Grant didn't have a fit?' Roy persisted.

'No, Skip,' Marc said. ' I am sure he didn't. I was awake most of the night with Grant, as he didn't go to sleep until after 3 a.m. and I dozed off to sleep just before you came in.'

Marc wanted to look after Grant all day, but as he was so tired Roy insisted that he go for a sleep. Marc cried, saying that Grant was his charge and he wanted to look after him. Roy insisted and following a few hours sleep Marc was all set for the next night.

The next morning Roy called to see them, again in the early hours, only to find Marc sitting on a chair by the side of Grant's bed. He was balanced on the back two legs of the chair with his head resting against the wall. Roy queried why he wasn't in bed and Marc said, 'Skip, you didn't trust me. I sat like this so that if I fell asleep then my chair would fall and wake me up!'

Roy explained that some of the children were deprived of love at home and now had the chance to care for others, therefore having a purpose to their lives. He was giving them responsibility and they respected this and wanted his trust more than anything. In fact their backgrounds were similar to those of the families with whom I worked on the community in Reading, consequently I understood the problem. It therefore increased my admiration of the way Roy was dealing with these young lads and the opportunities that they were being given.

Camp Mohawk could now be included as another entry on the summer holiday list and I joined them on their occasional outings to theme parks. This provided me with much needed support, particularly as Grant was now growing rapidly and his strength and speed were superior to mine.

Roy contacted me in the winter before Grant's fourteenth birthday and asked if Grant and I would like join a trip to the Netherlands. This was quite a surprise as Grant had had his last camp with them that year, but was still eligible as he wasn't yet fourteen. It is something they had done several times in the past, but not for a year or two. I would be useful to the group as a nurse and supervisor and, of course, would be there to help with Grant, who by now was much larger than most of the scouts. Roy's daughter, Joanna, and friend Jane, who were trainee nursery nurses, would be going to help too. We would be staying as guests of a Dutch scouting group in Heelen, in the south of the country. Roy was very friendly with many of their group leaders and suitable arrangements had been made to make the trip enjoyable and suitable for the disabled youngsters.

Roy had been presented with an old bus, which a firm had refurbished and converted into an ambulance bus. It was painted black and had a hospital unit at the back, kitchen in the middle and seating at the front. This was to be presented at London City Airport and then we would journey on to the Netherlands. The purpose of the visit was to visit the Carnival, an event held annually in many parts of Europe and heralding Lent. It is a three-day affair in which the whole family participates. It is an extremely happy time with everyone dressing up in colourful costume and playing anything that makes music.

I agreed to go and welcomed the opportunity for Grant. I

Julian, Grant (centre) and I frequently sat inside the playpen on the lawn, reading together

Grant (right) and Julian at the seaside, aged three and six. Grant's sense of mischief came out in many ways

Grant (aged four) sharing a moment with Paul. Grant's harness enabled us to enjoy many outings

Story-times played a large part in Grant's life and often gave him a few minutes' peace and calm

Zoë, Jean and David's little girl

Facilitated tricycle riding!

My 'toy boy' aged seventeen and I
at Fuerteventura

Eyes as the windows of the soul: communicating with Grant

Grant looking dapper in his DJ
at the Chilterns' New Year's Day
celebration

The Gentle Giant

packed a large rucksack and holdall with thick woollies, Ladybird books and the cassette-player and tapes.

The weather was freezing and the bus proved cold and unreliable, but nevertheless we had an enjoyable and interesting time. We were made very welcome by our Dutch hosts and soon were joining in the party atmosphere, which discos, food and a warm scout-hut created. Joyful singing and dancing seemed to be the order of the day and our children were warmly encouraged to participate in everything.

There were eight scouts and eight handicapped youngsters of varying degrees of disability. Each scout was entrusted with the care of a handicapped youngster and had to stay with his charge for the whole of the trip. This meant eating, sleeping next to their charge (after they were asleep) and changing wet or soiled pants.

Being in the extreme south we crossed over into Germany on two days and were met at the border by the German police, who escorted us to a street in Aachen where we were given a prime position from which to view the Carnival procession. Roy had brought with us a collapsible stand and the scouts soon had it erected. Scouts and their charges sat side by side watching as the floats went by; sweets, packets of popcorn and biscuits were hurled at the crowds. Grant thought this was wonderful and carrier bags were stuffed full, as were his cheeks. I don't think he could believe his good fortune as these goodies rained from the sky. Our Dutch hosts were amused and delighted at his reactions.

On one occasion an elderly lady saw the stand and thought she would like a seat. It was very full. Roy told her it was a private stand, but she didn't understand English, so with frantic sign language he tried to direct her away. She was not to be put off and refused to understand and, determinedly, she climbed the stairs to the top and squashed herself next to a scout, who had to push the others up tightly together. When the sweets came raining down, she fought with the rest of the group to obtain her share. Grant, seeing her looking away, decided to help himself to the sweets on her lap. Her face was a study, and with the laughter of those around she had begun to doubt the wisdom of her chosen seat and, staring, bewildered, around at the group, gathered her goodies and left!

In the evening, we were taken to a restaurant where our hosts had arranged food, drink and musical entertainment. Roy was particularly amused when he viewed from a distance a waiter who passed by carrying an order of drinks. His eyes looked straight ahead as he focused on the table to which the order was bound. Grant espied the passing tray on which sat a large glass of orange juice. As the waiter and tray passed, Grant raised his hand and deftly removed the glass and its contents without the waiter noticing its loss! I should add that we were guests at this restaurant so that Grant's total lack of social awareness did not amount to stealing!

We dressed our children in the bright and colourful costumes we had brought with us and painted their faces to look like clowns. This matched the tremendous trouble that most of the population took to make carnival time go with a swing. They all had a very happy time and we made many friends among our Dutch hosts.

The boys slept in a large hall, where their mattresses where placed side by side, and a scout and handicapped child lay in alternate positions. It was a long time for one so young to have such an assignment, but they loved it and carried out their work with care, enjoying the whole experience and hardly expressing a single moan. I felt honoured to be with these youngsters who were still children and enjoyed a cuddle before they settled to sleep.

We brought the creaking, drafty bus back to England with a lot of lovely young people who had warmed my heart.

Fourteen

As you may have appreciated in my story, 'Holding' is a therapy that I believed helped Grant more than anything else. It strengthened the bonding between us and improved our relationship and his security. Maybe by this enforced holding I had made him realize that human contact was good and comforting. The stories we shared at this time gave him his interest in books and, even though this led to obsessions, they were not negative ones as they gave him interest in life and introduced him to other preoccupations such as tapes and videos.

Holding is not new and has been a recognized way of giving comfort probably since time began. A child who is very frightened will be comforted by the parent when held tightly; the fear is shared until it is has gone and the child can proceed independently without the adult. Children with autistic behaviours usually shun touch and comfort from another person, making them prematurely independent. Insistence on comforting the child by holding him firmly will increase the feeling of security, alleviate fear and therefore aid in achieving more communication and compliance.

Some of the fears that autistic children experience are ones that we cannot comprehend, as their senses can change the natural input of sight, sound and touch, giving weird sounds and pictures that we don't understand. This can throw them into unbelievable tantrums that can happen in embarrassing places. In an ideal situation, the parent or care-giver could use physical restraint, holding the child and sharing the fear until he is calmer. However, the circumstances are not always such that this can be done and the extra strength of the child makes it difficult. Throwing your whole body on top of your child in the middle of a supermarket might cause something of a scene!

There was a case involving Grant which showed very clearly how an acute fear can be worked on and relieved by holding. We bought a greenhouse and sited it at the far end of the garden. Grant would go down to it, but could not pass over the doorstep. He stared at something just on the left of the door and fought and cried if I tried to take him in. As I wanted him to help water the plants I tried to insist on his entry, but it got worse and he panicked and screamed with fear if I attempted any move to get him in. He developed a morbid fascination and would be drawn near to the doorway, but would go no further.

One day on reaching the greenhouse door I took his hand and held it inside to the point where he stared. I have never seen fear so marked on the face of anyone and I would not like to see it again. His eyes expressed acute fear, his face went pale, he trembled and sweated profusely. I threw my arms around him, holding him firmly and took him away from what to him was traumatic beyond endurance. Whatever he saw was not what we were seeing. I looked for odd reflections in the glass or a different way of interpreting an upturned flower-pot on the slatted bench, but there was nothing that through my eyes could look frightening. It brought home to me how his vision was reflecting different images from our own.

Despite all this, he was determined to return to the scene so I decided that I should try and show him how, through his mother's love and security, I could diminish fear. I took him there and held him firmly, talking to him constantly and telling him there was nothing to be worried about. I always talked to him normally as if he could understand everything and there were many times when I think he did understand much more than we ever realized.

We stepped with some difficulty over the metal rim of the doorway as he was trying to struggle free. Once inside and still holding very tightly I held his arm out to the spot that he stared at and moved it around reassuring him constantly that there was nothing to fear. We then left the greenhouse, but he returned several times that day and each time I would do the same thing. With each visit he struggled less and the fearful look was subsiding. After two to three days he was going inside himself and by the end of the week he was seated on the floor sifting the stones, soil and baby tomatoes through his fingers!

I had eliminated a fear by enforced holding and the security of a mother's love. Through this protection, whatever he saw had either disappeared or he viewed it differently.

Like the greenhouse, in the past vacuum cleaners and food mixers caused him to run and cry, but later these, along with carpet sweepers, became obsessions.

When Grant was nine or ten the official 'Holding Therapy', which Dr O'Gorman had tried to teach me in years past, was brought over from the USA and was now being advocated as a method of treatment. Dr Martha Welsh in America declared her method was a 'cure' which angered many in the field of autism who said she did not have substantiated proof and was giving false hope to parents. Nevertheless, children had been helped and communication achieved, even if for only short spells following the treatment.

There was also some confusion over her explanation of 'faulty bonding' between the mother and child, giving the impression that she was indicating parental fault for the child's condition, which had been mistakenly suggested in the past. This kind of exposure does nothing to aid parents fighting to help their children. It only adds guilt to already tortuously stretched emotions.

Martha Welsh's method was for the mother to hold the child, sometimes for hours, talking to him, shouting at him, questioning him for his reasons for not wanting to learn in order to make the child angry and bring out her own feelings too. The child usually struggles with the mother who continues to hold on tightly, instilling the message that her love is so strong that whatever he does, whatever his feelings, she can take care of him and she is in control.

His anger eventually turns to sadness and this is known as the breaking point; she shares his tears and consoles him tenderly. He allows his mother to comfort him and gives eye contact. Having achieved this break the child then allows the mother to play with him and often communicates with some spontaneous language if there isn't normally any. I found the idea fascinating, particularly as I felt I had already achieved quite a lot through adaptations of this method.

I attended a talk on the subject by Dr John Richer who recounted his experiences of watching Martha Welsh in New York successfully achieving heart-rending communication between mother and child, after an hour or two of holding. After that I felt compelled to investigate further. I arranged an appointment to see Jasmine Bailey who was the only therapist in holding (at that time) in the country. She had set up The Mothering Centre in London to show parents what to do, and offer support.

I watched the mothers working on their children by holding which continued for at least an hour. The results did produce some improved interaction between mother and child at the end of a session, though on this occasion it was not to the dramatic degree that I had been led to expect. Grant was now eleven, large and strong and the only way to 'hold' was to involve the father too. The whole family was encouraged to participate; in videos of the New York clinic we watched sessions of terrible screaming and crying alternating between mother and child with frightened, bewildered small siblings watching. I was very uneasy about children being involved at such a vulnerable age. Surely they couldn't reap anything positive from this situation and I worried that it could be psychologically harmful.

Paul wanted to try the method. Julian showed interest but wasn't sure he was happy about the effect on Grant. Julian was now six foot (and growing) and a strapping lad at not yet fifteen. He decided that he would demonstrate how he felt 'holding' might not help his brother. He picked me up and flattened me on the floor, sitting on top of me and pinning my arms to either side of my head!

'Struggle!' he commanded. I tried, but no way could I be released from his grip. 'Now,' he said, 'what do you feel like?'

'Trapped and frustrated,' I breathlessly replied.

'Quite,' he said, and released me!

Despite this I felt we should go ahead. Surely the idea was to make the child angry and frustrated so that you break down their barriers, thus producing eye contact and speech. What had we to lose? If the method appeared detrimental in any way we would discontinue it.

Our attempts had to be done in the evening, and now Grant was older, an early meal on Paul's return from work, followed by holding about an hour later, seemed the best way to proceed. We found the hall the most convenient place as this interfered least with Julian's studies or the television. Julian stepped over us all as he passed through!

I started the session off while Paul helped hold him down, but soon we took turns of either holding down arms or legs while the other gave the input so that the long, continuous and arduous task was kept up. I think our longest session was an hour and three quarters.

Sometimes I would hold alone if Paul was out and Paul would do it if I was out. We had varying degrees of success, but never the dramatic 'break' that Martha Welsh had claimed would happen. Most of the time Grant would look in any direction than into our eyes and go deep into himself, refusing to let out any angers or frustrations. He had a resigned air of patience with a 'you can try all you like but I can stay shut off from what you are doing until you are fed up' attitude. I think it let out oodles of our own emotions if nothing else. If you spent nearly two hours to get this kind of reaction you finished up feeling frustrated and downhearted at your lack of achievement. On the other hand, there were good sessions that might have been shorter, but much more satisfactory and made you feel that it was all worthwhile.

We both experienced better eye contact on our good sessions and the fact that we increasingly managed individual holds without needing the strength of the other was proof of some success and less traumatic for us all.

Now I think we had slipped into our own version of holding that was more akin to the one which I had done some eight years previously. I couldn't help thinking that it was the very close and direct language input that was helping.

There were still so many constraints inhibiting continuation of this therapy to the degree that I would have liked. I had long toyed with the idea of taking Grant somewhere remote so that life's pressures were mitigated and I could concentrate fully on working with him. I had read an article in a magazine a couple of years ago where a mother took her autistic son to an isolated croft in Scotland and worked on him to the exclusion of all else, achieving some quite miraculous breakthroughs with his autism. She didn't have any other children to consider, but her husband did come some weekends to join them. She was away with him for some six months. I still had the article and I re-read it many times wondering if there was any possibility of doing anything similar. I had so much to consider – Paul, Julian, work, Grant's schooling. I looked at schedules ahead and then discussed the idea with Paul and Julian. They both readily agreed that if it might help Grant then I must go and they could manage by themselves.

I decided on three weeks to start with and, if it showed good results, then I could always do it again. I planned to write a daily diary and assess the results at the end. Paul and Julian decided they would join us in the last week which, from our planning, would be the spring half-term. Grant's school was not too happy about my decision, but understood my need to try as I think they were worried about my ability to cope with Grant without any support at all.

I planned it all with infinite care in order to anticipate all conceivable dangers and thus eliminate them. Wherever I chose had to be beautiful, mountainous, remote, but not so much so that I couldn't be in touch with people easily. I needed to have medical facilities such as a local doctor for epileptic emergencies if they should arise.

I studied the map long and hard together with brochures on Scotland. The need for beautiful scenery was essential for me. I needed rewards and relaxation and the tranquillity of mountains and streams as well as a certain amount of solitude. The ideal place seemed to be the west coast. I looked for the shaded areas of natural beauty where the mountains neared the sea. Having chosen the area I then looked for large holiday caravans sited singly near crofts. In this way I could enjoy solitude, yet still have someone nearby and a phone for emergencies.

I rang a few advertisers, then came to one that sounded perfect. It was on the edge of the sparsely populated village of Diabaig, opposite the north end of Skye, and in the Torridon mountains. I explained to the owners what I was looking for and it appeared to meet all my requirements. They were an English family who had escaped the rat race of London to live a quieter and simpler life. They said it was very beautiful around them and that the caravan was situated well away from the house so we would be undisturbed. There was a doctor in the village and a district nurse who covered a wide area. I booked it for three weeks in May.

I was excited about our trip as it was another chance to help Grant. I was not expecting miracles, but maybe some further chipping of that invisible barrier. Possibly a last chance, as I would never be able to hold him when he was Julian's size.

I filled the freezer with well-planned meals and organized the others with Edna who was only too pleased to help. Julian would go straight from school to his grandparents on designated evenings, where he and Paul would dine and then return home together.

I packed up easy-care sheets, incontinence pads and mattress protectors. We had bags of audio tapes and books galore. I took crayons and jigsaws and bought Grant walking boots and clothes for comfortable walking in the mountains. I made a list of my objectives for our two weeks alone.

1   To encourage speech, with signs.
2   To obtain an awareness of the need to go to the loo when he first awoke, in the hope of achieving a dry bed.
3   To observe and note the reactions of Grant after 1:1 attention for two weeks.

4   To join Grant in his solitude and experience his feelings.
5   To have time to slowly complete everyday tasks such as
     washing, dressing, teeth-cleaning, etc., without the everyday
     pressures that often impede completion of the task.
6   To give him loads of unrestricted space for two weeks, free
     from the worries and many dangers that surround him and of
     which he is totally unaware.

We set off at dawn on a mild May morning and, as the journey
promised to be long we used the quiet, early hours when the roads
were empty. This proved its worth by our reaching a motorway
café, a few miles short of the border, by 9 a.m., where we stopped
for breakfast.

I had packed lots of suitable distractions for the journey such as
books, tapes and snacks and these were all put to good use. At the
service station I began my unhurried but firm discipline, insisting
on Grant eating properly, going to the toilet and washing his
hands, and giving the minimum of assistance. Grant seemed happy
to oblige at this stage, but patience had to be the name of the game
as to complete any task was laborious and needed masses of verbal
prompts.

We were to meet up with an elderly friend in Edinburgh who
used to be the matron of the hospital where I worked in Malawi,
and she would put us up overnight. I had explained to her that it
would be difficult to talk and catch up on old times, as with Grant
my every moment was taken up. However, we did manage a short
chat when Grant was in bed. Unfortunately, he wouldn't settle so
I found it easier to join him in our twin-bedded room where,
once he felt the security of his Mum's presence, he fell asleep.

The next day we travelled on and it surprised me that, despite
the roads being really quiet, the journey lasted longer than I had
planned as it was so far north and the roads nearer our destination
slow. We made frequent stops to eat and stretch and lingered with
an ice-cream at Loch Ness to scan the waters for the monster!

By late afternoon we were travelling on single track roads and
looking with awe at the towering mountains of the Torridon

range. The landscape was breathtakingly beautiful and Grant was subjected to a continuous flow of words from his mother expressing her pleasure at seeing such scenic delights.

We reached the small community of Torridon where there is a post office and shop and wonderful views over the sea loch of the same name. Diabaig, our final destination, was ten miles on from here along the loch side, over the mountains and down again to the coast.

We followed the loch for a couple of miles, then the road narrowed and twisted up the hillside, delighting the eye as we rose higher, gaining peep-show views between the gaps in the pine trees. Here the loch stretched below, with the Applecross peninsula and the islands of Rona, Raasay and Skye forming a most wonderful trailing backdrop. The sun, sinking lower now in the west glinted on the water and speckled the nets of the salmon fishers.

The road climbed high and snow-topped mountains seemed within easier access, their peeks majestic and silhouetted against the evening sky. There were small patches of snow remaining within reach and the powerful sound of rushing streams could be heard above the engine. Melting snow had filled them to overflowing and they seeped into the boggy uplands. Onward we travelled, over the wilder heath land and past a lake where highland cattle grazed, so much more grand and rugged an animal than a Friesian and so suited to the land we were covering. We topped a hill and the ground fell away suddenly and surprisingly to our left. This was a road to be respected and definitely not one for the unwary! It followed a deep gorge down, and wonderful waterfalls cascaded from above us and passed under the road to fall in spray-tossed torrents hundreds of feet below.

Down we went with small properties coming into view and I realized we had almost reached our destination. The steep road rounded the bend and there below lay the bay of Diabaig. It nestled beneath steep cliffs that surrounded it in an almost complete circle. Beyond it lay the sea, the coast and the hills of the Applecross peninsula with dark shadows of distant islands. I don't think I have seen anywhere more beautiful and it never failed to take my breath away. My choice couldn't have been more perfect. Our caravan was about half a mile from the bay up the hillside, but protected from the winds by trees. The croft was a short distance beyond the caravan and was surrounded by a stone-built wall. The whole of the property was double-gated and therefore was ideal for our needs. Grant could be free here.

We met the family who told me that they would be going to London at the end of the week, but they had been in touch with the district nurse and one or two other locals who would be happy to keep their eye on us and leave their telephone numbers for emergencies. They offered us tea, but Grant was very restless being in strange surroundings and it was becoming too difficult to remain in the house, so we were taken to the caravan.

Our home for the next two weeks was spacious enough for our needs. It was a large mobile home which had two bedrooms, one with a double bed and the other with bunk beds. There was a large living area and a small porch, which was excellent for storing wellington boots, essential footwear for the surrounding land.

Grant took immediately to a carpet sweeper, which became his companion throughout the whole three weeks, even when the handle came off! I did put the obsession to good use whenever I could, but unfortunately he could never put enough effort into the action. He always needed at least my hand to give some support and guidance in order to have any effect on the crumbs.

I decided Grant should have the room with the double bed as I felt the space would be more conducive to sleep than the narrow bunk beds and when Julian arrived it would not be very satisfactory to have them together. The window in this room was a fixed one and this was essential for my peace of mind. I made myself a very comfortable arrangement on the bed settee in the living-room.

From the beginning Grant had to do everything for himself, however long it took. So on this first night after approximately one hour he was ready for bed and, as it was now late, he settled quickly and slept quite well, waking only with a bright cockerel heralding the dawn. Looking from the large window I saw we were surrounded by happy clucking hens who had come to have a look at their new neighbours.

With Grant's awakening I leapt from my bed to take him to the toilet and, finding him dry, showered him with praise. The toilet was an integral part of the caravan, in a small bath-less bathroom. After using it Grant snuggled down into my bed and was content with a cuddle and a few stories.

The first week we were there it was cold and we were grateful for some good safe heaters. One morning we awoke to a light fall of snow and the surrounding mountains had beautiful white peaks. It did warm up later in the day and mostly the sky was blue, setting off the scenery at its best.

We completed our morning chores of washing, dressing, then preparing and eating breakfast, making up a picnic and washing up the dishes. I would encourage Grant to help me wash out wet pyjamas and bedding, if there was an accident. Doing this without a machine and in the caravan was not the easiest of tasks. When we had rinsed the washing I insisted he carry the bucket over to the house to use their spin-dryer. All these chores took up a large chunk of the morning, and this was good, positive work.

I alternated my days with one day of walking in the mountains and the next going for a scenic drive around the coast of Wester Ross. I talked with him constantly about the all-embracing beauty and he appeared to be interested and pleased with his surroundings. We would stop and have picnics and an occasional ice-cream or other treat and I would read stories to him against the beautiful backdrop.

We found a municipal shower room at a casual camping site just on the edge of Torridon and it appeared clean and adequate for our needs. Fifty pence bought us a long shower so I took towels on our outings and we washed clean before returning back to base. During the first week, when it was cold, it was so hard taking off our layers of thick woollies in an unheated brick building, but the pleasure of the lovely hot water and the feeling of being clean all over made it all worthwhile.

To begin with, my holding therapy was limited as I felt we were working in such a close situation that the constant attention would be enough. At first Grant used some spontaneous language like 'thank you', when given food, or 'drink', 'gaggy' and 'Julian' (when we were ringing home). Towards the end of the first week he began to slow down and little was heard in the way of language. I then re-started the holding and it improved again. He seemed to be helped by that very close eyeball-to-eyeball contact.

As we progressed through into the second week I felt that we were gaining much closer contact and I was learning much more about the inner depths of my younger son. My previous feelings that 'there was a normal boy deep down that couldn't escape' were heightened and whatever anyone said to contradict this did not make any difference to this belief.

Our days walking in the mountains were so peaceful. We set out fully equipped with a rucksack each and all the right protection for emergencies. We never walked very far and kept strictly to the main path. I carried rectal Valium for the unlikely event of an uncontrolled epileptic attack and I always left full details of my walk on the window of my car. I also reported back to the family whose grounds I shared, as a sprained ankle from either of us could leave us isolated on the mountainside until someone walked past. I always prepared myself for these sorts of contingencies so that I could enjoy our exploits to the full.

One day I felt Grant would have walked for ever – he strode out as if with the intention of conquering Everest! This was super and for once we made a few miles with ease. He hadn't accounted for the length of the walk back so by the end of the day he was exhausted. This did tend to make him less enthusiastic on future walks.

The second week became delightfully warm and we gloated over the fact that for once Scotland was warmer and dryer than the rest of Britain. We chose a beach forty miles away by road (six miles by stony coastal path) for our day out. This proved to be a great success. The long drive there was full of scenic beauty and our final destination a delight. I told Grant how very lucky we were to be on a Scottish beach when the sky was bright blue and the mountains behind clear and magnificent. There was one other person and a dog on the stretching expanse of silvery white sand, washed firm and smooth by the retreating tide and marked only by the webbed footprints of the wheeling seagulls that landed lightly by the water's edge.

We walked the length of the beach, Grant leaving me only to leap, skip and flap his hands in reaction to this wonderful freedom. He ran to the sea and I had to follow just in case he should run straight in as he had on occasions in the past. I hated that I should have to put any restriction on this child, released as he was at this moment.

We later returned to the sand dunes that flanked the beach and offered pockets of warmth from the wind that still held shades of winter. We ate our picnic well-peppered with the blowing, fine sand. It was the epitome of tranquillity.

After lunch Grant took to the sand dunes and found inestimable pleasure in crawling around and around the wind-rippled hills. He rested briefly and sifted the fine, warm sand through his fingers and lay drinking in the sun's rays before he turned over and scampered off again in another direction. It gave me such joy to witness this obvious pleasure of freedom. Our heartaches were many with Grant, but a moment such as this was one to savour for ever. I vowed to bring Paul and Julian here when they came the following week and hoped the weather conditions would hold out.

From our caravan you could see the road climbing up the hillside from Diabaig and then, rounding a large outcrop of rock, disappearing from view. Paul and Julian were due to arrive late Saturday having spent the night with Paul's cousin and his family in Glasgow. I suggested to Grant that we walk up the road to meet them.

Our two weeks alone were almost over and, although we had not had any miraculous breakthroughs, I had confirmed my opinion that he was a person who was just locked in, and he was expressing this by his new awareness of eye contact as a form of communicating. We had had a little eye contact in the past, but I believed that as a result of this time away he had learnt something different and understood that looking into someone's eyes was a way of communication. Certainly it was with me and I believed at times that I was peeping into his inner being.

He had learnt how to put on and remove his wellington boots by using the lip of the outer door. As the ground was so wet and the caravan small, every time we entered or left it, wellingtons had to be taken off or put on demonstrating that if an action is done frequently enough it can be learnt. He became better at carrying things as I never did this myself if I could get Grant to do it for me.

I am sure that I understood him better from our two weeks alone. I became more capable of analysing his behaviour as I studied him so closely, uninterrupted by the family en masse and their constant demands. On one rainy day, he helped beautifully with the washing-up and with dexterity fitted together a large piece jigsaw quite freely and happily with me by his side handing him the pieces. Previously the jigsaw would have been knocked to the floor or the pieces waved aimlessly in the air as if to say 'I'm far too stupid to attempt a puzzle such as this'. He didn't want to walk up a mountain in the rain and, if he refused to help his mum in the van, she might make him!

Each evening when we had cleared up the pots from our meal I would walk Grant down to the harbour where there was a telephone box and we would ring home to Paul and Julian. He always walked freely and happily down the hill and would stand patiently by my side waiting for his turn to hear his Daddy speak to him. One night my money ran out before he had had his turn and he glared into my eyes with a cross and hurt expression. Fortunately Paul had the box number and rang us back so Grant got his much needed, one-sided, Daddy chat!

After the phone call we would sit ourselves on a small shingled beach facing the sea at the harbour entrance and watch the sun go down over the distant mountains of the islands. A small dog would join us most evenings and Grant always showed an interest in him and would give him the occasional passing stroke. The little dog seemed to appreciate Grant's disability and would sit calmly by his side. The scene set a tranquil end to our day and after sunset we would walk back up the steep hill to the caravan accompanied by our little canine friend who would leave us at the top and go back from whence he came. Grant would always walk the hill backwards as I think he felt it was less steep that way!

Saturday afternoon saw us walking up the hill from Diabaig and settle ourselves on the roadside to await the rest of our family. We could see the road around the corner trailing onwards up the hillside and also the road below us. Cars passed so infrequently that we were well warned of anything coming from either direction. We waited and waited and I talked to Grant constantly of their ensuing arrival as he sat patiently by my side, now relaxed and 'laid back' from his calming two weeks. We strolled up and down the road but they didn't appear.

By 5 p.m., and now nearly an hour and a half later than they had been expected, I suggested to Grant that we return to the caravan and have a drink until they came. Just as we reached the van I saw their car appear over the hillside. They had had to leave later than they hoped from the relations.

Later, over a cup of tea, I looked up at Grant and holding his gaze said, 'They did come at last didn't they?'

'Yeah,' he replied, smiling into my eyes.

Our week in Scotland as a family was a success. The weather continued to improve and the temperature soared above 70°F. Julian complained he was hot! One day Paul and Julian walked to our beach and Grant and I drove the forty miles to meet them. With the weather being hot I don't think there could be any more picturesque beach in the world and we compared it to a South Sea Isle. The sea, however, could not be equated as it was freezing!

Once together as a family it was so easy to see how very difficult it is to insist on the completion of a task or stick to any strict routine, to which autistic people are most responsive. To leave the van for a day out meant that tasks had to be hurried along and an hour over a dressing programme was just not possible nor was a long session of holding therapy. During our second week alone Grant was beginning to sleep for longer and in the third week, when we were all together, he slept until seven-thirty or eight, allowing us all welcome rest. It was as if he was slowly running down. It was interesting that he didn't have a single epileptic attack during those three weeks.

Fifteen

It was almost June when we returned and Grant started back at school for what would be his final few months at Smith. In the late autumn Grant was to change schools and move to weekly boarding at Hope Lodge School in Southampton. He had been well prepared for his move as I had been invited to take him in to participate in first a half day and later a full day in the new school, while I shopped in the town centre.

Hope Lodge was situated in a suburban street in Portswood, a district of Southampton. It was a cosy school which had a homely feel to it. The classrooms downstairs were small as were the bedrooms, but it was clean and comfortable. They had an excellent cook who had worked as a chef aboard ship and proved his worth with a couple of lunches that I ate there while visiting to either view the school or help Grant through an experimental day. Food quality was a necessary mark out of the allocated ten for Grant when choosing suitable placements, food being such a source of pleasure to him.

The house matron was a lovely lady with motherly qualities who I could see would offer lots of love to her charges. I also met other members of staff who were all pleasant and friendly. The principal was working her last half-term before retirement after being at Hope Lodge for many years.

As usual I worried about many things including the road and high windows that didn't lock. I was reassured about the front door, which was their only entrance and exit and was always kept doubly secure. The first room was the principal's office so that door was always guarded anyway. Since Grant had been at Smith school he had become used to not having the opportunity to escape and his obsession to do so was now greatly reduced but from my past experiences I found it hard to believe he would not let an opportunity go if it were there, and his road sense was still non-existent.

We hated the thought of having to board him because we had spent so much time drawing Grant close to us and making his life as secure, loving and fulfilled as possible. I had learnt from our time in Scotland that the need for continuity of care was essential for his progress as was a structure to his day which could not be offered within the family. But, equally, Julian was coming up to crucial school exams and deserved to have parents who were not physical wrecks by the end of the day and who could offer him support.

Grant still needed much help with simple self-care skills just to make him acceptable for any future long-term care he should need. A boarding-school would have staff who came on duty fresh in the afternoon and after school had finished. They would go home later in the evening to sleep for seven or eight hours. Only in this way, we thought, could care be consistent.

The principal of one school I visited to assess asked whether Grant was dry at night and finding that this was not the case she told me, in no uncertain terms; 'You parents just have to get your act together! Get him out of bed and take him to the toilet at hourly intervals for a fortnight. He will know what to do then and you will have him trained.'

Maybe we would, but would we still be sane after all those sleepless nights? Needless to say we didn't choose this school or any other with such an unsympathetic attitude. We needed guidance, help and encouragement, not a put-down demonstrating little understanding of the gruelling home conditions and the need to fight for just a few hours sleep.

I made my usual photographic plans to prepare Grant for this big move. I took my camera into school and took pictures of his classroom, his bedroom, the house mother, teachers, the dining-room and a smiling chef. I took the outside of the building and the large and comprehensive playground at the back. I mounted it all up into a large photograph album and clearly labelled each picture so that whoever read it to him would be using the same words.

We read it through with him on several occasions but I never knew if he really understood until one day when Claire had called to see us and I was telling her about the move. 'Let's show Claire where you are going to school, Grant,' I said. We picked up the book and started to make our way through. We looked at his face and it was a picture of misery. Both Claire and I took his unhappiness to heart. If only he could tell us what he understood, and felt. To see that look filled me with sadness because I shared his confusion and pain. We were his security and he could see something was about to threaten it, but what was it? He probably didn't know.

He was to start a day later than the other children so that there was a calmer feel to the day. I packed his suitcase and we set off early on the journey to Southampton. I imagined that we would be slowly eased in but this was not to be.

'Leave your suitcase there, Mrs Robinson. Susan will take Grant. See you on Friday.'

I kissed and hugged a bewildered Grant and left. I was split in two, the part under the skin of Grant had been torn away. He had to stand alone supported only by those who as yet didn't know him. He would be confused and frightened especially as with other partings he had always had his family at the end of the day. Today he would go to bed in a strange place not knowing what had happened to us. When he had stayed at Heathcroft, he had learnt to know we always returned. He had been slowly weaned into leaving us so that he understood it.

I returned home up the M3 feeling bereft and unhappy. At least someone could have offered me a cup of tea as this was no usual early morning journey. It seemed so strange returning without my usual silent companion by my side. Friday seemed an eternity away and life felt strange without him. We still didn't sleep as we were too used to our nights being disturbed and were still waiting for the sounds of the door opening, a tinkling musical box or, worst of all, the haunting noise of the first whoop that announced the start of an epileptic fit.

On Friday I arrived back at the school and went in, in eager anticipation of a reunion. My arrival was announced and Grant was brought from his classroom. Nothing could have prepared me for this meeting and, had I known, I would not have been able to send him away. He saw me and immediately burst into tears. He put his arms tightly around me and trembled and cried. Then his tears turned to laughter as he hugged and clung to me as if to never let me go. He looked into my eyes and laughed through his tears, then squeezed and loved me again. It was as if he had thought that I was out of his life for ever and he just could not believe I was there again. He must have clung to me desperately for five minutes; then, after having a brief chat about the week with his teacher, we happily made our way home, his hand grabbing mine when I lowered it from the wheel to change gear!

The weekend went all too quickly and we had to return him on Sunday evening along with a suitcase of washed and ironed clothes. Doing this laundry was not easy when Grant was around and I resented having to do it as it took up the precious time that I could be with him. Paul would often take him for a walk while I sorted out his clothes and repacked his suitcase for the return journey.

We had to leave by 5 p.m. on Sundays, having given Grant an early tea before we went. None of us liked this as it disrupted our day and the afternoons were sad as we knew the departure was at hand. I would sometimes walk with him down by the river. It was a wonderfully peaceful walk that started by Shiplake Church ending up at Shiplake Lock and was just the right length, being roughly a mile and a half return. It altered with the seasons as the summer brought the visitors with their boats that lined up patiently to pass through the lock. The winter was quiet and the river often calm, with water birds swimming nearby hoping that a crust of bread might supplement their sparse winter diet. The spring and autumn brought their own special beauty, and both Paul and I enjoyed using our cameras to capture a scene, usually with Grant patiently in the frame. He became so used to having to stand in front of a view that he knew he had to stand and smile. He was very photogenic as he didn't get the self-conscious look that most of us manage to show on a picture!

I didn't need to try and talk much with him on these walks as we had a deep understanding and knew that these precious moments had to last as a memory for the following week. He just held my hand, occasionally squeezing it or stroking the back with his thumb. Paul would have these special walks alone, too.

Grant seemed to settle well and the care staff appeared to be very fond of him. They told us about an amusing incident that happened one night after he was given strict instructions to go to sleep and not leave his bedroom. They were finding it hard to keep him in his room especially as they all were settled for bed early. After being returned to his room for the third or fourth time, a shuffling noise was heard in the corridor. The carer looked from the staff-room door only to see a duvet moving along the ground and the glimpse of a peeping toe as Grant hoped to make his escape unseen by all!

The staff at the school used to gather together on a Friday to see our reunion which for the first six weeks or so was just as frantic as the first. Our reunions became less intense as Grant realized that I would come to fetch him each week.

The following year, the school decided it would be more satisfactory if they could arrange a taxi to pick him up on a Monday morning, along with another boy from Wokingham. This was a better arrangement, but did make for another worry. What if the taxi were to break down? Grant looked so normal and each time there was a change of driver I had to give them clear instructions never to leave him alone in the taxi and to hold his hand very tightly when they got out, as he was unpredictable, with no road sense, and could run very fast. One taxi-driver didn't believe me and was seen one morning heading off down the footpath at great speed returning soon after having caught his charge. He wasn't the slimmest or fittest of men and, fearing for his own health, took tight hold of Grant's hand thereafter!

Half-terms, summer, Easter and Christmas breaks came round quickly and these had to be organized in advance in order that everything would go as smoothly as possible. However, as Grant's week was now filled by school in term time the things I had planned for evenings could now be done at the weekends or holidays.

Grant was calming down quite considerably and therefore becoming more manageable. The occasional words that we had forced from him were reducing even further. Our firm insistence on a word or sign had been productive, but he was now not stimulated as much in this area. He was always ready to look as if he were totally stupid, therefore the teacher, not realizing his capabilities, had taken him back to basic things he had been doing when he was four.

The first year he was at Hope Lodge was a total unwind for us all and I am ashamed to say that I tended to let things drift as far as Grant's schooling was concerned. The weeks went quickly and when his first school report came through a year after his entry to the school, we saw that the work he was doing fell far short of that which he had been achieving at Smith or for us at home. It was very upsetting, but Grant lacked any ability to self-motivate at all. By this time it was very hard to prove to anyone that he had achieved the things I knew he could do. He was growing rapidly and was getting too big for the classroom. He needed space and this was recognized by the new principal and staff. He didn't fit into any of the other class groupings as his ability wasn't high enough.

One notable achievement at Hope Lodge was night-time dryness. The night staff would take him to the toilet at roughly 11 p.m., again about 4 a.m., and upon waking, at whatever time in the morning. We would use the same routine being rather scared at first of disturbing his sleep. We didn't worry so much about a disrupted night at the weekends as we knew we could catch up in the week. Consequently this more relaxed state of affairs rubbed off on Grant who began to have increasingly dry nights and we soon dispensed with any protective padding. By the time he was fourteen we were experiencing completely dry weekends.

At this point I must reiterate that all autistic children are different and many will become toilet-trained at the normal time or maybe just a little later. I have also heard of others who suddenly decide to be clean and dry when it is least expected. On the whole Grant was later than most autistic children with whom I have been in contact.

When Smith Hospital School closed, Caroline Simmonds was made Educational Adviser for Autism for Oxfordshire Education Department. When I contacted her to explain that we were not happy about Grant's placement she was very anxious to help as she too felt sad about the reversal of his progress. So we began another painstaking search for something more suitable.

This time, finding something to fit Grant's needs proved difficult as his age was now against him. There were more places available for the younger child. We also were very anxious not to go any further away from home. We didn't want to go to termly boarding, which was a condition for several National Autistic Society schools. It was now becoming increasingly difficult to obtain funding for 'out of county' placements. This affected not only the chances of the child receiving the correct education, but had repercussions on NAS schools as they were not getting the pupils or the necessary funding to maintain their schools from the counties in their area. Dedisham school was in West Sussex some six miles from Horsham. It was reputedly a good school run by the National Autistic Society. I had dismissed it as a possibility as they took only termly boarding pupils. Caroline Simmonds was anxious to get Grant resettled and one day rang to see if there was any chance that Grant could attend the school on a weekly basis because Grant received a lot of stimulation and benefits from home life. She arranged to have Grant assessed for a place as a fortnightly border.

The school was very spacious, though rather old with an

institutional feel in places. The dedicated and loving staff counteracted this and the classroom that Grant would have was one which was light and bright. There were many facilities to make life as varied as possible for him with workrooms, kitchens, sensory room and an outside swimming-pool for the summer. It was situated in the countryside of West Sussex and only farm traffic and visitors to the school passed on that country track.

I was to take Grant along for an interview with the school. This time I had no photographs to show him, but his understanding was somewhat better and I told him all about the possibilities of another move. Paul and I now had much more communication from him by eye-contact. If he wanted a cup of coffee in the morning he would come into our bedroom and look deeply into Paul's eyes and raise one eyebrow when asked if that is what he wanted. He knew his father was in charge of coffee making. If Paul didn't respond immediately then Grant would go to the kitchen and start taking cups from the cupboard and line them up or bring an empty cup to the bedroom.

Our interview at Dedisham was scheduled for eleven in the morning. I drove down to Hope Lodge and picked up Grant, who looked smart in his school uniform chosen for the school by the new principal. This not only made the school smarter, but life much easier for us parents with our laundry and clothes planning at the weekend.

I sensed that Grant was very restless and uneasy; the house mother agreed with me. Being a carer within the school, she saw Grant in much the same way as we saw him and often expressed the opinion that his understanding was much higher than his abilities ever showed.

I had told Grant at the weekend that I would be coming to fetch him to see another new school and I was certain now that, although he didn't know exactly what it was all about, he had some idea and it bothered him. How understandable to someone who found life so frightening and confusing.

Our journey took about an hour and we arrived with time to spare. We were welcomed into the school by the secretary who showed us into a quiet room in a gable end of the old building. We were given some welcome tea and told we would be collected when everyone had gathered for the interview. I had brought favourite stories, but Grant became increasingly edgy and restless. I talked to him about anything that I could think of, and tried to read to him, but he wasn't interested.

The secretary came to tell us that the interview team were all gathered, and we followed her through the rambling building to a smallish room where several people were sitting in a circle. There were two empty chairs left for Grant and me. The chairs had arms and he clutched these tightly, looking desperately uneasy, his head bowed. I felt so deeply for him.

The team consisted of the headmaster, Mr Pickering, and his deputy, Mr Buglass, who had a distinct resemblance to the actor James Robertson-Justice. There was the head of care, a family group care leader, George Flint, who would be in charge of Grant's family group if he was accepted and there was also the local doctor who attended the school.

We were welcomed and a few questions asked while Grant looked far from happy, but now made no attempt to leave his chair. Mr Pickering turned to me and said, ' If Grant could speak, what do you think he would want to say to us at this moment?'

I answered without a second's hesitation: 'This is the most dreadful situation I could possibly be in. A small room full of strangers and all talking about me, I can't bear it.'

Mr Pickering smiled with understanding and said to George, 'Take Grant upstairs and show him around while we finish talking to Mrs Robinson.' Turning to Grant he said, 'Would you like to go with George, Grant, then come back to us in a few minutes?'

Grant eagerly leapt to his feet, looking at me for agreement to this arrangement. I gave his hand a reassuring squeeze as he passed and said, 'I'll see you soon.'

We continued the interview and about twenty minutes later the door opened and George led in a completely different young man. His shoulders were squared and his back straight. He came up to me and put his hands on to the arms of the chair and lent forward gazing into my eyes and smiled a confident smile.

'Grant says he likes this place and will be happy to come if you want him!' I translated.

Grant then turned around and looked at the room's members and went over and plonked himself firmly on to the lap of James Robertson-Justice and pulled at his thick beard! The group laughed, but Grant had passed his test, as had the school!

Sixteen

Grant had undergone a metamorphosis from an active and pretty caterpillar into a large less active, beautiful moth. At fifteen he was strong and tall with thickset shoulders, though fortunately not as tall as Julian who was now way over six foot.

We had been warned that adolescence could be difficult with behaviour problems getting worse, but that was not what we were experiencing. He was so much calmer and at times he became so slow he almost stopped! Between twelve and fifteen he had become much more manageable and his problems now were due mainly to his unpredictability, height and weight, which greatly exceeded mine. It was now difficult to stimulate him into any kind of activity including the simple self-help skills.

Paul gave him much more time as Grant needed his strength matching; I often found I was exhausted trying to keep this strong young man, with only physical interests, constantly occupied. Paul now found the same closeness I shared with our silent, gentle and loving companion.

This changeover from boy to man is another stage of coping for a parent. The socially odd behaviours seen in the autistic child can be overlooked, but from an adult these strange ways can appear threatening to society, although in reality nothing could have been further from the truth with Grant. An ice-cream knocked from the hand of a small child, an adult reading a Ladybird book, or a bout of excited hand flapping made people stare. I reacted differently, depending on my mood, and sometimes wanted to scream at them, 'Turn around – it could be your child or your brother or sister.'

An incident when Grant was eighteen amused us. I was walking hand in hand by the gently breaking waves on a beach in Devon. The sun had bronzed Grant's body which accentuated his perfect physique. We walked past two women who, like me, were in their late forties. They watched me pass by with their mouths hung open and the realization dawned that they thought I had a toy boy. I smiled and squeezed Grant's hand harder, looking up at him proudly and giggled inwardly at his mistaken identity! Paul, too, held his hand with the same pride, oblivious to what anyone thought, and ignoring the other implications of a man holding a young man's hand. He had just one wolf-whistle and that was in France!

We were now finding that we could take him to places that we couldn't take him before, when he was too active and restless. He liked to go to church, the colourful stained-glass windows still attracting his attention and holding his gaze. Frequently I would have to leave early if I couldn't hold him in place any longer and often many weeks would pass when we couldn't go as his mood was insufficiently calm. These calmer moods were becoming longer, enabling us to take advantage of a much greater range of entertainment opportunities. There was more chance of success if an adult was available to restrain him on either side. This showed again the benefits of increased security through human closeness (akin to holding).

There was a delightful annual event held at regatta time in the grounds of Shiplake College. It was a concert run by Henley Symphony Orchestra. The audience were encouraged to bring their own refreshments and to picnic in the beautiful grounds surrounding the college before taking a seat for the performance. Grant loved music and we had introduced many different types to give him the chance to appreciate not only what we enjoyed. He had shown much interest in silver bands playing in the open air and sat still without restraint enthralled at the loud and swinging sounds emanating from the glinting instruments. Grant loved James Last and his orchestra and we had many of his light classicals on long tapes for playing in the early hours of the morning, in the hope that they would lull him to sleep.

Could Grant cope with a whole concert? It was a good chance to experiment – the college venue was ideal for quiet withdrawal if he got too restless. If necessary we could still walk with him around the picturesque grounds and listen to the music.

It was a warm and pleasant evening and we picnicked in the grounds, reserving a seat close to the entrance to the marquee. When the performance began Paul and I sat close to him on either side and through many pieces he sat still, enthralled with the music. He did get restless at times, but not to the extent of spoiling it for others, and much to our delight, we did not have to leave the marquee until the end. We had now opened up new horizons.

We looked for other suitable shows. We took him to the circus, taking lots of photographs to make up an album for discussion afterwards. We needed to develop them quickly, of course, so that we could relive the excitement as soon as possible. Paul tried a Furies concert at the theatre in Reading as Grant always enjoyed listening to their lilting Irish folk songs on tape, particularly the appealing earthy baritone of Davey Arthur.

Pantomimes and excellent productions of *Postman Pat* and *Fireman Sam* were among the many pleasures we shared with him.

He had not been long at Dedisham when for a fifteenth birthday treat we booked up the London production of the musical *Starlight Express*. I rang the theatre and explained Grant's situation, asking for a seat, if at all possible, with nobody behind or in front of him. Thinking I was asking for the moon I was overjoyed when the box office clerk said, 'I think I have the perfect place. It is a seat to one side of the theatre with a skateway in front of you and nobody behind for three rows.'

It was an afternoon performance and we drove up allowing loads of time for parking the car and eating before the show. We were hardly off the M4 motorway when we met the queues and very slow traffic. Further into London the jams were solid and we were sure that we would miss the performance. Miraculously we found a place to park around the corner from the theatre on the roadside and arrived thinking that we were late. We were quickly told to relax as a bomb scare had frozen Central London and the start of the show had been delayed to give people time to arrive. We bought sandwiches to eat and settled ready for the excitement of a West End production.

Although Grant was somewhat restless at times, on the whole our treat was a success. Our position on a skateway could not have been better. *Starlight Express* is all performed on roller skates and skateways run throughout the theatre, where the skaters pass at great speeds throughout the show, supposedly as racing trains. It is all very colourful, active and musical.

At the end of the production the skaters pass through the audience more slowly to wave goodbye. The actor playing the role of the British train skated past us waving, then came to a halt, turned and returned to us, stopping at Grant and shaking his hand. We were touched to the point of tears at this involvement and it added to the pleasure that the whole day had brought to our family.

Many changes in our family life occurred during 1989 and 1990. Julian left for university, Grant started fortnightly boarding and Paul began a new job following redundancy when his company was the subject of a reverse takeover. It was as if my whole family had been snatched away in one go as Paul seldom arrived home from his new job before 8 p.m. It was a strange adjustment. Then when Grant's weekends at home and school holidays arrived I was thrown back into a situation of hardly coping again, probably made worse from having an easier time.

Julian had sailed through school, finding work easy and planning his study well. The extension we had built all those years previously, for the seclusion it had offered from the difficulties brought about by having an autistic sibling, had paid off.

Julian loved the challenges of life and had hoped for a career in the RAF as a pilot. He had experienced flying already with the Air Cadets and had piloted a power glider solo and loved the freedom of the skies. At sixteen he'd applied for a scholarship with the RAF. He was offered a two-day assessment at Biggin Hill, but was warned that if for any reason he was an unsuitable candidate he could be returned home at any time. On the evening of the day he went I received a phone call to pick him up from Reading station. He had excelled in the exhausting set of tests undertaken throughout the day, but had failed in the first half hour as a degree of colour blindness had been detected. His eyes had been tested by a local optician before he went and colour identification was not a problem, but the RAF tests are more exacting and the eyesight of the candidate has to be perfect.

He had been desperately disappointed. He had to rethink his future and we sought help from the careers advisory sessions held at school. Eventually he decided on geology, as his favoured subjects were science orientated. When university days were on the horizon he looked for those that offered gliding among their extra-curricular activities.

In sixth-form college he had studied geology and obtained top grades in this and the three other maths and science subjects also studied at A level – the level necessary for university entrance. He accepted a place at Durham University.

Paul settled in his new job and enjoyed his fresh challenges. This time his work was in the construction industry which was beginning to suffer from the recession. He had two and a half years with them until they went under like so many other companies at that time.

Although my hours were still somewhat limited while Grant was at Hope Lodge, I had completed a course extending my role in family planning into that of a specialist nurse in that subject. This course had been mainly in London and it had been good to get out and meet nurses from other areas, particularly those working in the isolating job of domiciliary family planning.

Once Grant was established in Dedisham I decided to do a City and Guild's adult teaching course which lasted for a year. This involved a considerable amount of work, but it was to prove invaluable for the teaching with which I was becoming more and more associated.

I put my nursing, teaching and parenting skills involving learning difficulties to good use, often combining all three within a teaching assignment. My work was varied and interesting.

I was much less active in MIDCAS (the local autistic society) now and Paul was taking over here with a lot of involvement in the new home the society had acquired, Dyson's Wood House. This was just three miles from us, and hoped to provide long-term care for many of our member's children. When Grant was thirteen or fourteen my role as leader of the local group and welfare officer for Mid Counties Autistic Society ended abruptly as, following a long and difficult, school summer holiday, I flipped!

Lack of sleep and having to keep Grant completely occupied during his seven weeks' holiday had taken their toll on me. On top of this there were the pressures involved in working for the autistic society. My family was important and a significant event for Julian became spoilt by my having to devote my immediate attention to demanding work for the society, as well as the other pressures. It all became just too much – Paul insisted that I take a back seat and I had to pass on responsibilities.

I was learning the importance of asking for help. Outings needed two people to assist. Help was often needed with shopping trips and I found that supermarkets would offer this willingly if asked.

Grant, now sixteen, had been at Dedisham nearly a year when we had ten days away in the caravan, staying in a most beautiful spot in central Wales. We introduced Grant to fishing for tiddlers, which he really enjoyed, but he still needed nearly all our help in holding the net and trying to scoop the slippery elusive fish. It was obvious he wanted to do it, but he still had no motivation to make any attempt alone.

I had noticed that he was very aware of bicycles as if he would love to be able to ride one. He would go up to Julian's and touch it and if we passed a bicycle shop when out he would pull me towards it. I would take him in and talk to him about the bicycles, their colours, size, handlebar shapes and tyre thickness. I enquired about the possibility of big stabilizers, but nobody was ever very helpful.

The tricycle had been redundant in the shed for some years so I decided to bring it out and clean it up. Our lane had not improved and its roughness did nothing to help Grant's motivation to keep the pedals freely moving. What we needed was a large expanse of smooth concrete like a disused airfield, but I couldn't think of anything in the near vicinity and how would I transport the trike anyway? I considered a tow bar and trailer, but that would be expensive and he might not enjoy cycling anyway.

My small Citroën car was a hatchback and quite spacious when the seats were flat, so perhaps I could manage to get it in. I negotiated it into the back with some difficulty and tied the tailgate in place. 'Get in the car, Grant,' I cried. 'We are off to find somewhere to ride your tricycle.'

I remembered a long stretch of concreted road that was a good half mile in length and ran from some houses at the back of a wood nearby to another minor road. It was quiet and the few cars that used it came slowly and could be seen from a distance with the road being so straight.

We reached our destination and unloaded the trike. 'Right, Grant, now here's your opportunity to ride. You can't manage a bike like Julian's, but lots of people ride these.' He clambered on to the seat and enthusiastically placed his feet on to the pedals. With a small push on his back he set off and continued, with just the occasional rescue from the hedge when his steering went a bit wonky. He looked so pleased with himself and we went up and down the road four times meaning that he had completed two miles on his first cycling trip!

His mood was bright and happy all evening and when he went to bed he was singing (in his own way). I went into him and said, 'You are happy that you had a long cycle ride, aren't you?'

He looked deep into my eyes and answered with a broad smile, which said it all.

I was excited about this as it opened up another physical activity which he needed so much because of his size. I spent a lot of time thinking of suitable places. But such are the unfathomable ways of the autistic mind, we could never get him to show as much enthusiasm again despite struggling with the trike in and out of the car. Sometimes he would ride it for a hundred yards then get off and run. Eventually I gave up.

I arranged days out with friends to widen my supportive net. Caroline Print, sadly for me, had moved with Norman and their family to a new Parish at Balcombe in West Sussex and we arranged to meet up for walks around some of the beautiful gardens in that area. It might seem a strange occupation for a youth to walk in gardens, but autistic children and adults are super sensitive to others and if Paul or I were doing things that made us relaxed then he was too, and appeared to get pleasure from his outing. If I was at peace in a beautiful garden, so too was Grant. He would walk between Caroline and me, often with his arms looped over our shoulders appearing to listen to our continuous flow of catch-up chatter. He appeared perfectly content.

I was a member of the Royal Horticultural Society and their extensive gardens at Wisley made for many a day out, often just the two of us. Grant had few restrictions there and loved the open spaces and most especially the restaurant!

Paul got his relaxation from long walks with Grant and from his aviation interests. Mutually happy days were spent on the viewing terrace at Heathrow where Grant loved to run around, usually to end at the café or the nearest ice-cream vendor. He was quite a tease, but they both enjoyed these special days together.

Another favourite venue was the beautiful airfield at Popham in Hampshire, where they would enjoy the convivial atmosphere helped in no small way by the excellent barbecued burgers!

Jan Howland, the wife of Gary, who ran the youth club (Grant was now too big for the youth club as he was liable to flatten 'the small youths' when he got excited and ran) often joined me on outings. We took days away together to relax and unwind from our families. She would often accompany me on a journey to and from school, which helped to ease the intolerable separation which happened each time I left Grant. Jan and Gary and their two girls, Sally and Vicky were always there to support us, be it a fund-raising function or a summer trip out. They had become fond of Grant and interested in his welfare.

Towards the end of this school holiday I heard about Chilterns outreach and respite care centre, recently opened in Henley. They offered parents support not only within the unit but also in their own homes with whatever was required to help them cope with their problems. This might mean dressing and caring for the normal child or children in order to allow the parent to attend to the problem child. Their new manager, Jo Jackson, was well known to us as she had worked at Heathcroft, as had some other members of their staff. Angela Bedford, whom I also knew as she had worked at Smith Hospital School, came round to assess our needs.

There was only one week of holiday left, but we were into our seventh week and I was getting exhausted and found it hard to face the last few days. I still had plenty of ideas, but not much strength. I told Angela that I needed someone to accompany me on outings. I wanted to be with him, but needed physical and mental support.

After going through ample form filling Angela told us our case would be processed and ready for us to have help at half-term. When the next day dawned complete exhaustion had set in and I didn't see how I could get to the end of that day. I called Angela back and asked apologetically if I could have help today, explaining that I didn't think I'd get through it unaided, and the end of the week seemed so far away.

Two hours later a strong young man called Ray Williams came round to join us for a long walk and a pub lunch. He was only two or three years older than Grant and made a suitable companion. We went to a trout farm and lake so that Grant could fish out of the tank and take home his tasty catch to cook. It was a beautiful day and the walk around the large lake was calming and relaxing. We watched a few people out fishing in small boats and were then taken into a shed where we were given large samples of smoked trout on buttered bread. This went down very well with Grant and gave him even more pleasure than his tour of the trout farm. He helped to catch large trout from the huge tanks heaving with silvery fish. These were gutted for us and we took them home wrapped in lots of paper to cook for our supper.

Ray was impressed with his day and was determined to return another day to fish, the harder and more conventional way, and from a boat.

Dedisham was good for Grant. He adjusted quickly and had few settling-in problems. The buildings were rambling and it took me a long time not to get lost when I visited. Grant, however, found no difficulty. Predictably he found the kitchen with speed. If Grant went missing it could be guaranteed he would be found there.

It was emotionally traumatic when he first started and I had to leave him for two weeks, with only constant spoken reassurance that I would return to comfort him. The staff were very good and sensitive to my feelings and were happy for me to phone for the first few evenings to ask how he was settling.

When I took him to his room with his suitcase I had the impression that he knew what it was all about and was happy. His bed was in a family group room and was one of seven. As he was epileptic they had put his bed against a wall with a long chest boxing it in. This not only gave him protection from a seizure, but also a degree of privacy and a place to put his books and cassette-player.

Most nights they found him missing on their hourly tour and had to search the rambling building to find him. He became a challenge and double handles appeared on doors just as they had done in schools and other places where he had stayed previously.

He was befriended by a large, more able, autistic boy called Aaron, who shadowed Grant and took him by the hand and led him for meals, or anywhere else he should be. The staff felt it was a good friendship which Grant tolerated and probably enjoyed. It was helpful for the staff too as Aaron stopped Grant wandering where he shouldn't.

When school finished in the afternoon the key care worker would collect her charge from the classroom and take him or her upstairs to the respective family group. They would be taken out into Horsham, or go for long walks in the West Sussex countryside.

Grant was still totally handicapped by his condition, needing someone with him at all times to protect him from the dangers of life. Also he was still reliant on someone else for his complete care. But he had matured and, from this maturity, there came a lovely human being who touched his care-givers. He now actually gave to them some of his inner being. He could radiate a loving calm that influenced people and make them feel better. We knew his love, but he was now extending it to others; messages came to us that he was becoming special to a lot of people because of the way he behaved with them.

One such was the lady who worked the night shift at Dedisham. When she was on duty Grant would quietly make his way into the staff-room, find the biscuit tin and, after helping himself to a few, would sit on a comfortable chair and look at his book. He made it more than clear that he did not wish to return to bed and he would be even happier if she made him a cup of tea. He usually got his tea too as, while she put the kettle on to make tea for herself, he would be standing behind her with his hand gently stroking her arm. If she said, 'Grant, you really should go back to bed!', he knew that a look deep into her eyes with a pleading smile would do wonders. He had the power of charm and along with his good looks, he made it work for him!

This sounds as if it would not bode well for good nights at home, but this was not so for two reasons. Firstly, autistics tend to learn behaviours associated with a place so he didn't expect tea from us at midnight when he was at home. He was also getting disturbed nights from the younger members of the family group, so he was inadvertently sleeping deeper. When he returned at the weekend he slept long and deeply and we were feeling all the benefits.

Grant was acquiring quite a fan-club among his care workers, not only at school, but at Chilterns too. There were some staff, I know, who had a soft spot for him, but also he was gaining friends from the young people who were in care. Even if Grant appeared to take little notice of them, those who could talk said they were pleased to see him.

Chilterns tried to offer two outings in the week for the holidays and split the children into two suitable age groups, typically those under and over twelve. I would usually join the older group to help with the outing and to be with Grant. The staff, helpers (who were often interested students) and the young people with different mental disabilities, made a pleasant group with which to be. One talkative, more able girl, called Joya, decided Grant was her boyfriend and never let him out of her clutches! Sometimes I think Grant found her a bit too much, but for the most part he accepted her advances, even her amorous approach when she sat on his lap and threw her arms around his neck and kissed him. The staff were most amused and said that Joya loved Grant, but Grant really preferred peanuts!

Grant loved going to Chilterns; he enjoyed their outings and his occasional overnight stops. He was treated as an adult and enjoyed the physical things they did, which were good ideas and offered new outlets. One of these was a trip to the cinema to see *Robin Hood, Prince of Thieves*. They took a picnic in with them and he ate his lunch seated between two staff and watched the big screen enthralled. Having recently seen the film on television, it amazes me that it held his interest and again we were left with wondering just what is going on in the autistic mind.

Celebrations around Christmas and New Year were often a round of parties, so wanting to be different and respect the age group in their care, Chilterns sent Grant an official invitation for a formal, black-tie dinner. The staff were to prepare a multi-course dinner and wait on the diners. There was a predominance of males so to make the mix even, the staff produced daughters to fill the gaps.

Dad's dinner suit came into use again! We never thought that Grant would need to wear it and it made us very proud, and happy. We took photos of what we knew would be a very rare occasion. We showed him his dashing image in the mirror and he squared his shoulders and stood up straight, obviously pleased with what he saw.

We drove him in our 'carriage' to the door, just taking him inside to hand him over and admire their beautifully laid table. They had spared nothing and gave our young and special people a tremendous evening. With their friendship, security, and the jovial atmosphere I reckon they did better than an evening at the Ritz!

I heard later that Grant had behaved himself well apart from one incident when a member of staff had sat down next to him with her chocolate mousse pudding, her waitressing role complete. She turned to someone on her other side to say something and when she turned back Grant was just scraping the last spoonful. At times it pays to be autistic!

Seventeen

At sixteen, in the UK, our special children are due for monetary allowances of their own granted by the state, but I will not attempt to try to describe these here as they constantly change. Working out what money Grant should be receiving took some time so when eventually it came through, he received a substantial back payment which arrived just before his seventeenth birthday. We put it in a separate building society account in our own names, but for his use. We wondered if there was anything he needed that would improve his life, but we had no ideas. Then, we considered a holiday as he thrived in the sunshine, loved the sand and swimming and was always happy when he was with us.

We selected Fuerteventura, an island in the Canaries, which guaranteed sunshine. We chose the location very carefully, as it had to be safe. Having selected a small development of apartment blocks close to the sea, we asked the travel agent to check that what looked to be ideal in the brochure was indeed suitable. We needed the sea near, but not too close, and a swimming-pool was essential.

Until Grant was fourteen, contemplating a holiday such as this would have been beyond our wildest dreams and we were still rather apprehensive about the four-hour flight. We phoned the airline to make arrangements with them, explaining our special circumstances. They were very helpful and our seat was booked so that we could be together and would not have to wait at the check-in desk.

We prepared Grant for his holiday in our usual way through

pictures. The holiday brochure was used to show him the resort, apartment and swimming-pool. We found photographs of the inside and outside of a plane. (Paul's hobby came in useful here!) I created a scrapbook and discussed it with him at home, and two weeks before we were due to leave sent it into school to continue the preparation.

The day dawned and he appeared excited when I helped him to shower and dress, though when we arrived at Gatwick I wondered whether Grant thought he was just out for another day watching planes.

The flight was our first hurdle, but we need not have worried. The aircraft roared into action and taxied down the runway, paused briefly, then on the all-clear from the control tower thrust forward ever faster and took off into a clear blue sky. Grant went pale and I reached for the sick bag, but once the plane had levelled out his colour returned and I thankfully replaced the bag.

We had packed our hand luggage with books and his Fisher Price tape-player, but we hardly needed them. He watched with eager anticipation as the stewardess approached giving out drinks, getting closer by the minute. When he had finished his Pepsi cola and all of our nuts he saw her approach again, this time with food, then coffee. He was in paradise!

He hardly fidgeted at all throughout the whole flight and even showed a little interest at my explanation of what he could see through the window.

We arrived at our destination where our excellent accommodation, typical of the Canaries, consisted of one of many small bungalows situated near (but not too near) an unheated pool and a covered bar where they served food. This area became a source of great pleasure to Grant, sitting on a bar stool, watching Spanish television and slowly munching free bags of crisps which he charmed from the non-English speaking barman with his usual smile. We had worried about him escaping or jumping into the pool, but neither of these problems arose. Although hot, he preferred not to cool down in a very cold pool. On two occasions we pushed him in, but he just swam furiously to the other side and got out, choosing to lie on a sunbed, hands behind his head, lapping up the sunshine with large iced colas to cool him down.

His love of food was satisfied by nightly visits to the assorted restaurants of the small town nearby. Long walks along the footpaths that ran over the lunar-type landscape near the shore and sifting the warm sand lazily between his fingers gave him exercise, relaxation and pleasure during the day.

On the last night of our holiday we joined an organized barbecue and a coach took us to our destination further down the island. Our tour representative had arranged a place for Grant at the end of a table, so that he would get the best view of the cabaret. By now he was so relaxed that we didn't need to worry that he might leap up from the table. With so much delicious food piled high on his plate and cola filling his glass as soon as it was empty, he had no reason to move! The Spanish dancing girls were colourful and the music lively and fun.

Despite very full stomachs Paul and I danced with Grant, participating in his style of movement, which consisted of mainly jumping up and down. This was totally compatible with some of the odd dances that others were doing! After consuming plenty of wine who cared anyway!

The evening ended with the usual slow smoochy dances. Grant danced beautifully and touchingly with me, even moving his feet in time to the music. The band was playing the popular song, 'I Just Called to Say I Love You.' This moment was magical. As the singer crooned out the words he held the top of my arms and gazed into my eyes.

Paul and I were over the moon and could only say that at long last his presence with us was pure pleasure.

Grant's face lit up upon seeing the aeroplane for his return flight home which offered more stewardesses, food and drink. This time when the plane's engines roared for take off he reached out and for the first time sought comfort from my hand.

The summer that followed our holiday in Fuerteventura was filled with an assorted programme of interesting events and outings.

The Sunday prior to Julian's return to university saw me finishing the final batch of ironing. Paul had taken Grant out for the day as it was the Farnborough Air show and although they were not actually going to the event he planned to walk by the edge of the airfield.

It was early afternoon when the telephone rang. To hear Paul's voice from a telephone box immediately stopped my heart as it indicated trouble. Paul's voice sounded tense. 'I hate to tell you this, but Grant has had an accident. He was hit by a car.'

'Oh no!' I cried. 'Is he all right? What happened? Where is he?'

'I'm with him at Frimley Hospital and they think he has only broken his arm, but he ran straight into the road in front of a car, was tossed into the air and hit his upper arm and his head really hard when he landed.' Paul paused for breath.

'Where is he now? He can't be left alone!' I had visions of him so confused and scared by his situation.

'Don't worry, Dave is with him while I'm talking to you.' (Dave is a good friend of Paul's who shares similar interests and often accompanied them on outings.) 'Can you come over with his night clothes and wash things…?' Paul explained how to get to the hospital.

I gathered together a small suitcase containing nightwear, a washbag and his medication. I packed books and his faithful tape-player then changed myself into a comfortable tracksuit that would serve as day or night wear.

My recollection of the next two days is hazy as sleeplessness and concern combined to muddy the memory of the horrors that followed.

I drove, and Julian navigated the forty minute journey to Frimley, where we found they still hadn't left the casualty department. Grant was on a trolley with a generously bandaged arm and a neck collar. He looked pale and in pain.

I have always said that I lived life with Grant one day at a time with his unpredictable behaviour. Although he was so very much calmer (at times almost to the point of lethargy) he was still prone to running off unexpectedly in any direction, particularly if there was something more interesting nearby. In this case it had been some parked cars on the opposite side of the road. He was bored and must have thought that sitting in the car would be more pleasurable. He wasn't aware that our car was not among those to which he was running. He was now so strong that if he wished to go he would detach himself from your grasp with one flick of his arm. That could be quite painful, and briefly delay the reaction to chase.

X-rays had been taken of Grant's skull and arm and a clean, high fracture had been detected on the humerus (the bone that forms the upper half of the arm). His skull, thankfully, showed no evidence of damage. The doctors decided that, because of his autism, the most successful way to heal the fracture would be to insert a steel pin and plate joining the two bones, done under general anaesthetic. This would eliminate the need to plaster the arm which, due to the fracture's position, would possibly also include plaster to his upper body. This he might find hard to tolerate. He was to go to the operating theatre the next day.

I explained to the staff his condition and they soon realized that it would be essential for me to remain with him for the whole time, therefore a room needed to be found where I could have a bed by his side.

Paul and I discussed our arrangements and I was happy to spend the first night with him, as I felt my nursing experience could only be of benefit in what was not going to be an easy night. If Paul had the next day off he could either come in and help me or give me a break.

The night was long and gruelling as, despite the strong painkillers, Grant was very restless. I had to sit by his side all night to prevent him hurting himself even further. I played him music, but he was motivated enough to put a hand out and switch it off himself as his discomfort was such that any sensory stimulus was an irritant.

The night staff were excellent and very supportive. Because of the worry over possible head injury they came in to do hourly checks on his pulse and blood pressure. The day staff were short in number and exceptionally busy and we were left for hours on end.

Paul came in about nine in the morning, after leaving Julian at Reading station as he had an appointment in London. I desperately needed a break as I had only had an hour's light sleep all night so left Paul to cope with Grant's trip to the operating theatre. Once the pin and plate were in position there would be less worry over further harm.

I returned home much less concerned and soaked in a bath before sleeping deeply for approximately four sweet hours. Much refreshed I prepared a large cottage pie for whoever was around to eat, at whatever time, then with fresh magazines and suitable clothes in which to change I got ready for another night's battle.

My good friend, Jan Howland, had heard of the accident and called round briefly to deliver a lovely get-well card, beautifully made by Vicky. It had teddies and balloons saying, 'Get well, Grant!' and was very bright and colourful. I packed it into my holdall along with a big bag of Maltesers, the chocolate sweets which he loved.

When I arrived back, the ward looked active and busy and Paul was relieved to see me. The day had been extremely difficult in many ways and most of the time he had been left alone. There had been further trips to X-ray and the arm had been pinned in theatre. Since then Grant had been awake, but restless.

I went over to Grant who I thought was sleeping, but found this not to be the case and didn't like what I saw. His eyes looked glazed and didn't seek mine, his back was arched and his good arm stretched downwards with his hand at the end stiff and claw like.

'Oh my God, how long has he been like this?' I cried.

'What do you mean?' asked Paul, bewildered and tired from his awful day. He stared at me with concern, saying, 'He seems to have gradually gone downhill. I have asked nurses to come and see him, but nobody has been near for ages. I think there has been some sort of emergency and they have been frantically busy.'

I felt scared. Grant appeared to me like cases I had seen of severe head injury and I dashed from the room to find a doctor or sister. I didn't need to look far as they were both only yards from our room at a nurses' station. I gabbled at them, 'Please come and see my son as I hate how he looks and I am really worried.'

Sister stared back at me briefly, then quickly putting two and two together, made four. 'You're Grant's mother, I'm sorry I haven't seen you before.'

I apologized and instantly took to this pleasant, efficient looking sister.

'We didn't know what he was like normally,' she gently said. 'We knew he was autistic, but that could mean anything. I believe you are a nursing sister too?' She smiled understandingly and looking at the doctor said that they would come immediately.

I explained briefly what he was like normally and said I was very worried about the spasticity that he was now displaying. The house doctor examined him then immediately called for the Senior Registrar who came to us within five minutes. He made a full neurological examination, testing reflexes and other signs that could give him any clues to his condition. I had already made it clear that I thought that he was displaying signs of brain damage. He had ignored my comment and continued the examination. Then he looked up at Paul and me and said, ' I don't think it is brain injury. I have seen this once before and it could be a severe reaction to one of the drugs we have given him during the anaesthetic. There is an antidote and, if this is the cause, then once we have administered it he should show signs of improvement within twenty minutes.'

There then began a search throughout the hospital for the antidote. Every medicine cabinet on every ward was painstakingly searched for the precious drug. While this was happening, they struggled to open up a suitable vein in which to attach a line to administer the drug quickly once it had been found. The intravenous line had to be very firmly fixed so that Grant could not remove it if he was restored to his former self.

Time seemed to stand still as the search continued on and on through the hospital, but just as they were about to contact outside help the drug was found in some unlikely cupboard.

Paul and I stood by as it was slowly administered into the carefully prepared cannula on the back of his hand. Then we waited and watched, watched and waited, the seconds ticking slowly past. There seemed to be no change and at least twenty minutes had now elapsed. We were giving up hope and beginning to think that brain damage from that severe blow to his head must be the only answer. Were we not to see his sunny smiling face again?

A few minutes later I noticed that his hand was no longer stiff and fingers were beginning to relax. Slowly his spine began to uncurl and the rigidity that caused the awful arching slackened. Could it really be working? We held his loosening hand and talked to him; as we did so slowly we saw awareness come back into his eyes. The doctors had won and we were so grateful. The delight was written all over their faces too. With the crisis over I searched into my bag and brought out Vicky's specially made card and held it high for him to see.

'Look Grant! Vicky has made you this lovely get-well card.' He looked at it with interest then started to chuckle. He either saw something in the card that really amused him or maybe it was pleasure that the get-well card had worked! He became quite helpless with infectious laughter. It was music to our ears and we hugged each other with pleasure in the knowledge that our gentle, happy young man was back with us again.

The next day we saw the consultant who operated on him and asked when he could be released home. 'Oh I would like him to stay another two or three days,' he replied. 'We must be certain there are no head injuries and any such problem would need immediate attention.'

'I do understand,' I said. 'But it is far from easy to manage him here. He can't bear the restriction and he is almost impossible to control.' The sister backed me up, explaining that I had but a few hours sleep in the last two days. However, the consultant was adamant he should stay and the hours of the day stretched way ahead. Paul would be coming in the late afternoon.

I thought about the situation and what I could do to improve it for both of us. Then it came to me: 'Chilterns (our wonderful respite care centre) – they offer outreach! I wonder whether they reach out as far as Frimley Hospital?' I walked Grant to the phone and rang them. Needless to say they were upset and shocked to hear the news and felt sure they could manage some help.

They had to make some adjustments to their days' arrangements, but soon after one in the afternoon, Kathy Langdon arrived with a large get-well card and two more bags of Malteser chocolates and some crisps. She also brought some inset puzzles she knew Grant liked doing and appropriate books. What a wonderful sight to see Kathy walk through that door with a friendly smile. I warmly welcomed her with a hug, as with her assorted wares she offered support and she knew and understood Grant's needs. Grant looked pleased to see her too as by now another familiar face was as welcome to him as it was to me!

I was tremendously relieved to have her there, if only to have company to walk the corridors, which by now I must have covered over twenty or more times. The passages interlinked around the building forming a square and goodness knows how many times I had nodded to the same people throughout the day! I went off for a while by myself and had a drink in the downstairs café and examined the books they had for sale in the foyer.

I chatted to the ward sister who was concerned that I had had so little sleep. I told her my husband was coming in around five, but would need to leave later as he was extremely busy at work. She made arrangements for a bed in a side room on the next ward and suggested that I slept there while Paul was around, as I would be near enough if I was needed.

When Paul arrived he was delighted that Kathy had been to support me and, when he heard of all the difficulties, said he would stay the night in the hospital, getting into the bed when I left it, then we could both get maximum sleep and support each other if necessary.

I explained to Paul about the corridor walk, then went off to my side room and a very welcome sleep that came the instant my head touched the pillow. I borrowed Paul's watch which I set to bleep at ten forty-five. After five hours sleep I felt very much more refreshed, and washed and prepared myself to take over my night task.

Returning to the ward I found Paul looking extremely fraught. He had walked the corridor square seventy-two times! Grant still had on his size ten leather-soled shoes and they were none too quiet in the silence of the settling wards. Paul tried hard to stop long enough to change him into trainers, but it was an impossible task. If he stopped then Grant went frantic and threw himself around the room. He hadn't slept now for over two days and nights, and surely he couldn't go much longer without sleep.

I assured Paul that I was now fighting fit and ready to cope again and it was his turn to sleep. He went off to our temporary bed and I surveyed the scene. My sleep had left me alert and ready to take over. Grant must need to rest and, as he couldn't get home to his own bed, something had to be arranged here.

If I took him anywhere near the bed in the room he used all his strength to resist any action to put him in. Maybe he was in pain, but now he was also suffering considerably from his autism and this whole situation was overpoweringly frightening. I somehow needed to offer him security and comfort, but firstly I had to be sure he was free from pain.

I spoke to the night nurse, 'Is Grant due for pethidine? I want to ensure that he hasn't got any pain.'

She examined his records and said, 'It is just a bit early for it, but by the time I have it all together it will be just about due.' She looked as if she would do anything to ensure he calmed down, as already he had disturbed the whole ward on several occasions during the evening.

The ward opposite was closed for cleaning and I eyed the pile of mattresses stacked high at the end of the corridor leading to the darkened ward.

'Do you think anyone would mind if I borrowed some of those mattresses?' I asked her. 'I want to create a padded cell!'

She laughed. 'Do what you like if you think it will help. I will get someone to help carry some over.'

I was talking to her standing outside the door, holding it shut while Grant was trying very hard to open it from the inside. Returning to Grant I stared around the room deliberating on how much could be moved out into the corridor. I left Grant's bed, which I pushed up against the window, and a comfortable chair. There were cot sides on the bed and I removed the side facing the room while the one on the other side helped shield the window. The nurses brought me the mattresses and I placed these side by side on the floor and against the wall. I then took Grant along to the toilet so that he could be as comfortable as possible once the pethidine had taken effect. There was a window on the door covered by a sliding panel so that it could be shut across for privacy. I asked the nurses to leave me to my own devices, but perhaps to check us every so often. Then taking Grant inside and shutting the door I placed the armchair in front of it and there I sat with my magazine and tried to ignore Grant as he flung himself around the room from side to side, back and forth. Occasionally he would drop to the floor and look as if he was about to sleep, but this didn't last long and he would leap up again and pace the room. He kept this up until two in the morning when at last he dropped to the floor and stayed there and I gently placed a blanket over him and lay down by his side. He slept for a few hours and later I dozed too.

When the sister came on duty next day I told her that I wished to take our own discharge and she said she didn't blame me! It took some time to make arrangements, but by ten in the morning we were on our way home. Grant was always happy in the car so the drive home brought a peaceful relief beyond compare!

Paul returned to work and, in the afternoon, Angela Bedford, our social worker, called on her way home and said she would do anything to help and suggested that she prepared an evening meal, as Grant was taking up all my time. She proceeded to make an extremely tasty tuna and pasta bake, which she left in readiness in the oven to reheat later.

Chilterns had prepared a series of helpers so that I would have some support daily as Grant was still very restless and constantly moving. His arm was in a sling that he couldn't undo, but this aspect caused few problems as movement caused pain. I had been told that we must encourage use of his arm so that his shoulder wouldn't stiffen and even seize up altogether.

His activities such as swimming and horse-riding were restricted and we had little to do but walk and watch old faithful videos such as *Postman Pat*, but at the moment he was too restless for these. The school summer holidays were only just over so I was at a loss to know how to occupy him. Paul and I had seven days holiday booked in Crete in just over two weeks' time and we wondered whether we should cancel. I had spoken to Dedisham and they were not prepared to take him back until after half-term, at the earliest, as they rightly felt there were a few disturbed children who might damage his healing arm by inadvertently knocking into him.

Chilterns said that they would like to have him for the week. They wanted us to recover from the terrible trauma and they fancied the challenge of making him move his stiffening shoulder. They booked him in, but emphasized that if we really felt he wasn't ready to be left then they would understand if we cancelled last minute. They stressed how Grant would have lots of attention because of the fact that all the children were back in school.

We were all so traumatized by this incident: Grant, as he was the victim and his autism had blown up the experience to one of horrific proportions; Paul, as he had watched helplessly while Grant was hit and tossed by the car and became racked with feelings of guilt that he had put Grant into the situation which had led to this accident and to his ultimate suffering; I, for having had to cope with the nightmare, that as yet was still not completely over.

I tried to help Paul realize that the same thing could have happened years ago and it really was most surprising that he had received only minor injuries in the past. My own words did little to comfort me, as now as I worried more about his safety, knowing that what I had feared could and probably would happen again.

Just before we left the hospital Grant had had a minor epileptic fit. It was more like an absence. He was standing near his bed at the time and his eyes went glazed, he went pale then slowly sank down on to the bed. When we were home he had two or three other similar incidents. This was not surprising after the awful events of the last few days. Prior to these episodes he had not had a seizure in the last two years and we were hoping that he could start the gradual reduction of his medication. As his dosage had not altered in this time (but his height and weight had considerably increased), we felt there was a good chance that a lesser dose might be successful. However, when we visited the paediatrician a few weeks later he dismissed the idea, as Grant had to be completely fit free for two years, whatever the circumstances, before he would consider any safe reduction.

We left Grant for our week in Crete and, although hard, the decision could not have been better. We slowly unwound throughout the week and by the end of our break we had begun to relax. We talked through our feelings and by our return could face life again with renewed spirit.

Grant was thoroughly spoilt for his week, except for the necessary remedial treatment. He was not allowed a cup of anything to drink unless he reached for it with his healing arm. The same went for any in-between meal treats such as biscuits. I had demonstrated to them a series of exercises shown to me by the physiotherapist and they dutifully worked on him daily putting him through his paces. As their staff changed shift they came to him with renewed enthusiasm, so by our return the movement in the arm and shoulder had improved considerably. When eventually Grant went back to school, their care staff also kept up the exercises.

It took a long time for full movement to return, but because of the continued perseverance of care staff including those at his final care home in Devon, the arm and shoulder almost completely returned to normal.

It was strange, but only a few days after his painful accident and operation we took him for one of our favourite walks by the river Thames at Shiplake. Paul took a few photos of him and he looked extremely happy, probably glad to be back with us in a normal situation again. Yet these lovely pictures are sad to behold when you see his arm in a sling.

Just a few months later Grant ran into the road again. This time it was while out with Dedisham staff in Horsham. They were crossing over a zebra crossing when he turned and shot back across the road, the cars now moving. This time he fortunately hit the car sideways on and was thrown back onto his bottom receiving no more than a few bruises.

The shaken staff member, Liz, rang me later with Grant by her side and told me of the incident, which must have been an onerous task for a young woman to undertake.

'What was on the other side of the road from where you had crossed?' I asked her. 'No, don't tell me. Was it McDonalds or Burger King?'

'Yes, McDdonalds,' she said. 'We were on our way back to Dedisham for our supper, so he was hungry.'

'Let me speak to him,' I said and once the phone was put to Grant's ear I admonished him, saying, 'I told you to never run into the road again! We love you and we don't want to see you hurt like you were before. Cars are dangerous!'

I spoke to him further and then returned to Liz. 'What was his face like when I spoke to him?'

She told me he looked pleased when he heard my voice, but when I scolded him he looked as if he was going to cry.

I came from the phone frightened and sad as I was convinced that we would not have him much longer. He couldn't help these excited spurts. He didn't see dangers, only his needs of the moment. But he couldn't be kept in a bubble and away from the realities of life – it wouldn't be fair. He had to live life as normally as possible, and for as long as he was able.

The thought that he could be further damaged or severely maimed was almost impossible to bear, so I dismissed it from my outer emotions and it gathered deep down inside me along with all the other hurtful thoughts I had to dispel for the sake of sanity.

Eighteen

When Grant reached seventeen we were being advised that we must start to consider his long-term care. In the UK, education is funded by the county authorities until nineteen, after which the Social Service department is responsible for long-term care. If a suitable place was found before he reached nineteen, which would meet with educational and care needs, funding would be shared between them until then. If he had suitably settled and the care home was satisfactory, it would be more than likely that the placement would be maintained.

Our first priority was to look for a home as near as possible to our own; as far as Education and Social Services were concerned, this should be within our own county of Oxfordshire. We then had to assess what each place had to offer and what we required for Grant. Our primary need for him was a home where the staff had a clear understanding of autism and its associated problems so that he would be fully understood and cared for in the best way. Needless to say this eliminated the majority of care homes available locally.

Dyson's Wood House fulfilled most of these objectives. We had worked vigorously over the years to raise funds to enable it to open and it was only four miles away. They were having teething problems, but that was to be expected. Getting a new home up and running, particularly one for autistic people, is a complex and delicate operation. However, we had never viewed it as an option for Grant, because of his propensity to escape. The grounds were open with shared road access to several properties. I was sure

Grant would be happy to join the neighbours any morning for breakfast!

It became apparent from visiting Dedisham, when delivering and collecting Grant from school, that he appeared to be one of the most severely handicapped pupils. There were many others who were much more disturbed and disruptive, but our strapping lad, though happy, was lost, deep in a world of his own. He was content to watch others work or play games, but preferred not to join in. Dedisham staff were now calling him 'the Gentle Giant' and loved our quiet boy who contrasted noticeably with many of the others.

When the care staff arrived to take over from the teachers at the end of the afternoon, they came to the classroom for their charges. One day Grant was duly collected by his key worker, Liz Mitchel, who after leaving the room stopped to talk to someone. Grant sauntered back into the classroom and found himself a book, which he took to a corner of the room, and stood quietly turning the pages. The teacher, who was still in the room, had a visitor to whom she was showing some work, so ignored Grant's return. A few moments later Liz rushed into the classroom in a fluster thinking she had lost Grant. She collected him and hurried from the room.

Later the visitor enquired about the excited *pupil* who had come in, grabbed the *teacher* and dragged him from the class!

So we had to find somewhere that would suit our Gentle Giant, but would also be homely and safe. As Caroline Simmonds was still advisory head for autism in Oxfordshire and at the moment we were looking for a pre-nineteen placement, we asked her to help find the right one. Angela Bedford, Grant's social worker and a friend of Caroline's from their days at Smith Hospital School, was also involved as Social Services would be sharing the funding. The ensuing search for a suitable home in the company of one or both led to some very enjoyable days out, with stops for lunches at pleasant country pubs.

Angela had a list of all the residential care homes in the area and went through these methodically. There was absolutely nothing that fitted the bill in Oxfordshire which meant we had to look 'out of county'. Many counties now insist that placements should be provided within their boundaries and, if these are unsuitable, then a case has to be made to convince the authorities of the need to look elsewhere. Autistic people are expensive as they need a high staff to client ratio and, once the diagnosis is acknowledged, which can in itself be difficult, parents are usually faced with an uphill battle to receive the correct management for the education and care of their child.

We looked at Reading and saw something we liked, but they were having internal difficulties at the time so we passed them over. We looked at a newly opened home in East Sussex, but some of the rooms and the garden were small. Grant needed, and thrived on, space.

I read in the National Autistic Society quarterly news bulletin about a home soon to be opened at Cullompton, Devon. It was called 'Forge House', and advertised itself as a home for autistic people and those with challenging behaviours.

It was the summer before his accident and I telephoned to ask what they had to offer, bearing in mind Grant's inclination to do nothing, not even the simplest of life skills, such as washing or dressing. Would his behaviour be classed as challenging? I certainly found it so!

I spoke to Sue Green who was the wife of the owner, and she explained their set-up. Chris, her husband, was a builder and she had worked for some time within the field of mental health. Chris had become interested in our kind of young people and saw that there was a real need for good and caring homes for life. They acquired an old farmhouse on the edge of the village and decided to convert it by extending each end of the building, thus forming a spacious, purpose-built home that still retained some of its original character. It had land to the front which provided a garden and car park, while the back had a reasonable area that was to be mostly concreted, but was spacious enough to offer some outside freedom and, as it faced south, got the benefit of the sun. They also owned an adjacent field which could be used for growing fruit and vegetables. Cullompton was ideally situated, not too far from the north and south coasts of Devon. Dartmoor and Exmoor were also close so there were many beautiful and interesting places to visit on their outings from Forge House.

One young man, Jon, had already moved into the home and he sounded remarkably similar to Grant. My interest aroused, I asked Sue if I could be sent full details as it sounded very promising. It was a shame it was so far away.

Grant's accident delayed further looking but, once he had returned to school in late October, we began to think again.

A few places had recently become vacant at Stroud Court due to parent authorities taking back their clients, as suitable facilities had been provided in their own county. Since the opening, now over ten years ago, many friends had children happily placed there. It was secure and spacious and the residents were organized into small groups to suit their ability. There were many workshop facilities and they even took autistic people for day care. We had been so closely involved that a placement here would be pleasing. But, in the final analysis, the most important consideration would be what was in Grant's best interests.

On a cold and very snowy January day in 1993 Angela Bedford and I set off up the M4 motorway to assess both prospective placements. We were first to visit Forge House, stay for lunch, then call at Stroud Court on the return journey. Unfortunately, Caroline was unable to join us, but had visited both places on a separate occasion.

A recent case conference at Dedisham had highlighted the fact that Grant was ready to move on to a residential placement. He was not going to gain anything further by staying on longer in an educational establishment. It would be best to try and settle him somewhere that would not only offer good care, but also meet his ongoing educational needs, which was the policy of all specific autistic units.

The snow fell with increasing fury, thickening, swirling, settling and drifting in the brisk wind that drove it hard at the car. Just as we were contemplating turning back at the next exit the car began to splutter and, fortunately for us, decided to cough and chug itself into the Membury service station that miraculously appeared a few hundred yards ahead at just the right moment. As we pulled to a halt the faltering engine finally died.

Angela turned to me, only to see a smile on my face. 'I don't know what you are looking so happy about!' she retorted.

'Can't you see,' I said, 'we could have been standing on the side of the motorway, frozen and turning into snow-women, but here we are at a service station where we can ring the AA. [Automotible Association] and have a nice hot drink while we wait!'

'I see your point,' she said, but I would have preferred to be speeding on our way to Devon.'

We decided that we should ring Forge House and assess their weather conditions and, if they were all right, let them know we would be late.

I rang the AA while Angela rang Forge House who couldn't believe we were stuck in the snow as it was a lovely day in Devon, and the sun was shining brightly.

'Hum, exaggerating a bit, isn't he?' Angela mused disbelievingly, as we shared our phone conversations over a cup of tea. 'He just wants to impress us that their place is best. Come to sunny Devon and all that!' We looked from the window and maybe, just maybe, the snow was easing up and the sky a little lighter.

The AA were coming, but because of the suddenly deteriorating conditions we had been warned our wait could be long.

'Do you think it is worth talking to that AA man standing in the doorway looking rather pathetic as no-one is interested in signing up with him this morning?' I challenged Angela. 'We have been waiting an hour and you are good at chatting people up!'

Angela gave me a long look. 'Good idea,' she said and off she went.

Sitting in the window of the café I saw Angela leave the building with the AA man and approach her car. After no more than a few moments under the bonnet and an obvious try of the engine, they returned. Angela joined me smiling. 'The plugs gave up with the wetness of the driving snow. We've dried them off and it sounds much happier. Let's go! The AA man will cancel our call. He says I should join the association too as I might not always break down with you on board!'

'You joined, of course?' I questioned.

'We-ell,' said Angela, 'I took his leaflets and smiled and thanked him very nicely!'

We duly arrived and were immediately given an enjoyable lunch, sitting with the manager and a resident. Paul and I had already visited last August when we were in the area and had liked what we had seen. Angela was equally impressed today and the few residents who were already in situ looked settled and happy. Forge House had a very homely feel, with a standard of decor that equalled any illustration in *Ideal Home* magazine. Yet the whole place was large and spacious.

Forge House felt warm and comfortable despite the lack of residents and staff as they were building up both slowly in order to try and get the right mix. They were also very anxious that residents were chosen well for suitability and given the chance to settle before introducing the next. They selected their staff very carefully to ensure that they were up to the job of providing good loving care and coping with the extremely difficult problems that could arise within their new family. When full they would have nine residents and high staffing levels with a full programme to maintain interest and stimulation throughout the week. They offered horse-riding (always popular with Grant) on Exmoor, swimming, cooking, pottery, music and drama. They would continue to work on developing communication skills, personal hygiene and self-help and they would have educational outings and group holidays.

They also encouraged parents to be involved with their son or daughter so as to allay any fears and worries they might have. They hoped to assist in home transport in order to help maintain continuous contact with the family. Their aim was to involve the local community in the home so that they would be accepted into the spirit of the town. They planned that a social life consisting of visits to pubs, local discos and clubs, would allow their clients to develop interests that most people take for granted.

Angela and I left, after staying longer than we had planned, and a further delay on the motorway made our arrival at Stroud Court very much later than expected. This was most unfortunate, but we still had time to scan what we needed to see to decide which of the two possible homes might be suitable for Grant.

Stroud Court had a lot to offer but on the way home Angela and I agreed with little hesitation where we believed Grant would fit in best. Forge House had a homely, intimate atmosphere that felt right for him. I could picture him settled there, with the bustling centre of the small town just 200 yards along the busy street. My only concern was for his safety as the busy road was all too near. If I were scoring out of ten Forge House most certainly would make nine! Angela pointed out that wherever he was, unless he was kept under wraps, the roads would be a danger. If their security was good it would make little difference.

Angela now had to discuss the whole situation and the home's suitability with Caroline and then they both had to make reports and applications to their Social Service and Educational heads to see if the proposed placement would be accepted and the appropriate fundings offered. Approval and paper work took some time to complete, but eventually the go-ahead was given and Grant was to move into Forge House on 1 June, 1993 aged eighteen.

That spring we had another wonderful and successful holiday with him in Minorca. Like many of us he thrived in the sun and would lie back happily for many an hour soaking up its comforting warmth. The only distraction to this contentment was the added delight of Spanish omelettes and colas or shandies.

There was one incident here that made me realize two facts. One was that Grant was a man inside and the other that at most times he looked very normal!

Sexual problems can materialize from puberty, but with autistic people it is often less of a problem than for those with other mental handicaps. Autistic people have an inability to socialize and therefore close relationships are rarely formed and sexual ones are even rarer. Most problems usually amount to inappropriate touching of their own body in public places and guidance to suitable privacy for these satisfactions can usually rectify their anti-social behaviour, although it may take some time.

So far Grant had shown only one such behaviour – he was a boob man! When we changed for swimming he was always interested in viewing my breasts and even with clothes on would try for a quick feel! I would say nothing bar a firm 'Don't, Grant!' and remove his hand. As with past difficult situations, reacting would only have made things worse.

However, sitting on the sun-baked beach in Minorca on our final day, I watched a man close by stare at Grant. This was nothing new, although staring was usually brought about by Grant doing something odd. At this moment Grant was sitting quietly by our side enjoying the last moments of the sun before we left for our return journey and looking nothing more than a very handsome, bronzed, eighteen-year-old youth.

The man started to look quite angry and I was not happy now at the way he glared at Grant. Looking back at our son and following his eyes I realized what he was looking at and why this man looked so angry. Grant's eyes were locked on a very large pair of firm brown breasts that belonged to this angry man's wife, sunbathing topless. A few more minutes and I think Grant might have received a black eye! To retrieve the situation I held Grant's hands and spoke to him, as I often did, by putting a hand on his cheek to redirect his gaze into my eyes, and the man realizing there was a problem looked away.

By the time Grant returned to Dedisham School he had only two weeks of term left. On his last day I learnt with surprise how much Grant had touched the lives of so many who had worked with him there.

I was met at the classroom door by Wendy Thomson, Grant's

teacher, who told me that all the staff were in tears. I entered the classroom and was both touched and amused to see at least four adults mopping their eyes. These staff were so caring and dedicated to their difficult job and from this scene I really saw how each child mattered. They told me how Grant had been so special and, although he couldn't speak, he had given them something that words couldn't describe. They were so anxious that I should keep in touch and inform them of how he settled into Forge House. On the way out, George Flint, who had been the head of Grant's family group, ran after me. 'I know I have already said good-bye,' he said. 'But I must tell you this ... Grant is unique. I have been here for nearly twenty years and there has been no-one like him and probably never will be. He has something that none of the others had. The staff learnt so much from him and I enjoyed watching a member of staff blossom from his or her association with your son. It was not just the staff but the children too. At the case conference it was said that it might be better if he was with older ones in the evenings, but I don't agree. Grant was always very happy to watch the little ones playing games. He would sit quietly behind them with his worn book turning the pages and watching the more able children with their game, jigsaw or Lego construction and offer them a certain peace. I can't emphasize how much we will miss him.'

I took Grant home so touched at the sentiments expressed about our son. He couldn't talk, or look after himself, or socialize in the conventional way, yet he was offering love to people.

I had frequently wondered about the purpose of his life when he couldn't look after himself, work for a living or even socialize unless someone else helped him. The Dedisham staff were showing me his purpose by their words and tears that day. Grant's main role in life was to offer love and at times, comfort to others. This love was pure and unconditional. He bore no grudges and saw no faults.

We had a few days at home before we left for Devon. We had booked a caravan at a site near Cullompton where we could have a day or two of holiday followed by leaving Grant overnight at Forge House. The next day we would call in for coffee and to see how he had settled then make our way home if all was well.

Having the couple of days in the caravan was not the best thing to do mainly because it rained and this increased our depression. We walked around wet gardens open to the public and drank tea in dank cafés, our misery increasing as the day wore on.

Grant's mood echoed ours and, though we tried to be cheerful, we just exuded unhappiness. Forge House insisted he was still ours, but at this point I felt that passing him over to his life care home was transferring all our responsibilities of the last eighteen years.

When Julian went off to university it was hard because you knew that your child had flown the nest, but we all have to endure these heartbreaking moments of parenthood. Julian, however, had taken responsibility for his own life for many years. He knew what he wanted to wear and had had an allowance so he could make his own choices. He thought for himself and would consult us on decisions only when desperate. He knew where he was going and had expectations of life. We eagerly anticipated his future with its many discoveries yet to be made and experienced.

Grant, however, had always been fully dependent, as a baby would be. Up to now it had been my responsibility and pleasure to choose his clothes and when with him to know his every need. I was passing all this over to others along with part of my heart and soul. It was here I entered my second state akin to bereavement for this child.

This was how I felt at the time, but later I realized how much he did still belong to us and, although we saw him less often, our times with him were extra special and usually very good.

The day we left him was Bank Holiday Monday and we arranged to return a week from the following Saturday, but like Dedisham we would ring and have one sided-conversations, heavy breathing replacing dialogue from Grant's end.

Liz Campbell was to be Grant's key care worker and she was of a very similar age to Grant. There were two teams who worked opposite shifts and their system worked well.

Grant's room was lovely. It faced south, overlooking the garden or pathed area and, as a high bank backed this, he looked straight out onto a field in which a horse lazily grazed. Flowers had been placed in the room to welcome him and familiar things brought from home had been nicely arranged.

Chris, the owner, had cut down the bed's legs in order to offer safety in the event of an epileptic fit. There was a washbasin in the corner and Grant's dressing-gown hung nearby. Next door to his room was a very attractive bathroom which would be shared by a few residents.

Grant appeared very much at home when we called the next morning and after a coffee and chat it was agreed that it would be better if we didn't linger too long. So we hugged him tight, and collected our caravan and trundled our way rather sadly back down the M5 and M4 motorways to Reading and on home.

The two weeks went slowly, but we rang Forge House and they rang us and we were happy that Grant was settling in well and there were only a few teething problems; these were mainly linked to the night and his wakefulness and wandering. As time went on he became more at home in his new surroundings, so his sleeping patterns improved. We sighed deep breaths of relief that Grant was settled in such a good place where he was obviously happy and they were giving him lots of stimulation.

A week or so later we were to travel to Durham for Julian's graduation. The ceremony with dinner on the previous evening was an enjoyable and memorable occasion. The actor Peter Ustinov, the Chancellor of Durham University, presented the degrees and gave an amusing speech that enlivened the proceedings.

So 1993 saw formal education complete for both our sons. Grant would continue to be educated and the simple life skills he still had to master would be lovingly re-enforced daily. Julian, following a break, would return to learning in a different way – he had accepted a place in Cardiff to complete a PhD in Geology.

Nineteen

Paul and I loved our trips to Devon. There were so many beautiful places to visit. The nearest seaside towns and villages were delightful and offered wonderful coastal walks. We would leave home at dawn so that we could be with Grant by 9 a.m. and enjoy a long day out, usually walking many miles along by the sea or exploring inland areas such as the heather clad moorlands of Dartmoor, where wild ponies grazed and rocky tors could be climbed. We would end the day in a country pub with a hearty Devon meal and wicked, home-made puddings topped with clotted cream. We wanted Grant home on a regular basis, but the journey was long. We usually managed to bring him home every third week, his stay lasting about five days. Five days were a more suitable stretch of time than just a weekend, giving him a chance to re-adjust and enjoy his visit. It also made a reasonable time lapse between the two long car journeys. Grant did get restless on the drive, but story tapes and savoury bits to nibble helped to pass the time.

After the first few months Paul shared these journeys by driving down to Devon from work. The round trip was over 300 miles, but he was not daunted by this as he enjoyed the pleasure of Grant's welcome and his silent company on the return home. It was also good for us both to have the link with Forge House and with the staff working there.

Jan Howland would often accompany me on my journey, which would be helpful as well as companionable as she could pass things to Grant when he became restless. If we talked too much he would give us both a meaningful look and hold my hand; this told us very clearly that it was his silent time with me before leaving him. We respected this and with difficulty kept quiet! Grant would squeeze my hand and stroke it with his fingers until I needed to change gear, which was usually not until I came off the motorway at Cullompton.

We often broke the journey at a large Asda supermarket store near Bristol that was roughly halfway and only hundreds of yards off a convenient junction. It had a restaurant on its upper floor with an excellent range of food and from here we could watch the customers do their shopping. Even if I had not planned to stop, Grant would get excited if he saw the large Asda sign from the motorway. Sometimes Chris Bolt, the manager of Forge House, would meet us there in the minibus along with other residents and pass Grant over. Grant's companions all enjoyed having a good place to stop for a cup of tea before they returned.

Two others joined Grant at Forge House from Dedisham and one of these was Joanne, who had been in the same class. Joanne could talk, in fact she never stopped! A lot of her speech was very repetitious, but she was always bright and bouncy, asking the same questions over and over again. As she was chatting madly to you she would turn and throw her arms around Grant and say she loved him. She used to miss him terribly when he was home, asking frequently when he would be coming back. She would sit close to him on the settee and link her arm with his, proudly. On the whole Grant just accepted her and her amorous advances with a respectful calmness and shared his (still loved) Ladybird books with her.

Forge House gradually filled to maximum capacity of ten residents. However, it quickly became apparent that the needs of these people were different. Those with a higher level of ability and better communication skills required less supervision and more encouragement to develop their independence. The less able often needed the protection of a locked door, such as into the kitchen, thus inhibiting the independent lifestyle of the more able. Therefore the need to split the residents became more than obvious and it was not long before Chris Green purchased a second, smaller, house in the little town. The opening of the new unit freed rooms for other new residents with similar abilities to those already there. Grant's week was busy and with the others he was kept well occupied. Along with the simple life skills of washing and dressing, which improved continuously as a more stable routine became established, other occupations, such as carrying the washing in a basket and making his bed, were added to his schedule. He swam twice a week, went horse-riding on the edge of Exmoor, was taken to a weekly club, had a half pint of beer at the local pub and helped, and was helped, with simple food preparation, particularly sandwich making. They walked a lot and shopped daily in the town for the requirements of the home and went further afield on clothes shopping sprees. He was taken to a country church on some Sundays, which pleased me as I knew that he enjoyed the music and the stained-glass windows, not to mention the coffee and biscuits at the end of the service! One day a week they had an excursion to various places of interest or to the coast for the day and it would be a pleasure to hear what new place they had found to visit.

The September after his admission to Forge House they had a holiday in a country farmhouse in France. Unfortunately, the channel crossing was very rough and most of the party, including Grant, were sea-sick. The weather remained unkind, being wet and windy for much of the week, which made the holiday difficult and tested the patience of the staff.

The choice of sunny Minorca the following year was much more successful. They rented a villa, which proved to be quite luxurious, with its own swimming-pool. Here Grant's favourite activities of eating and sunbathing were well indulged and he caused much amusement by continually walking around the edge of the pool reading his book. He continued this dicey exercise until he fell into the cold water in all his clothes, but not put off he kept up this occupation until he fell in again!

Poor Liz Campbell, who was very fond of Grant and extremely

patient, had suffered the effects of Grant's sleeplessness and returned to England extremely tired, with many hours of sleep to recoup.

Grant's life continued in a much happier, well-constructed way. He liked his routines and I could plan for his five or so days at home well in advance, arranging my clinics and lecture days around these – though I had to plan my life carefully. Also within these arrangements I had my parents to consider. My mother had had both legs amputated, as a result of Raynaud's disease, a condition which had caused almost complete restriction of blood to her limbs with gangrene setting in. Her determination to regain a certain amount of independence was admirable, but the restrictions imposed by her handicap became unbearable and mentally she was tortured by the necessity to be dependent on others. My mother and father needed support although there was little that could be done, and my father did well to keep her life as stimulating and interesting as possible.

Paul's circumstances at work had changed and, as we had suspected would happen, he was made redundant again. Following six weeks out of work he gained new employment just before Grant's entry to Forge House. He was to work for almost a year as an accountant at Bisham Abbey, the national sports centre where, although he found it interesting to meet famous sports personalities and teams, the work was not what he enjoyed. He resigned, having been lucky enough to be offered a directorship in a busy local company engaged in scaffolding hire and sale and he was happy to be back in the construction industry in which he thrived.

Grant's first year at Forge House had gone well and he was happy and settled and we were relaxing more and enjoying some of our own interests. Paul's ensuing birthday reminded us of that awful first parting now almost a year ago. My birthday present to Paul was tickets for the London show *Buddy*, the story of Buddy Holly. We wondered if it would be suitable for Grant and established that it probably would since it was a lively musical show with little straight talking. Remembering our disastrous and worrying journey to *Starlight Express* we decided that this time we would go by train and make a complete day out, with lots of interest for Grant.

Grant loved dressing well and being admired for his handsome looks. I helped him into a smart shirt and bright tie and he donned his seldom worn Jaeger sport's jacket, in which he really did look fine. Upon seeing himself in the full length hall mirror he smiled broadly.

'Don't you look super,' I told him. He chuckled and stood up straighter, obviously agreeing with me! He was excited, as we had talked for some time about the day out and he knew it was something to be anticipated with pleasure.

We drove the car as far as Heathrow where we could park and take the underground train to our destination. The train was packed and there was only the odd single seat. We settled Grant then stood by his side holding the rail for support. He was happy and his lack of social awareness became apparent when he started to chuckle and kept it up, completely oblivious of whatever anyone else would think. We talked to him, asking him what was funny, even though we didn't expect an answer. In the end we decided that possibly the fact that he was travelling backwards was the reason for his mirth. We spoke to one or two people near him who were taken by his natural and infectious merriment, explaining his condition of autism and his inability to communicate.

Our first port of call was a large Burger King in London, which we knew was a necessary part of his day and his Jaeger jacket was removed to protect it from this greasy pleasure! Then with his tummy satisfied by an extra large burger, chips and cola we decided that we had plenty of time to visit Piccadilly to satiate Paul's liking for Tower Records, one of the largest compact disc and cassette outlets in town. For Paul, the prospect of a rare CD not available from our local shops would be an added birthday treat. To arrive at our destination required several changes on the underground. We walked and danced through the endless subways, passing buskers playing lively music that could be heard from some distance away. When we eventually reached the large store we climbed four floors to the CDs of interest. The windows overlooked the busy, fascinating landmark, Piccadilly Circus, where red buses and black taxis vied with each other, people jostled and dodged cars, preoccupied by their shopping or sightseeing. Grant loved watching a busy scene, particularly in suitably safe surroundings, as he was now, seated at a quiet window with his mother close by his side.

We listened to music through headphones and looked at the tapes for children, eager to see if anything new had come on to the market recently that might capture his interest in the story line. I knew most of what was available and was always searching for fresh material that might hold his attention.

Eventually it was time to re-negotiate the London underground system and dance past the same buskers in order to reach the theatre on time.

We had seats on the end of a row in the front circle so it was only the people behind who might be disturbed if Grant became restless. They turned out to be a family with young children and *they* worried in case *their* children troubled us, so we quickly established a mutual understanding.

The show began with the opening scene of a skiffle group in the fifties, which is how Buddy Holly first started. The music pounded out, bright and melodic, and Grant's feet tapped the floor with pleasure. As the show proceeded, the lively songs, that were hits in the late fifties and early sixties, became even livelier and we swung and clapped along with the stirring music produced by the excellent impersonators of Buddy Holly and the Crickets. The whole audience was taken up with the show and the music, and Grant enjoyed every moment. By the interval many people on the front row spoke to us commenting on Grant's obvious pleasure and wanting to know more about him. We gave simple explanations of the condition of autism and described the enormous pleasure we were getting from his enjoyment of the show, as there was so little in his life in which he could participate. To see his happiness in a show like this was so satisfying.

During the next half of the production the front row of the circle was more intent on observing Grant's pleasure than the show, and at the end they came to us to express their delight at what they had witnessed. Grant really had enjoyed every minute.

It was a wonderful, unforgettable day that we will remember forever.

Although Grant was now settled in a home for life, it did not deter me from investigating anything new to help our children, though it did restrict what I could actually do myself. I attended a workshop in Oxford on Facilitated Communication. This is a method that involves hand-over-hand or hand on forearm support of students as they communicate through pointing at pictures, letters or other objects. The amount needed and the amount achieved is very variable, depending on the need and the motivation to communicate.

Reports of successful breakthroughs again raised the hopes of many parents who felt compelled to put yet another theory and process to the test. Like other theories it evoked controversy and the need for full research and evaluation. As a parent I didn't want to wait for written reports and analyses, but was happy to try it out. Did it, or would it work for our son?

My conviction that Grant was normal, deep within his shell, was still there. If there was a way to reach him I would continue to try, even if the balance of opinion among the professionals was that the chances of success were small.

I had seen for myself that Grant needed facilitating in order to ride his tricycle and that just the lightest touch on his shoulder would keep him pedalling; if I removed that touch then he came to a halt. Why? I don't know, but I did know that for some inexplicable reason he needed motivation through me, as if I was his electrical charge. Would it be the same through communication? I knew he had the ability to say some words, as evidenced years before when he clearly said to the shop assistant, 'I can!' when I had declared that he couldn't speak.

The fact that it needed quite a bit of input was frustrating, but I told Forge House of my interest in this method and acquired a simple laminated 'querty' letter sheet to see if he would point to any letters that would form words. I was anxious not to pester him too much as he was very contented and I didn't want an enjoyable long weekend spoilt by introducing added frustrations for him.

Making a choice is usually a very difficult undertaking for most autistics. Facilitation might help, although their autism could still hinder them as their love of sameness, which brings order to their lives, could intervene. Grant always chose Bovril beef sandwich-spread when asked to choose between that and marmalade or honey. Was it that he always had Bovril, or did he really like it best and made his own choice?

I made the decision to facilitate, initially with the sole intention of helping him make personal choices. If this proved successful we could go on to letter sheets or typewriters.

One day while out walking on Dartmoor, we came across an ice-cream van, much to the delight of Grant. His ice-cream always depended on what we fancied, or the price, but what would Grant really choose. I put facilitation to the test. Lightly holding his arm and standing in front of the large display picture on the side of the van which showed the many varieties available, I asked him to point to the one he wanted. Grant rarely pointed to anything except something in a book, and that was only if he was asked and pestered to do so. With my hand lightly under his elbow and the other supporting his hand at the wrist he pointed, quite definitely, to the picture of a frozen fruit coated ice-cream, something I would never have chosen myself. Not believing that he had made a definite choice, and thinking that it was not what I would like, I asked him again, and again I facilitated the action. He was not changed in what he wanted and pointed confidently to the same ice. We bought it and handed it to him. The excited and joyful noises and the smile on his face when he ate, were enough to convince me that this was indeed *his* choice.

Liz Campbell at Forge House was excellent at helping with this method and she too had some good results, but she was also brilliant at encouraging words and got more from him than we did at home.

Grant had a formal annual assessment held at Forge House along

with a new Oxfordshire social worker. We had come to the end
of Grant's educational input from Oxfordshire, with its associated
funding, and now the expense of his care came solely under the
auspices of Social Services. They had to be happy with his
placement before agreeing to pick up the bill. Thankfully,
following the case review and reports assessed by appropriate
bodies, it was decreed that he was suitably placed and we all
breathed sighs of relief. Grant was well established and we had
seen progress in a few areas. He had matured in many ways. There
were times at home when we were ready to go to bed and he
wasn't. We would lock the kitchen door, where he might just be
distracted, and leave him in the lounge. He would be all ready for
bed with his teeth cleaned and would usually have spread himself
across the settee looking through one of his favourite stories. It was
lovely just to see this hint of independence and recognize it. We
would say goodnight and get ourselves into bed and switch off the
light, the door wide open so that we could see what happened.
We couldn't go to sleep as we had to check he had settled and turn
out the lights. Usually after a short time he would wander through
and get into bed.

If Julian was home we would leave the two of them together
(Julian usually watching sport) and when Grant took off for his
bedroom he would check that he was settled. What a difference
from those early years!

It was a rarity for Grant to wander off now so I was surprised
and panicky one day when I found he had disappeared from the
garden. The gate was open and after a quick garden search I stared
up and down the lane. Would he still make for his usual port of
call which was Joan's house up the lane and opposite? I checked
her garden and there was no sign of him and started on down the
lane not knowing where to look next.

Suddenly I heard a call from Joan: 'Wendy! Are you looking for
Grant, he is here.'

I turned back, relieved, and Joan was leading him down her
front path, looking a bit dishevelled in her tracksuit.

'Are you all right ?' I asked her.

Passing Grant over she replied, 'A bit shaken, actually.' Then she laughed. 'It was my own fault, I was getting dressed and still had little on. The front door wasn't locked, just on the latch. From the bedroom I heard the front door open and called out, asking who was there. As there was no reply I was rather unnerved to say the least! I looked from the bedroom only to see the very hulking form of a fair young man, in a dark tracksuit, passing down the hall! I didn't know whether to scream or if my luck was in! It took a few desperate seconds before the identity of the intruder dawned on me – Grant – and thankfully it was!'

There was a pub in the centre of Binfield Heath which has unfortunately been shut down recently, but for a couple of years, after a change in stewardship, it became an ideal venue for a summer evening stroll. The landlord and his wife were interested in Grant and I used their setting to help with his independence. As we usually called in the early evening, often to fill in a gap before Paul returned from work, it was a time when the pub was very quiet. I would give Grant the money and send him up to the bar to obtain his own drink, which was usually a Coke or Pepsi. The landlord would be aware of his need and would help to free the sweaty coins from Grant's tightly gripped fist in return for his much desired drink. Gradually Grant was happier to release the money, but many a time he would attempt to obtain his own cola from behind the counter, not really realizing the need to exchange money for goods. The landlord, amused, patiently directed him to the correct side of the bar.

The pub also served good food and we often called there to eat to make life more interesting for Grant and less problematic for me, freeing my precious time so that we could all enjoy his days at home to the full.

When Grant was home he was still very much ours and I bought clothes for his use when he was with us. This helped to make life easier for the staff when packing for his home journey and still gave me the pleasurable task of choosing clothes that were my taste! I had always seen this as one of the benefits of having a son without the ability to make choices; unlike mothers of 'normal' teenagers, I could keep him dressed in the image that pleased me! Grant usually showed pleasure if anyone admired how good he looked (which was frequently), so I couldn't have got it too wrong.

One day, in the summer of 1994, I had one of those annoying phone calls from a photographic centre offering a special deal on a family group photo. Instead of politely dismissing the caller I considered that having a family group picture was a lovely idea, though, bar Easter and Christmas, it was seldom that we were all together and arranging it might prove difficult. I accepted the offer and waited to receive the details.

It was late August before the boys were home at the same time and a football match between Julian's team, Reading, and formidable opposition, ensured that we could guarantee his visit and book the appointment with the photographer!

I had explained Grant's condition in advance and our brave and experienced photographer was very confident of his ability to succeed with his task of making this a memorable shot. His antics to get Grant to smile were enough to merit him an award! He peeped around his camera, jumped and danced, pulled funny faces, made weird movements and bounced teddies on his head. Our usually photogenic son was not in the mood to smile for this very silly man. Paul, Julian and I had laughed helplessly at his efforts and the missed shots of us three must have been most frustrating. Hot and exhausted he looked desperately at us for inspiration. 'What would make him happy?' he pleaded, his hand wiping the sweat from his forehead. Suddenly I came up with a thought.

'Ask him if he would like a c-u-p of c-o-f-f-e-e.' I spelt it out, not to spoil the reaction. I had also remembered the café next door, where we could get what we were promising.

'Grant, would you like a cup of coffee?' the photographer questioned hopefully.

'Yeah,' said Grant with a big beam and click went the camera.

Since my near collapse after a summer holiday my involvement in the Autistic Society had, of necessity, reduced. Dyson's Wood

House was up and running and a new group had begun with younger parents, who had had children recently diagnosed, and now needed support. Early diagnosis was improving, particularly in Berkshire owing to a specially trained team who understood and recognized the problem. This led to there being many parents with similar worries and thankfully they saw the need to get together. After introducing them to sources of help, I took a back seat to be consulted when and if they needed me.

I still taught about autism, giving information to groups that requested a speaker on the subject, and was happy to continue in this role.

The new parent's group became known as the Berkshire Autistic Society and they developed quickly into an excellent alliance, offering considerable help to many. Speakers at their monthly meetings were of a high calibre and gave the parents, teachers and care workers insights into all aspects of autism and methods of treatment and care.

They arranged outings, holiday entertainment and educational support, particularly with 'Needs Statements' and challenging local authorities to ensure appropriate placements were secured. The Berkshire Autistic Society is currently very active, giving out information and gaining new members daily, and many other similar societies have been formed throughout the country.

The group worked closely with Roy Howgate from Camp Mohawk, and younger children if accompanied by parents could benefit and gain support from the facilities offered at the camp. This was a boon in the endless summer break. Camp Mohawk obtained, through fundraising, a superb sensory room which I had the pleasure of using with Grant. A sensory room is designed to soothe and gently stimulate senses. It is softly cushioned and is full of equipment that stimulates, delights or relaxes the senses with its gentle music, water beds, floating sea-gulls and twinkling lights. They fill the room with peace and tranquillity and overcome the body with soporific sensations. It has a most wonderful calming effect on most autistic children, not to mention their careworker or parent in with them! Many schools, homes and special units now boast a sensory room, which does wonders for soothing a child or adult through a traumatic tantrum or experience.

Another method of treatment that was becoming popular and interested many parents was 'Auditory Integration Training', which aims at normalization of hearing. It is believed that the hearing of autistic people has regions of hypersensitivity. These areas are first assessed by an audiogram, then filtered music is played through headphones and the ears are 'exercised' to achieve as normal hearing as possible. The music is played on a CD player which has a specially devised amplification and filtering device, developed by Guy Berard, and is responsible for the altered soundwaves which reach the ears of the recipient by headphones. To date there is little scientific research to validate its success, but there are many recounted stories of improved behaviour and speech.

Grant's earlier hypersensitivity to many sounds made this method appear very plausible and, of course, something I considered would be well worth a try.

London has a Light and Sound Therapy Centre, but this held a long waiting list and was very expensive. It would involve ten days of treatment requiring us to stay in the city, or make long journeys every day which could be traumatic for our children.

The opportunity to purchase a system was looked at jointly by Berkshire Autistic Society and Camp Mohawk. A suitable room was provided at Camp Mohawk and the treatment could be purchased by a parent for as little as £300. An audiologist was needed who was trained in the use of the specialized equipment; happily the society knew of someone newly trained and anxious to practice the method and research the results.

After a fairly brief discussion with Paul, we were in no doubt that we wished to give Grant the opportunity to have this method of treatment, and his name was one of the first to be put on the list. All being well, they hoped it could begin in July 1995, as soon as all the equipment and arrangements had been finalized. We would arrange a couple of weeks for Grant to be at home so that he would gain full benefit.

The epilepsy that had dominated his life in those early years of adolescence had now been controlled for four years. Paul, particularly, was anxious that we discussed reduction of his medication as he worried about the long-term effects of strong drugs on his body. This was discussed at his case review and it was arranged for him to see the local consultant. There had been some activity following the trauma of his accident, but two years had now elapsed since that dramatic event.

Grant was generally of excellent health, apart from the colds that the staff and residents alike picked up and passed around. This is one of the hazards of group living. Depletion of staff, when their charges need them most, will always cause agonizing worries for managers. They will be faced with the decision of whether to bring in agency staff, who are unaware of the foibles of the residents, or to struggle on with the small number of staff left, running themselves down to the ground with the extra work.

One evening, in February 1995, Liz rang as she was worried about Grant and couldn't understand him. 'He is getting very angry with us and looking so fierce. We have never seen Grant like this before and wonder what is the matter. We are concerned that he could be in pain, but have pressed most bits of him and have no clues. Have you any ideas?'

As I have written before, an autistic person who cannot express himself and explain a pain, causes a parent or carer the worst of worries. All they can do is observe very closely. We suggested toothache as he must be due to cut molar teeth, but apart from that, without him by my side to observe, how could I say more?

Liz said that he had been rubbing his head, but sometimes if he was a bit distressed he would do this anyway. She said everyone had been notified and would be watching him closely. Tomorrow morning someone would call me to report on his condition.

The next day the message was good, but they had arranged an emergency dental appointment and again we would be informed of the result.

The dental surgeon proclaimed his mouth A1 and could see little evidence of new molars, but he took great interest and showed sympathy with their problem, asking to check him again if there was any further worry. This was all very reassuring, as was the fact that he appeared much happier.

Twenty

Grant's twentieth birthday, on 26 March, fell on Mothering Sunday that year and two weeks before Easter. Paul fetched him as usual on Thursday the 23rd so that he would be home to celebrate the day with his family.

Liz at Forge House was also very anxious to give him a party. The house had good birthday events and as his key worker she was not going to allow Grant to miss out on his celebration tea. She asked us if we could bring him back on the day after his birthday, Monday, then stay to the tea party she would organize.

Thursday was a clinic evening for me, so when I returned from work at 9.45 p.m. Paul had collected Grant and they had just arrived back. Grant welcomed me, but wasn't as bright and responsive as usual, and smiles were few. I hated it when he was in this mood as I felt cheated, wanting to take pleasure from his short time at home and anxious to know that he was enjoying it too. He hadn't been in this quieter, withdrawn state for some time; he seemed depressed. Paul hadn't had his usual responses that he liked so much, and had found him sombre on their return journey.

Although only March, we had been having some lovely sunny days and I had spent several hours in the garden prior to his coming home. The daffodils were bright and cheerful and the early weeds that surrounded their base needed clearing to highlight their spring beauty. As I worked happily exposing the small clumps of forget-me-nots that had taken over the shrub border in front of the house, I thought about the springs long gone and how those many, very difficult, lonely and frustrating years had faded. How lovely it was to anticipate Grant's visit home with pleasure. We would have good days walking in the countryside or by the river and maybe call at the garden centre and walk around the plants, planning what was needed to make this year's summer display. We would enjoy a cup of tea or hot chocolate in the centre's pleasant café, surrounded by exotic houseplants that gave off heavenly perfume. When we had finished, Grant would probably wander around the table displays, stopping to run his fingers luxuriously through the gravel or bench pebbles, loving the tactile quality and ending up with filthy hands, which I would wipe clean on the screwed up tissue found at the bottom of my pocket.

Paul would take him out and gain equal pleasure from his company. They would either visit the local airfield and eat hot burgers from their outside barbecue stand, or leave the field and take the beautiful walk down to the nearby farm to watch a barn full of squealing baby pigs being reared for the food chain. These fascinated Grant and he would study them for some time. Or, they would walk, Paul holding his hand, over the fields to Henley to visit Paul's parents, taking time to stop and talk to a donkey, dog or horse that they passed on the way. Edna would provide Grant with a tasty home-made cake and a cup of hot tea before they made their way back. Being six miles in all, it would take some time, but they would come back tired, and ready to relax for the evening.

Friday dawned wet, making the garden centre a suitable venue and we walked around the large greenhouses full of colourful polyanthus and looked at the newly prepared hanging baskets, planted up with delicate busy lizzies flowers, ready to plump out into delightful summer displays.

We lingered in the café, as the weather outside gave us little alternative. When we returned home we sat together watching an episode of 'Postman Pat'. Grant was still rather sombre and he stood, legs pressed against the radiator and his bottom resting on the windowsill, with a friendly Ladybird book in his hand. He was flicking the pages, not really interested in the contents.

'Come and sit down with me,' I encouraged. 'It's nice to have a few moments together before I get up to make our dinner; your Dad will be home soon.' I patted the empty space by my side and he looked at me over his book before sidling towards me. Instead of sitting, he lay across my knee and cuddled close, like a baby. He looked so miserable and tears filled his eyes. I hadn't seen tears for many a year and knew, for some reason, he was very unhappy. I talked to him and tried to offer comfort, but who knows what lies behind the unhappiness of someone who cannot express himself?

Paul was surprised and amused to see his position, but sad when I told him he was upset.

Paul took him out on Saturday and came back disappointed with his day as Grant was not good company, being quiet and remote. However, they did return with Grant clutching a beautiful, pink azalea plant, which was a favourite flower of mine.

'Grant has something for you for Mother's Day,' Paul said, following him into the kitchen. Grant came over to me with one the first smiles that I had seen this weekend and happily gave me the plant.

'Oh Grant,' I cried, 'that is beautiful, you know how I love flowers.' He looked so pleased at my reaction. To receive the beautiful plant was pleasurable enough, but to see Grant's obvious delight at giving me something made it extra special.

The next day, Sunday, was Grant's birthday and as usual we had put a lot of thought into his presents. It is so difficult to think of things to buy for someone who is not really interested in anything. Liz had said Grant liked listening to music in the morning while they were getting him dressed, and his Fisher Price cassette-player that had lasted all these years was not loud or clear enough now that he appreciated music more. So we bought him a combined radio and cassette-player.

I was also delighted to find a shop in London where they sold wax lamps. When the bright orange wax warmed up it started moving up and down the lighted tube, forming fascinating patterns and creating a pleasing sensation for the eye. Liz had requested a night light so that he could read his books in the early hours and the lamp not only filled this criteria, but was also pleasurable. It would be necessary to site it high as after a time it became very hot.

We gave him his presents in our bed in the morning. As usual sweets and new books gave him the greatest pleasure. When I showed him the cassette-player and put a new tape in to play, his reaction was strange. He looked at it sadly and shook his head, lying back on the pillows.

After twenty years I was used to strange reactions and Christmas and birthdays were, more often than not, an anti-climax. Sometimes months of looking for new idea would culminate in a reaction of complete indifference. It needed time for him to adjust to something new before he accepted it. More often than not he would look briefly at the unfamiliar or unwrapped goods, then grab at an old, well-thumbed Ladybird book and insist that it was the only thing he wanted at the time. We learnt to be patient and not to be too disappointed.

Paul, Grant and I all walked together on Saturday around a local nature reserve. This was a favourite place of ours, with a wide variety of interest. The trees were showing signs of budding, shadowed with the pale green of new growth. Grant was slow and somewhat lethargic so we didn't walk too far, but enjoyed a lazy and pleasant stroll through the woodlands and fields of the reserve.

Julian arrived home on the train in the late afternoon and Grant was delighted at the large box of Cadbury's Roses chocolates handed to him from the back seat. Julian got an immediate response!

We celebrated Grant's birthday enjoying a pleasant meal, as a family, at Paul's 'local', a pub in the Oxfordshire countryside. Grant became excited at the background music and I asked the landlord for the titles, as it was always good to know of fresh songs that appealed to him. One of the numbers he particularly liked was Steely Dan's 'Have a Little Faith'.

Julian was going on to London the next day for a conference and we saw him to the train. Later in the afternoon Paul and I drove Grant back to Forge House to celebrate his birthday, yet again, this time with his friends. What a welcome met us on our arrival! The residents from both homes and most of the staff were there to provide a wonderful birthday party. The table held an array of party treats: sandwiches, crisps, sausages, sausage rolls, cakes, chocolate biscuits and a very chocolatey chocolate cake, made by Liz, which made Grant clap his hands in excitement when she carried it through the door, lit up by candles.

Later, when everyone was full and very sticky, and hands had been washed clean, Liz staggered into the room, this time with a huge pile of presents. There was a new shirt, after-shave, a pair of smart, black shoes and books, to name but a few.

This was then followed by some loud music and dancing, in their large lounge, until Paul and I decided we should make the long journey home; we were both due at work the next day. We kissed and hugged Grant and said good-bye.

Grant could not have been given a better birthday or a better send off from all his friends. He died suddenly, from a severe epileptic fit, in the early hours of the following Sunday ...

For some reason on Saturday 1 April, although a sunny, spring-like day, I woke up depressed and stayed in that state all day. I couldn't explain my feelings and they were unusual. We went out for dinner that evening with some good friends but despite the jovial atmosphere the depression didn't lift. That night I slept fitfully, waking on many occasions, and just before dawn I awoke scratching desperately at my throat which had become very itchy. In my dazed state I considered looking at the cause of the itching, but returned to sleep.

Just before eight Paul went to the kitchen to make some welcome tea. The phone rang out, all too early for a Sunday morning. 'Hello Chris,' Paul said brightly, but then there was silence. Leaping from our bed to the kitchen I witnessed the horrific look upon Paul's face and a desperate, 'Oh no, Chris!' He listened for a little longer and with tears welling in his eyes, broke the news to me. Our lives were shattered.

Julian came straight home and the family were informed. Jan and Gary Howland came round instantly to support us. We were all in a daze and found it hard to take in our tragedy.

Heartbroken, devastated and shaking with shock, I needed to tell people and rang close friends immediately. It gave me something to do as our lives had suddenly halted in an appalling way and we were in a void.

Jean and David Denham, were among the very first that I rang. Our closeness, engendered when Zoë and Grant walked together, sharing similar interests, would now be renewed by our shared loss. Zoë and Grant had become 'friends' and epilepsy had killed Zoë and now Grant; they were soulmates together. Jean and David didn't tell us that today was Sasha's birthday (their adopted daughter from Ethiopia) but, unselfishly, said they would come over in the evening. We valued their unfailing support, love and friendship.

Jean rang Caroline Simmonds, who later in the morning phoned to offer her condolences and her help, if we needed her. There was a way I felt she may be able to assist and that was with something which Paul and I had already discussed and did not know how to proceed with. We wished if possible for Grant's brain to be used for research. I had read in a National Autistic Society publication, some eighteen months previously, that research into autism was being undertaken at the Maudsley Hospital, London, and if families could bring themselves to donate the brain on the death of their autistic relative, then the research done could be invaluable. Bar accident or illness the life expectancy of an autistic person is similar to anyone else, so brains for research were not frequent. If good came from Grant's death it would give another purpose to his life.

Caroline said, 'Leave it to me.'

It was fortunate, for research's sake, that Grant died on a Sunday as he would need a post-mortem and this couldn't be performed until Monday morning. Caroline rang The National Autistic Society as early as she could the next morning and they directed her to Dr Anthony Bailey at the Maudsley. He immediately contacted the coroner in Devon and an agreement was made, but it was essential for Dr Bailey to leave instantly for Devon to collect Grant's brain.

On Monday evening we received a phone call from Dr Bailey to tell us tactfully that he had just returned from Devon; his mission was successful. We decided that, instead of flowers, we would ask for donations in aid of the invaluable research they were undertaking at the Maudsley into autism and epilepsy and the final total exceeded £2,000.

I wondered about Grant's depression of the previous birthday weekend and if his tears and sad rejection of his new tape-player had anything to do with his impending fate. Did his autism take him into another sphere of which we knew little? Did he realize he was leaving us? We will never know the answer to these questions – not in this world. My mind lingers on the title of the piece of music played on our last night together as a family. 'Have a Little Faith.'

My faith and comforting deeds and support from friends took us through the next few weeks. God had only loaned this special child to us.

One of our most dreaded tasks was to visit Forge House to talk with them and clear his lovely room. We didn't know how we could possibly face the other side of that bedroom door. Hand in hand we made our way down the corridor and entered the room. Instead of being bowled over by grief we were engulfed in an overwhelming feeling of peace and tranquillity. The room *was* Grant and we felt his presence there; we couldn't be sad, just comforted. His new birthday nightlight,

Shropshire), friends, neighbours, and relatives. The church was packed full. People who heard too late to attend the service wrote letters and we learnt more of how Grant had touched the lives of others.

It was not entirely a sad event, but a celebration of his short life and it brought us all together to talk about it. We stood or walked around our well-groomed garden for the occasion, catching up on Grant's friends of the past and present, all these many nice people he had brought into our lives. We had made so many lovely friends through Grant.

I spoke to my mother on the phone that evening and she was sad that she could not make the funeral. It upset her that through her disability she was unable to support her daughter in the saddest moment of her life. She told me she had had a dream and she wished I could have shared it as she clearly saw Grant walking through the room looking so normal. At a later date she told me that it couldn't have been a dream as she was sitting on her bedside commode!

Now more than ever I saw the purpose behind Grant's life, but also saw a certain futility in its continuation. He was still very handicapped by his condition and, despite all we had tried, was still locked deep down in his body, a body that would not allow him to rise to the surface and live a life of his own. He was so reliant on other people; he could make few decisions for himself; he could not express his feelings or understand those of others; if he wanted to go to the pub or for a swim or for a walk he had to wait until someone decided that that is what would be done. He couldn't go to a football match or climb a mountain like Julian, or even make a normal relationship with his brother.

We would have continued to try anything that came along to help free him. We still would have loved him dearly just as he was; he gave more to us by his unconditional love than we were giving to him by struggling to make him live to our social standards. His small actions said more than words, like when he stood immediately behind me when I was cooking at the stove

standing on a chest near his bed, offered solace as it bu[
patterns with its soothing orange wax.

The staff at Forge House said they also experienced the
feeling in his room and those close to Grant came here to
peace and comfort. We left most of the contents of G
room behind with clothes and equipment for the use of c
in the home. We liked to think that they would be used l
companions.

We felt sad for Joanne at Forge House who would mi
friend, though may not be able to understand where h
gone — like Grant ten years before, when Zoë died.

I felt Grant's presence again at the funeral at Sh
Church and knew he was with me and held me up throug
service, as I had helped him through many church se
there in the past. The stained-glass windows were l
reflecting light into the church as the sun shone on their
colours, colours and reflections that would have fasc
Grant. How appropriate that they should twinkle so tod

How often, long ago, had I sought help from C
Shiplake churchyard, as I wrestled outside the churcl
with an uncontrollable child. I had constantly called f(
and often prayed desperately for a way to get through a
day or weekend. I was helped when I reached into praye
supported when I felt it hard to carry on and the next
would come as if I had heard the words spoken clearly.

It was apt that Caroline Simmonds, who had giver
education, sorted and helped with his placements and c
points of suitability with me in order to make his
educated and comfortable as possible, should now read
at the service that would send him to his final place c
one which would offer eternal peace.

Grant's life was represented there on that sunny,
spring day. The sort of day in which Grant wou
blossomed. They came — from Bishopswood, Hea
Smith, Chilterns, Dedisham, Forge House, the Autistic
(old and new), Claire (who had moved back h

and fearing for his safety, and feeling restricted, I would tell him firmly to stand back. His arm would come round me and he would gently stroke my back and look me straight in the eyes, smiling deeply into mine.

Now this should be the end of Grant's story and for some it probably is but this depends to a large extent on one's personal beliefs and convictions.

When I was nursing I was often witness to patients near death and how they would see relations, long gone, seated or standing by their bedside, ready and waiting to take them over into the afterlife. I closely observed the action of two spiritualists who were present at a house I visited as a district nurse. The lady had been discharged the previous day from a hospice in London, where she had talked regularly with them. Since she had arrived home she had had a severe stroke and was very poorly.

I didn't realize who these two women were seated either side of my patient's bed, but seeing there was nothing I could do for my patient I said I would leave and call back at the end of my morning's work. Her death was inevitable and could happen at any time during the next twenty-four hours. One of the women said, 'Please stay! It won't be long now as they are all here.' She glanced around the room. She then turned to her friend and asked, 'Can you call her husband in now?'

The patient's husband was brought into the room and he was asked to hold his wife's hand and give her a kiss good-bye as she was about to leave her body – and thereupon this lady died.

After seeing to her, I left at the same time as the spiritualists and, as I packed my car, I questioned their obvious occupation. They explained to me that the spirits had told them that their client had had a stroke and, as they had promised to try and be with my patient at the time of her death, she and her friend were ready to travel from Essex to be here in Oxfordshire to see her over to the other side. The time of death had also been disclosed so they knew how long they had and planned their arrival accordingly. It was all very fascinating and being witness to the scene made a deep impression on me.

In the past I had some family experience of spiritualism from a relative on my father's side, so with these examples behind me I did wonder about contacting a reputable medium to see if I could be in touch with Grant after his death. I could never talk with him in life, only what I could tap from the closeness of maternal love by delving into the depths of his blue eyes or his gentle expressive touch. Could I possibly reach our beautiful Gentle Giant now in death? Was this my last chance?

I thought about it and asked a close friend, noting her reactions. She was scared that I may be hurt further by an unsuccessful sitting. I mulled it over for some time more and it was some ten months following Grant's death when I met up with Ana-Marie, a bright friendly girl and an old school friend of Julian's, who now worked in a local Building Society. She had known Grant as a child from youth club days. She had lost her sister Rosie, aged seventeen, only two years previously and on Grant's death sent us a beautiful and heartfelt letter that touched us all. We shared our feelings and for some reason I asked whether her mother had visited a spiritualist. She told me she hadn't, but that she, herself, had and how it had helped her. The spiritualist had said things that only Ana-Marie could have known about Rosie. Now she was certain that her sister was never far away and had just passed on into another dimension. She was convinced that one day she would see her again. Ana-Marie quietly told me of several others who had been helped by this spiritualist. I requested the phone number and called to arrange a sitting the following week.

Mrs Weaver was a blonde, slight lady in her late forties and she led the way to her tidy lounge, while she said goodbye to her previous client. She then turned to me saying she would have to have a cigarette to unwind. She had to have some space from one sitting before the next.

While waiting, my heart thumped deep within my chest at

the anticipation of what was to come. She smoked, leant up against her kitchen sink and we chatted briefly. However, I remained very guarded in what I said in case she picked up any clues to my life, or whom I might be trying to contact in death, which would compromise her credibility. She explained that her gift of communicating with the spirit world had been with her since she was four. Strange things had happened to her after her baby brother had died, but then she was not aware she was different from anyone else. We sat relaxed in a small room at the back of the house and she told me about my grandparents, gone before, that I only properly identified after the sitting, and these tentative connections continued for about ten minutes. Then suddenly she looked up and said, 'Oh! I have a young man here – aged 24, no – 20. He died suddenly. He says he is so pleased you have come to contact him as he has been waiting to tell you that he is all right now!' She looked up and said, 'Does this mean anything to you?'

The tears in my eyes and my firm nod said everything.

She went on, 'He says that you have been thinking of making contact for some time and he has been waiting. He wants you to know that he is much happier over here as he can do everything that he couldn't do in life and he says that you always felt that his life would be short.'

She went on to say that he wanted to learn and she wondered whether he was about to go to university. It was at this point I had to tell her that he couldn't talk, although I still didn't disclose much detail as I was still waiting to hear more that would make me completely convinced of her natural abilities.

Other spirits came through that gave me messages, but after some minutes she said, 'The young man wants to talk some more, but he is being very patient and just stands in the background, waiting for his turn. Oh! he has come over and is gently stroking the back of my neck; he has a lovely smile!' I thought of Grant's wonderful, cheeky smile that we had loved so much and of the way he gently stroked the back of our neck or shoulders. She told me so much, saying how close we were. She said there was something wrong with his brain and that the name Anthony came to her, did that mean anything?

'Oh yes!' I explained. 'His brain was removed for research and the doctor who is working on it is called Anthony Bailey.'

She told me that he had been happy watching others and was content to watch and not participate; that he liked preparing sandwiches and doing simple puzzles.

She then bent down and stroked her legs from the knee downwards and enquired, 'Was there something wrong with his legs?

'Only itchy feet,' I replied.

'No!' she said firmly. 'That isn't it.' And she stroked her legs again from the knee downwards.

Still getting a complete blank from me she changed tack and said, 'There is someone that concerns you a lot, a woman, and I think she lives up the country; am I right?'

'Yes,' I sighed, thinking of my mother and her amputated legs – below the knees. The leg strokes! It was her he was indicating, not himself.

'He wants you to know that she is all right, not to worry too much about her and that he visits her frequently.' I thought of my mother's words about seeing Grant walk through her room in the middle of the night and how she had said that he looked so normal and happy. My mother died six months after my meeting with the spiritualist, weary and ready to pass on.

There was much more. Although it was tremendous that I was getting so much from this sitting, it was sad that I had had to wait until Grant's death before he could talk to me.

The spiritualist gave me so much proof of Grant's identity that both Paul and I were given peace and comfort from each special message. Julian was fascinated by my experience, but possibly more sceptical. We all missed Grant desperately, and what more could we want, but to know he was happy.

My visit with the spiritualist was almost over and her final words in our sitting were, 'Your son says, "Thank you for looking after me so well in life – I will be waiting here until your time to come over."'

Epilogue

It is now almost certain that there is a genetic factor involved in autism and there are leads in the research being done that are taking them nearer to discovering the offending gene. There is, however, a possibility that there may be different varieties of autism which might need the identification of several genes.

It is still extremely difficult for the medical profession to assess the prognosis of their young patient once they are diagnosed with autism. All aspects of functioning need to be taken into account in order to have any idea on the future capabilities of that child.

My own advice on this would be to always think positively and optimistically about the outcome. Seek local societies who will hold up-to-date information.

Carefully assess your child and family before embarking on anything new. Welcome the support and friendship of others in similar situations. There are many articles or books written by autistic people and these not only make fascinating reading, but give a wonderful insight into the person deep down and why they acted in a particular manner. Books and articles like these can help with understanding the complexities of the autistic mind, leading to better management skills.

In reading Grant's story I hope you will see that we didn't fail. It is true that we never broke down the wall and retrieved the person that could live independently and be socially aware. However, we did give him as much love as we could and from deep within came a gentle affection for all who cared to try and know him. His gift was simple, but rewarded and humbled many.

Finally, love your children for what they are – and never give up hope.

Appendix 1

TWO POEMS

Autism in Our Family

A baby is born; happiness, love.
The baby grows; doubt, worry.
Where is speech? Where is comprehension?
Why so active?

The child is Autistic. What is that?
What does his future hold?
What will our life be?

Try out new treatments. Cling on to hope.
New methods of teaching, new theories.
How can I help him?
How can I break through the barriers
That hold my child within himself?
Why does he refuse to learn?
Why does he have no play?
Why does he wish to escape?

High fences, locked doors, frustration, aloneness.

Fears for his safety, constant attention.
Years without sleep. Always love.
Can I cope? Will I cope?
Can I give my family all they need? Who misses out?

Respite care, much guilt but relief.
He grows bigger, stronger.

Such strange behaviour; misunderstood.
What of his future?
Can I cope? Will I get through the years?
We all love him so much. He grows taller, stronger.
What is his life? He is happy, he knows no pain.

What will become of him?
Who will give him love when we can't?
Who will understand him when we are not here?
We must secure his future;
He must be cared for by people who understand.
We love him. He now loves us.
We need sleep, we need shared care;
We want his future secure.
He is a young man, so vulnerable.

(Written by the author half way through the long summer holidays
when Grant was 14 years.)

White Daffodil

At Easter God gave us a child small and bright
With the daffodils yellow he gave us a light.
So the years passed and our baby he grew
Like a daffodil tall with the fairest of hue.

At Easter we learnt God had given us more;
Daffodils bloom yellow, but here's what we saw.
Amongst the bright yellow there is one that stood out,
A flower that was white, of its beauty no doubt.

At Easter he took his flower back home
He had lent us His beauty to love and to own.
Our daffodil white had given such joy
He was God's special child and our own treasured boy.

Appendix 2

ADVICE AND INFORMATION FOR FAMILIES WITH BEHAVIOUR PROBLEMS

Some of these ideas are taken from a leaflet produced by The Family Fund Trust, PO Box 50, York, England, YO1 2ZX. There are also ideas from myself or members of the Berkshire Autistic Society. We hope they may be of help.

1   **Child constantly rocks; destroys chairs and other furniture by rocking and/swinging.**
    A secure swing, in or out of doors, can give much comfort. A rocking chair on a stable base may also help.

2   **Child constantly jumps up and down, destroying sofa, beds, etc.**
    A strong indoor or outdoor trampoline, securely anchored and well supervised. Firm handling to ensure that the child only jumps on the trampoline.

3   **Child has poor communication, screams and is aggressive, perhaps causing the child to become isolated.**
    Music can be very soothing. The child's own cassette-player turned low in an ear-level cupboard (locked if necessary) or his/her own Walkman. National Music and Disability Information Service, Foxhole, Dartington, Totnes, Devon TQ9 6EB. Tel. 01803 866701

4   **Child climbs curtains, pulling them down.**
    A Velcro strip glued to wall with backing sewed to curtain.

5 **Child throws bedding off.**
Warm night clothes with soft fastenings. An all-in-one sleep suit. A washable duvet with elastic ties at corners to draw it gently into position: this is lighter and less restricting than blankets. Or zip into washable sleeping-bag.

6 **Child wets and soils.**
Contact the local Health Service Continence Adviser and/or ERIC (Enuresis Resource and Information Centre), 65 St Michael's Hill, Bristol, BS2 8DZ. Tel. 0117 926 4920
Disposable nappies, plastic sheets, etc., should be available from the local health visitor or continence advisor. This will depend on the area.

7 **Child wets and soils on the floor.**
Cushionfloor covering – easily washed and tough, but warm to the feet and softer than Vinolay, etc. Or urine-proof heavy duty carpeting available from any good carpet shop.

8 **Accidents on carpet or soft furnishing due to incontinence or vomiting that smell even after clearing up the mess.**
Try a squirt from a soda siphon, or wash with a solution of bicarbonate of soda. A product for lifting odours from carpets, bedding, etc., called 'Well Done' is available in the UK. This comes in a spray-powder form and consists of enzymes that digest and convert the waste, thus removing the odour and leaving a pleasant smell in return. Suppliers: Certified Laboratories, PO Box 70, Oldbury, West Midlands B69 4AD, UK.
   These suppliers also produce a product called 'On Duty' which is a powder to sprinkle on waste to revert it to a pleasant smelling jelly, making cleaning an easier task. It is also useful for long car or coach journeys as urine in a potty or container can be converted to a pleasant smelling jelly!

9 **Child is messy feeder and has outgrown baby bibs.**
Plain adult pelican bibs with a trough can be provided by the Social Services department as equipment for daily living – see your social worker or occupational therapist, or contact local government services for advice.

10 **Child beats head and fists on walls.**
A safety helmet can be provided by the Health Service. Ask your family doctor. Line walls with polystyrene tiles or roll. Some parents add a layer of foam to shoulder level covered with strong attractive washable material. Carpet and carpet tiles adhered to the wall instead of wallpaper. Helps to soundproof as well as minimize damage.

11 **Child tears off wallpaper.**
Consider removing wallpaper and cover walls with Polyripple. Expensive but smoother than Polytex. Paint with vinyl silk. Use a frieze border for colour, or dangle mobiles out of reach.

12 **Child rolls about on the floor a lot. Needs safe stimulation.**
Covered foam wedges and cubes of various sizes, which interlock for stacking.

13 **Child interferes with fires. Climbs over fireguard.**
A large fireguard with a top cover that does not leave any space to allow access to the hearth. This should be fixed firmly to the wall with clipped hooks. Fires should be supervised at all times particularly if there is sensory disfunctioning.

14 **Child has hazardous behaviour in kitchen – climbs on stove. Pulls boiling pans over, etc.**
Ideally, ban your child from the kitchen. Lockable doors with security codes are a good way of restricting access to dangerous rooms. Wrought iron door between kitchen and living area means child can be seen and join in without interfering in kitchen activities. Ask Social Services for advice and help with this under Chronically Sick and Disabled Persons Act. Cooker guards are available from British Gas, Electricity Boards and Mothercare department stores.

15 **Child escapes from garden.**
A high fence or wall. Get advice and possibly financial help from Social Services. Make sure the garden has plenty of distractions within it, such as play equipment. Climbing roses and other prickly plants help to make fences child-proof!

16 **Child hits people and things.**
Make a punch bag from a cushion dropped in a pillowcase and tied with a string. Fasten to the top of the door frame with a hook as for a baby bouncer. The rest of the family might enjoy hitting it too!

17 **Child interferes with water and gas taps and electrical plugs and switches.**
Consult your local Social Services department or its equivalent or British Gas, Electricity Board or Water Authority. In the UK, protective covers are available for electric sockets from the Electricity Board, Mothercare department stores or the charity SCOPE.

18 **For advice needed about equipment.**
Contact your local Social Services department or its equivalent or the Disabled Living Foundation, 380–384 Harrow Road, London, W9 2HU. Tel: 0171 289 6111

19 **Child smears excrement.**
All-in-one-suits, either homemade or created from 'pull-on' type pyjamas sewn firmly together at the waist. An opening is made and re-enforced down the back and just wide enough to squeeze the child through. The hole is then secured with buttons and tight loops or hooks and eyes. Showering with cold water so as not to reward the action; this sometimes can have instantaneous results!

20 **Child tips furniture such as bed or cupboards in bedroom.**
Bolt bed and cupboards to the floor or wall. Often an obsession or behaviour that is prevented is forgotten.

21 **To prevent entry in or out of room/house.**
Double handles on doors; one as high as possible.

22 **To protect windows and glass.**
Safety film which can be bought from Mothercare.

23 **Miscellaneous.**
Picture and photo frames in acrylic can be purchased from IKEA.

Don't discard toys that are ignored – put them away and bring out again at a later date. Sometimes things ignored at three can be a source of great pleasure at six, eight or even much older.

Try not to let your child's obsessions severely interfere with the rest of the family – they are important too. Seek professional advice if this happens.

In the UK, hold a RADAR key for disabled toilets which is particlarly invaluable for mothers out with boys or fathers out with girls, but also for difficult small children where tantrums and unacceptable behaviour causes increasing frustrations to an already fraught parent.

UK key can be obtained from the local district council or RADAR, 12 City Forum, 250 City Road, London EC1 8AF. (Declaration of disability needed.) In other countries, contact your local government offices for guidance on what help is available.

Badges, T-shirts and sweatshirts – all with logo saying, 'Please be patient – I'm autistic' The badges wash well and are very effective on the front of a winter coat when shirts are not visible. They are available from Berkshire Autistic Society, 103 London Road, Reading, RG1 0BZ, UK. Enclose a SAE and cheque to BAS for £2.00. Details of clothing will be enclosed, or a leaflet about clothing will be supplied on request with a SAE to the above address.

Useful addresses

AUSTRALIA

Association for Autistic Children in Western Australia
987 Wellington Street
West Perth
WA 6017
Tel. (08) 9481 1144
Fax. (08) 9481 4223

Autism Association of ACT
C/-1 Charlotte Street
Red Hili
ACT 2608
Tel. (02) 6295 0207
Fax. (02) 6299 2444

Autism Association of South Australia
PO Box 339
Eastwood
SA 5063
Tel. (08) 8379 6976
Fax. (08) 8338 1216

Autistic Association of NSW
PO Box 361
Forsetville
NSW 2087
Tel. (02) 9452 5088
Fax. (02) 9451 3447

Autistic Children's Association of Queensland
PO Box 363
Sunnybank
QLD4109
Tel. (07) 3273 2222
Fax. (03) 3273 8306

Autism Tasmania
PO Box 1552
Launceston
TAS 7250
Tel. (03) 6343 2308
Fax. (03) 6343 2308

Autism Victoria
PO Box 235
Ashburton
Victoria 3147
Tel. (03) 9885 0333
Fax. (03) 9885 0508
Web. http://home.vienet.net.au/-autism/

BRITAIN

Allergy-induced Autism Support and Research Network (UK)
(affiliated to the Hyperactive Children's Support Group)
3 Palmera Avenue
Calcot
Reading
Berks. RG3 7DZ
Tel. (01734) 419 460

Autism Research Database

This database information is available to anyone who contacts the National Autistic Society Information Centre on Tel. (0171) 903 3599. E-Mail. (JANET). UK.AC.SUNDP.VI::LSOAHU (Prestel/CAMPUS GOLD): YSD043

Camp Mohawk

Roy Howgate
Camp Mohawk
Wargrave
Reading
Berks. RG10 8PU
Tel. (0171) 511 3000

The Family Fund

PO Box 50
York
England
The Family Fund Trust may be able to offer some financial help to families with a child with a disability that the Trust considers very severe according to its guidelines. The Trust can offer help with essentials that will improve the well being of a family under stress, such as provision of a washing machine, tumble dryer, fridge or telephone installation. For further information contact the Trust at the above address.

Mencap National Centre

123 Golden Lane
London EC1Y 0RT
Tel. 0171 454 0454
Fax. 0171 608 3254

The National Autistic Society (NAS)

393 City Road
London EC1V 1NE
Tel. 0171 833 2299
Fax. 0171 833 9666
Web site. http://www.oneworld.org/autism_uk/
E-Mail. nas@mailbox.ulcc.ac.uk
The NAS works with more than twenty-six branches and over fifty local

societies. They can offer advice and refer you, if required, to the nearest local support group. Helpline: (0171) 903 3555 (lines open 10–12 weekday mornings).

The NAS produces an excellent range of publications, bibliographies and videos, and runs short courses at a variety of locations around the country. It also holds details on schools, benefits, suitable holidays and toys. To obtain details of NAS publications, write to the head office address (FAO Publication's Department), enclosing a SAE.

Anyone with a more general interest in the condition – such as students and researchers – should contact the NAS Information Centre on Tel. (0171) 903 3599

Parents, carers and people with autism can contact the autism help line either by writing to the NAS Head Office address or by phone on Tel. (0171) 903 3555 (lines open 10–12 weekday mornings). NAS Services on Tel. (01179) 872 575 or Fax. (0117) 987 2576 will take enquiries about placements in local schools, adult centres or direction to local services.

The NAS publication *Approaches to Autism* includes information on most of the therapies that are discussed or used in this book, as well as other recently developed therapies and educational methods.

**The National Autistic Society
(Scottish Office)**
111 Union Street
Glasgow
Strathclyde G1 3TA
Tel. (0141) 2221 8090
Fax. (0141) 2221 8118

**The National Autistic Society
(Welsh Office)**
William Knox House Suite E2
Britannic Way
Llandarcy
Neath
West Glamorgan G1 3TA
Tel. (01792) 815 915
Fax. (01792) 815 911

Network 81
1–7 Woodfield Terrace,
Stanstead
Essex CM24 8AJ
Tel. (01279) 647415
Fax. (01279) 816438
Offers help with educational statementing.

News (USENET)
nntp://bit.listserv.autism
This news group gives availability to world-wide views on all aspects of autism
and alternative therapies.

Society for the Autistically Handicapped
199 Blandford Ave
Kettering
Northants NN16 9AT
Tel. (01536) 523274

Sound and Light Therapy Centre
90 Elizabeth's Walk
London N16 5UG
Tel/Fax. (0181) 880 1269

SOUTH AFRICA

Association for Autism
PO Box 35833
Menlo Park
Pretoria 0102
Tel. 012 345 3245
Fax. 012 664 2469

South African Society for Autistic Children
Private Bag X4
Clareinch 7740
Cape Town 8001

UNITED STATES OF AMERICA

Autism Research Institute Review International
Bernard Rimland, Ph.D, Director
4182 Adams Avenue
San Diego
CA 92116

Autism Society of America
7910 Woodmont Avenue
650-Bethesda
MD 20817
Tel. (303) 657 0881
Fax. (800) 329 0889
Website: htpp://www.autism-society.org/

Autism Society of America
Palm Beaches
805 Xanadu Place
Jupiter
FL 33477
Tel. (561) 746 1465

Autism Society of Pittsburgh
500-G Garden City Drive
Garden City
Plaza
Monroeville
PA 15146
Tel. (412) 856 7223
Fax. (412) 856 7428

Autism Society of Western Kentucky
PO Box 1647
Henderson
KY 42419
Tel. (502) 827 5805

Recommended reading

PERSONAL ACCOUNTS

Emergence – Labelled Autistic, Temple Grandin and Margaret Scariano, Arena Press, 1986.
In the Dark Hours I Find My Way, Birger Sellin, Victor Gollancz, 1995.
Nobody Nowhere, Donna Williams, Corgi Books, 1993.
A Real Person – Life on the Outside, Gunilla Gerland, Souvenir Press, 1997.
Somebody Somewhere, Donna Williams, Doubleday, 1994.

FURTHER READING

After Age 16, What Next? Services and Benefits for Young Disabled People, The Family Fund Trust, 1996.
Autism and Asperger Syndrome, Uta Frith, Cambridge University Press, 1991.
Autism – Explaining the Enigma, Uta Frith, Basil Blackwell, 1989.
Caring for the Carers, Christine Ledger, Kingsway Publications, 1992.
The Handbook of Autism, Maureen Aarons and Tessa Gittens, Routledge, 1992.
Siblings of Children with Autism – A Guide for Families, Sandra L Harris, Gazelle Books, Woodbine House Incorporated, 1994.
Son Rise: The Miracle Continues, Barry Neil Kaufman, HJ Kramer Inc., 1994.
Taking Care, Alison Cowen, Joseph Rowntree Foundation, 1996.

ARTICLES

Autism: A Personal Account, Therese Jolliffe, *Communication* Vol 26(3), December 1992.

'An Autistic Person's View of Holding Therapy', Temple Grandin, *Communication*, Vol 23(3), December 1989.

'Changing Social Behaviour – The Place of Holding', John Richer, *Communication*, Vol 23(2), June 1989.

'Dietary Treatment in Autism and Hyperactivity', Eric Taylor and Rosemary Hemsley, *Communication*, Vol 24(2), June 1990.

'FC OK ... – A mother's experience with Facilitated Communication', *The Challenger*, Vol 4(1) January 1994. [*The Challenger* is the publication of Berkshire Autistic Society. For a photocopy of the article send an SAE to The Berkshire Autistic Society, 103 London Road, Reading, Berks. RG1 0BZ Tel: 0118 959 4594.]

'Holding Therapy' Phil Christie, *Communication*, Vol 21(3), December 1987.

'I am drowning in loneliness...', a translation about Birger Sellin, *Communication*, Winter 1995.

'Viewing the World through Rose-Tinted Glasses (Irlen Glasses)' *Communication*, Vol 29(1), January 1995.